THE RING

Books by Stephen Fay

The Zinoviev Letter
(*with Lewis Chester and Hugo Young*)
Hoax
(*with Lewis Chester and Magnus Linklater*)
The Death of Venice
(*with Phillip Knightley*)
Measure for Measure
The Great Silver Bubble

Books by Roger Wood

Katherine Dunham, her Singers, Dancers & Musicians
(*with Richard Buckle*)
The Sadler's Wells Ballet at the Royal Opera House, Covent Garden
The New York City Ballet, In Action
The Theatre Ballet of Sadler's Wells
The D'Oyly Carte Album
Shakespeare at the Old Vic, Vols I, II and III
(*with Mary Clarke*)
Egypt in Colour
(*with Margaret Drower*)
Roman Africa in Colour
(*with Sir Mortimer Wheeler*)
Persia
(*with Sir Denis Wright*)
An Introduction to the Antiquities of Saudi Arabia

THE RING:

Anatomy of an Opera

by

Stephen Fay

and photographed by

Roger Wood

Longwood Press
Dover, New Hampshire

This edition first published in the United States in
1985 by Longwood Press (a Division of Longwood
Publishing Group, Inc.) 51 Washington Street,
Dover, N.H. 03820

Library of Congress Cataloging in Publication Data

Fay, Stephen
  The ring.
  Includes Index
  1. Wagner, Richard, *1813–1883*. Ring des
Nibelungen. 2. Bayreuther Festspiele.
  I. Wood, Roger. II. Title.
  ML410.W1F4 1985   782.1'07'3   84-27825
  ISBN 0-89341-532-4

Colour plates printed by Springbourne Press Ltd.
Phototypeset by Tradespools Ltd, Frome, Somerset
and printed by Butler & Tanner Ltd, Frome, Somerset.

Contents

Acknowledgments

Many people have helped with this book. Foremost my thanks go to Ruth Holden. She and Lady Solti had an idea in December 1980 for a book to record this production of the *Ring* at Bayreuth. They chose me as illustrator, as both Sir Georg and Sir Peter have known me for over twenty-five years. Later Ruth Holden edited all the photographs, and assisted in the final selection. When John Goodwin of the National Theatre mentioned that Stephen Fay already had had an idea for a written account, and as the publishers welcomed our collaboration, the two book projects became one. To all these people I owe unstinted thanks.

At Bayreuth the idea of admitting an outside writer and photographer inside the Festspielhaus was not well received, but Sir Peter and Sir Georg pressed vigorously for me to be admitted. During the months of rehearsals they and their assistants gave me unfailingly cheerful cooperation. To all of them I offer my grateful thanks.

After months of uncertainty, finally Wolfgang Wagner welcomed me on stage with a handsome commendation to the stage staff. Thereafter he brushed aside all the restrictions he had previously imposed. I greatly appreciate his generous cooperation in allowing me to work in the Festspielhaus. I am grateful to all the theatre staff who, without exception, welcomed and helped me, in particular Walter Huneke, the Technical Director and his assistants, and Dr Oswald George Bauer, the Press Director.

Before rehearsals started the principal singers had been asked whether they would object to my attendance at rehearsals. I am grateful to them all that not one registered a refusal. I thank them for their invariable good humour and patience throughout. It has been inevitable in such a small book that pictures have had to be eliminated; to any singers inadequately represented, I apologise.

Apart from the problem of photographing all scenes through the stage gauze and excessive smoke, in keeping with 'the curse of the *Ring*', I was plagued with mechanical failures in trusted equipment and with technical problems in films. I thank those who carried home packets of mine to be attended to in London. Susie Home, the designer, has presented the photographs magnificently. Finally, Frau Lavinia Rosenthal, a friend of many years and a member of the Bayreuth Konservatorium Committee, has encouraged and supported this venture from start to finish. Without all this help from so many people, the pictures in this book could not have been made.

R.W.

Introduction

No performing art I have ever watched strikes so directly at the heart as opera does. The alchemy of words and music can leave a spectator emotionally limp, or over-excited, or in tears. There is a corollary of this intensity: heightened emotions are not confined to the audience. Indeed, I now suspect that they originate during the preparation and rehearsals for the performance. There is nothing quite so operatic as backstage in an opera house.

The explanation is not difficult to discover. To begin with, there are more things that must go right in an opera house, and, therefore, more things that can go wrong. Besides the singers on stage, there is an orchestra in the pit. The presence of a conductor dictates that there are two well-developed egos in the house, because there is a director too. Moreover, the performers are unlike actors, simply because they must sing as well as act; they are as conscious of their physical state as the most finely tuned athlete. The opera house is not a place in which to expect sweet reason.

This generalisation holds true, to a greater or lesser degree, throughout the world of opera. But I believe it is more applicable in Bayreuth than anywhere else, for a number of reasons, the most fundamental of which is Richard Wagner himself. Few people visit Bayreuth, to work or to watch, without holding firm views about the man who not only wrote the repertory, but built the Festspielhaus. Since the audience arrives with such strong opinions, one of the prevailing emotions among the performers is fear – that they will be booed. This fear is mixed with expectation: a singer who performs in Bayreuth can be sure of regular employment in Wagnerian roles thereafter. Critics go there from all over the world, quite literally, and a singer can leave Bayreuth famous or notorious, but hardly unnoticed. The professional stakes are high.

The essential irrationality of the Festival is further nurtured by the fact that Bayreuth is a small town in Bavaria that becomes in the spring and summer months not unlike a desert island on which singers, orchestral players and the production staff are marooned for weeks, or months. There are other things to talk about besides Richard Wagner, his successors and his work, but they gradually fade. The conversation becomes obsessively dominated by the single subject. This is an observation, not a complaint. True, there are days when people would sell their souls for the sound of Mozart, or a dinner party at which opera went unmentioned. But most of the participants willingly embrace the obsession. Otherwise, there seems to be little point in being in Bayreuth in the first place. It is a Mecca, for its kind. The intensity of the shared obsession multiplies and magnifies the crises that are endemic in opera houses. After a summer in Bayreuth I felt I was incapable of being surprised by any eventuality in the opera world.

I had not realised this before I went. My reason for being there was to observe a man of the theatre I had long admired, grappling single-mindedly with a great work of art. Peter Hall generously understood what I hoped to do. His companions, Bill Dudley, Guus Mostart and Michael McCaffery, all became my friends. I have tried to write a true account of what happened in Bayreuth in 1983, and because Hall and his colleagues allowed me to watch their work developing I was in an uncommon and privileged position for a reporter (for I am that, not a critic). The consequence is that the account, which I believe to be fair, is not impartial. I was involved with them; I desperately wanted them to succeed. After we met, Sir Georg Solti was as generous with his time as his remarkable schedule permitted. Solti treated my ignorance gently, and gave me a lecture on conducting for which I am especially grateful. His wife, Valerie, was unfailingly kind, as were his musical assistants, particularly David Syrus, who continued my education. In Bayreuth itself, Wolfgang Wagner was never entirely convinced that this story could be properly told, but that intellectual conviction did not prevent him from granting Roger Wood and myself access to the facilities of the Festspielhaus, as well as the auditorium, for which we thank him.

Without the co-operation of these men, no account of the 1983 Bayreuth *Ring* would have been possible. Without the help of their assistants, the organisation of work would not have been possible either. In Bayreuth, Gudrun Wagner, Gabriele Taut, and Oswald Bauer each took time to help. Sir Georg's assistant, Charles Kaye, found gaps in the diary during which I could be taught. But the most unstinting help we had was from Jan Younghusband, personal assistant to Peter Hall, who performed above and beyond the call of duty, and remained delightfully good-humoured while doing so.

My greatest debt, however, is to none of the participants, but to my wife, Prudence. Not only was she remarkably patient with my absorption in the production during 1983, she edited the manuscript with her customary skill, though any errors are, of course, my own responsibility.

S.F.

1

A climb up Everest, without oxygen

Richard Wagner was an extravagant man. Having written both the score and the libretto for *Der Ring des Nibelungen*, an operatic cycle that takes four nights to perform, three of them demanding the audience's attention for about six hours, Wagner decided that there was no one in Germany capable of directing the production except himself. Since no theatre in the 1870s met Wagner's exacting standards for the sound and performance of his *Ring*, he built his own – the Festspielhaus in Bayreuth, a small town in northern Bavaria. And because he considered no existing orchestra or operatic company was qualified to play and sing the work, he became an impresario, persuading some of the most outstanding performers of the day to work in Bayreuth for months on end. Wagner described the *Ring* as a Festival Play, and he decreed that it should be heard in a festival atmosphere that offered no distractions. Writing the *Ring* took some twenty-five years, and was an astonishing musical achievement; performing the work in 1876 in the manner he thought it deserved was a theatrical *tour de force*. Richard Wagner invested his festival with such conviction and vigour that after his death it became a cult and the Festspielhaus his shrine. The Festival saw its 100th anniversary in 1976, and in 1983 the artistic and administrative director at Bayreuth, Richard Wagner's grandson, Wolfgang, honoured the 100th anniversary of the composer's death with a new production of the *Ring* that would be performed each summer for the next five years.

The conductor of that production was Georg. Solti, making his debut in Bayreuth; and he had asked that the production be directed by Peter Hall, the director of Britain's National Theatre. Both are men of such eminence that each had been knighted, for services to music and the theatre respectively. Each is at the height of his artistic powers, and yet Solti and Hall both had deep misgivings about producing a new *Ring* in Bayreuth. That had little to do with the conditions they would work in, for Bayreuth tempts singers of international reputation to perform, often in roles they are singing for the first time. The orchestra is composed of experienced German musicians, and the technical facilities in the Festspielhaus have been widely copied by other theatres.

What Solti and Hall found awesome was the *Ring* itself, which is, says Hall, the '*biggest* great work of art ever created'. Nowhere is the task of producing it more exacting than in Bayreuth. In all other opera houses a new *Ring* is introduced gradually, often beginning with *Das Rheingold* and *Die Walküre* in the first year; *Siegfried* and *Götterdämmerung* coming into the repertory in the following two years. But successive administrators at the Festspielhaus, all of them Wagners by birth or marriage, have been unfailingly loyal to the remarkable achievement of the founder; Richard Wagner produced the four operas creating the *Ring* cycle in a single summer, and everyone else there has done so too. Bayreuth is unaccustomed to compromise, and great men of the musical theatre go to the Festival on Richard Wagner's terms.

I first learned about the 1983 Bayreuth *Ring* from Peter Hall in New York in October 1980, when he was rehearsing *Amadeus*, Peter Shaffer's play loosely based on Mozart's life, before its Broadway opening. I thought I detected a whiff of melancholy in his announcement. Of course, Hall said, he was delighted to have been asked to direct the *Ring* in Bayreuth; he thought of it as a present for his fiftieth birthday, which fell that year. But he did not talk like a celebrant. Instead, he brooded on an account of Richard Wagner's leaving the Festspielhaus after the first performance of the Ring in 1876, turning to his wife, Cosima, and saying that he wished he were dead. Hall's version of the story is not completely accurate, for, according to Cosima Wagner's diaries, it was some days after the first performances were finished that Wagner felt life was no longer worth living, and that was not because of any failure of his own composition or direction, but because of poor performances from singers who had played Siegfried and Wotan, and because his professional ear was displeased by some flawed tempi from Hans Richter, the conductor. But strict historical accuracy was not relevant to Hall's story: he was telling it as a cautionary tale. The *Ring* is a peculiarly daunting prospect for any experienced professional director, especially when done in Bayreuth.

Hall's ambiguity about the Bayreuth *Ring* was out of character, and so, I discovered later, were Solti's uncertainties. Of course, it

4

was perfectly natural for both to display a proper respect towards a great work of art, and Richard Wagner himself is undeniably a particularly hard act to follow. His biographer, Ernest Newman, who is not one of the idolators who hold Wagner to be immune from criticism of any kind, wrote of the improbability of anyone's emulating Wagner's own 1876 production: 'Wagner was a far better conductor than any of his conductors, a far better actor than any of his actors, a far better singer than any of his singers, except in tone. Each of his characters, each of his situations, had been created by the simultaneous functioning within him of a composer's imagination, a dramatist's, a conductor's, a scenic designer's, a singer's, a mime's. Such a combination had never existed in a single individual before; it has never happened since, and in all probability it will never happen again.'

The forebodings of Solti and Hall aroused my curiosity, so I asked all the collaborators in the enterprise if they would allow me to watch their work on the 1983 *Ring*. With varying degrees of enthusiasm, they consented. (Hall was at the enthusiastic end of the spectrum; Wolfgang Wagner at the other.)

It occurred to me later that creating a new production of the *Ring* in Bayreuth is like an attempt to climb Everest without oxygen; the failure rate does not deter others from trying. An account of such an expedition should begin by describing the features of the peak to be scaled, and there is no better place to start specifying some of the obstacles the *Ring* presents than the very beginning, the first scene of *Das Rheingold*.

The libretto of the *Ring* is littered with detailed stage directions; Wagner never intended that his successors should suffer any doubt about his intentions. Scene One is set on the bed of the Rhine: 'Greenish twilight, brighter towards the top, darker below. The upper part of the stage is filled with swirling waters that flow restlessly from right to left. Towards the bottom, the waters resolve into an increasingly fine damp mist, so that a space, a man's height from the ground, seems to be completely free of the water, which courses like a train of clouds over the dusky bed. Craggy points of rock rise everywhere from the depths and mark the confines of the stage. The whole river bed is broken up by craggy confusion, so that nowhere is it completely flat, and on all sides, in the dense darkness, there seem to be deeper gorges. The orchestra begins while the curtain is still closed. The curtain rises, the watery depths are in full flood. In the centre of the stage, around a rock whose slender point reaches into the brighter area of densely swirling water, one of the Rhinemaidens is circling with a graceful swimming motion.' (Her first words, incidentally, are

Weia! Waga!
Woge, du Welle!
Walle zur Wiege!
Wagalawia!
Wallala weiala weia!

The exclamation marks are Wagner's and he started as he continued, with heavily alliterated lines, written for their sound as well
as the meaning.)

Most directors and designers have evaded this remarkably
ambitious stage direction. Naturally, Richard Wagner himself had a
good try at meeting it. In 1876 he built machines topped by cradles
in which the Rhinemaidens were to recline, gracefully. The cradles
could be raised and lowered, and (when set on a trolley) moved
backwards and forwards. Confronted by the machine, one of the
first Rhinemaidens, declaring it a device of the Devil, stated that
nothing on earth would persuade her to be strapped into it,
especially as she had just risen from her sickbed. But most singers
behave like prima donnas only part of the time; for the rest they are
susceptible to persuasion, and after much squealing all three
mounted the cradles, where they sang beautifully, and were all
pleased with themselves. Certainly, the Bayreuth *Ring* productions
for the next sixty-five years never improved on Richard Wagner.
And when the grandsons, Wieland and Wolfgang, took control in
1950, they did not try to emulate their grandfather. They dealt with
the problem by the subtle use of stage light and projections on
gauzes, concentrating on the psychological implications in the
work. This abstract solution was much admired, and widely copied.

By the mid-1970s, however, Wagner's method had become too
familiar and was passing out of fashion, and in the new Bayreuth
production in 1976 a French director, Patrice Chéreau, offered a neo-
Marxist interpretation of Scene One of *Das Rheingold*, inspired by
George Bernard Shaw's statement that the *Ring* should be seen as a
revolutionary document. Chéreau set Scene One on a hydro-electric
dam, and the production became known among the stage staff as
the 'dam *Ring*' – as few spoke English, no double meaning was
intended. The Rhinemaidens clambered out over the dam wall,
rather than swimming in the water, and the gold was plundered
from its power unit.

Confronted by such a radical solution, the Bayreuth audience was
at first scandalised; but it gradually became accustomed to the

message over the years, so much so, indeed, that the last performance in 1980 received a ninety-minute ovation. As the critics left Bayreuth that summer one or two of them told the resident dramaturge, Dr Oswald Bauer, that they pitied the director who followed Chéreau. Indeed after Richard Wagner's realism, the abstractionism of Wieland and Wolfgang Wagner, and Chéreau's politically provocative interpretation, there seemed to be very little unmapped ground.

Solti was not interested in making the *Ring* into a disparaging political tract for our times. He had only agreed to conduct at Bayreuth as long as Wolfgang Wagner accepted what Solti described as a 'romantic' interpretation; this made Peter Hall a compelling choice for director, and William Dudley ideal as designer. Solti felt Dudley had the abundant visual imagination necessary for the *Ring*'s thirty-six separate scenes; an Englishman in his mid-thirties, Dudley was a naturalistic painter by inclination, out of sympathy with abstract work and intrigued by the technology used to create the realistic fantasy of films like *Star Wars*.

Solti, Hall and Dudley wanted their *Ring* to be romantic and loyal to Wagner's stage directions; when he said 'fire', they wanted fire; when a man turns into a toad, they wanted a toad; when a character wakes to see her horse, she should see a horse; and when Richard Wagner has the Rhinemaidens making a graceful swimming motion, there should be water on stage to make this convincing. What Solti, Hall and Dudley intended was to tell the *story*, from its beginning on the bed of the Rhine to the destruction of the house of the gods in a great conflagration at the end.

The *Ring* is a gripping tale, based on the ancient myths and sagas of northern Europe, and a publisher's blurb might state with strict accuracy that it is about greed and power, sex and violence. It begins, as good sagas ought, in a state of innocence. The opening music in E flat major characterises primitive nature: it begins on a note from the horns, then settles down after a melodic transformation on the strings, and speeds up to become the surging movement of the Rhine. This is the fundamental musical theme of the *Ring*: the force of nature which will devastate the power of the gods. In the brief first scene of *Das Rheingold*, more of the musical themes that recur throughout the cycle can be heard: themes of the gold, the ring that will be made from it, and the renunciation of love as a prerequisite for the acquisition of power. Wagner described the themes as an emotional guide to the labyrinthine development of the plot, but they are more than that. As a guide to the characters, what they feel, where they are and why, and what the weather is, the themes are sufficiently illustrative to enable a blind musicologist to follow the story from the first E flat to the last D flat.* When that story sounds improbable, remember only that the *Ring* is a fairy story, which ends unhappily ever after, with tears.

The entire cycle tells how three generations of gods, Wotan, his daughter Brünnhilde and his grandson Siegfried, are destroyed by Wotan's corrupting desire to possess a ring which passes through many hands, bringing death and ruin to each who holds it. There are a multitude of subplots and characters, but the basic story emphasises that love is stronger than power, as do most religions. But because the *Ring* is rooted in ancient northern European mythology, and Richard Wagner himself was a most complex man, directors, critics and commentators have produced many contradictory interpretations of the great work. Someone earnestly explained to me in Bayreuth that the death of Siegfried represents the crucifixion of Christ. Cocky young men (I was one myself) see each of the main roles as representing different aspects of Wagner's own character. Others, Wieland Wagner foremost among them, who are much influenced by Freud or Jung or both, find in the *Ring* a story of psychological conflict. The story can be interpreted as a straightforward tragedy in the classical Greek mould or it can be seen as a revolutionary document demonstrating the overthrow of capitalism by the proletariat as Chéreau and George Bernard Shaw suggested. (Unfortunately, Siegfried, the instrument of this revolution, *can* be played as a model either of Lenin's dictatorship of the proletariat, or of Hitler's SS, never mind Christ crucified.)

Evidently, *Der Ring des Nibelungen* is all things to all men. In that ambiguity, and in the astonishing illustration of the story through the musical themes, lies its greatness. What an outline of the story makes clear is that there is no single 'correct' way to produce the *Ring*. Many have been tried, with varying degrees of success, though since 1950 the prevailing trend has been for directors to impose increasingly obscure and complex interpretations of their own, at the expense of Richard Wagner's text and stage directions, and, on rarer occasions, at the expense of the music too.

The weight of Wagner's work makes it a burden to most conductors and directors; only the most foolhardy are not afraid of the *Ring*. Mulling over the difficulties one day in the spring of 1983, after rehearsals had begun, Peter Hall said to me: 'When I do a work by Shakespeare or Mozart, I'm in love with them. I'm in awe of Richard Wagner.' But that is to run ahead of the story.

---

* An outline of the story of the *Ring* appears in the Appendix, since this account of a new production concentrates on the characters who brought it to life, not on an analysis of the plot. Readers who are unfamiliar with the plot might find it worthwhile to pause and read the outline so as to be able to identify the scenes and characters in the narrative that follows.

2

Bayreuth: a family business

Richard Wagner's biographer, Ernest Newman, claims that no artist in the world's history has endured such hatred. None has enjoyed such adulation either. The most striking example of this that I have come across is in a book describing the rehearsals of the *Ring* in 1876, written by a disciple of Wagner's called Heinrich Porges. Outlining the qualities demanded of the artists involved, Porges says: 'Such a company can be formed only when a number of artists share the conviction that *a divine creative power* has found paramount expression in one single individual, and accordingly regard it as their *mission* to give material form to the ideal images which this genius has hitherto conceived of only as possibilities.' (The italics are mine.) This is a tall order, but Wagner – the 'divine creative power' – would not have disagreed with a word. Wagner thought of the theatre as a place of worship; a temple as noble and uplifting as a great cathedral. Had Wagner believed in God, one feels he would have thought his proper place not far from His right hand. Instead, he believed utterly in his own genius, which he recognised himself a decade or so before his followers, though they soon made up for lost time. By 1850, when he was only thirty-seven, Wagner was already being compared to Aeschylus, Shakespeare and Beethoven.

Wagner was a nineteenth-century revolutionary; indeed, the part he played in one revolution, in Dresden in 1848, led to a fifteen-year exile from Germany. In modern political jargon, Wagner could reasonably be described as a neo-Marxist republican with anarchic tendencies (he was a friend of Michael Bakunin, the legendary Russian anarchist, and regularly quoted Proudhon's maxim that property is theft, though that never prevented Wagner from acquiring his own). But Wagner's most momentous revolutionary activity was as a musician.

9

He was born, in Leipzig in 1813, with an intolerant, restless, wilful nature and astounding energy. He regarded his poverty as unjust and never doubted his right to help himself to other people's money, particularly if they were his friends; he felt the same way about their wives, and fathered children on Cosima, the wife of his most devoted musical disciple, Hans von Bülow. Cosima eventually became his second wife, legitimising the succession, though that did not prevent Wagner in his late sixties from dallying with one of his Rhinemaidens.

His deepest scorn was directed at the music he heard in the opera houses of Europe, and Wagner resolved that the purpose and the execution of opera should be reformed radically. The result was what he called 'music-drama', in which he overthrew all the old operatic conventions of structure and performance, not least that applying to length. His stories were told in poetry, with music illustrating its recurrent themes, and the most remarkable music-drama of all was *Der Ring des Nibelungen*, a work so long, and demanding such virtuosity from the singers and players, that even Wagner himself recognised that certain conditions would have to be met before the *Ring* could be performed. 'I can imagine a perform-ance only after the revolution, for the revolution alone can provide me with my artists and my audience,' he wrote, in 1850, just before he began composing the *Ring*.

Since the outside world lamentably failed to provide him with the revolution required, Wagner launched his own, and the place he chose for it was Bayreuth. He is said to have gone there in the first place because the Margrave Theatre had the deepest stage in Germany; he then rejected it for the first complete *Ring* cycle when he discovered that the auditorium was small and unsatisfactory – though architecturally delightful. But this explanation ignores a constant theme in Wagner's own writing about his operatic revol-ution: his insistence that the *Ring* should be performed, complete, in a theatre that had been custom-built to provide the right acoustic balance between singers and orchestra; a theatre where the audi-ence would concentrate on *nothing* but the *Ring*. A small town lacking any special character of its own was therefore a convenient location. Moreover, the local mayor offered a site on a hill on the edge of town, free. Since Bayreuth was in Franconia, the northern part of Bavaria, Wagner could continue to milk the exchequer of his greatest benefactor, King Ludwig II of Bavaria (more commonly known as mad King Ludwig, and not least because of the sums he lavished on Wagner).

The theatre Wagner built on the green hill in Bayreuth, the

Festspielhaus, is not a thing of beauty. Dudley would claim, during the summer of 1983 (without ever being able to identify the source of his story), that the RAF had had a mission to bomb the Festspielhaus in 1945, but as the pilot flew over it the bomber did not release his weapons because he thought the building was a brewery. The building's exterior was of no concern at all to Wagner and its sole architectural distinction is that it was, at the time, the largest free-standing timber-framed building ever constructed, because of Wagner's belief that the acoustic improved in a wooden structure. It was dominated as it still is by the sloping roof of the stage tower, and there was little attempt at decoration. Since Wagner's death, a neo-classical portico has been added to the façade; the original brickwork covering the wooden frame has been replaced, and red brick offices and dressing-rooms have been added to the sides of the building. But Richard Wagner would still find the interior entirely recognisable.

On my first visit to the Festspielhaus, Peter Hall took me on a tour of the large auditorium, pointing out its virtues. Seating 1,925 on hard bentwood, it is modelled on the open-air theatre at Epidaurus, giving virtually every seat a decent view of the wide proscenium; six huge classical columns on each side decorate the auditorium; a ceiling canvas is painted so as to give the impression that the auditorium is open to the night sky; and there are no side boxes or overhanging balconies to interfere with sightlines or distract the audience (boxes and the balcony are placed discreetly at the back). One more feature makes the Festspielhaus unique among opera houses. To ensure that the conductor and the orchestra players never distract from the stage performance, they are tucked away in a sunken pit, hidden from the audience by a curved black cowl, with the brass and woodwind players actually underneath the stage. This cowl, Hall explained, created Bayreuth's distinctive orchestral sound. In all other opera houses, where the pit and the players are visible to the audience, the sound flows directly out of the pit into the auditorium, and consequently the sound of the singers on the stage follows 'behind' the greater volume of sound from the orchestra. In Bayreuth the opposite happens. The orchestral sound bounces off the cowl wall behind the conductor, then moves *away* from the auditorium across the stage before hitting an acoustic wall which sends it back to the audience. So the singers' voices 'precede' the orchestral music into the auditorium, and the contrast between the two is more evenly matched. The vocal athleticism of the Wagnerian honking tenor and strident soprano is not an imperative in Bayreuth.

Wagner intended that his Festspielhaus should be 'absolutely provisional' (an early fantasy was to burn the theatre down at the completion of the first cycle). At the same time he rather hoped the building would eventually be transformed into a national monument. Although this has not happened, the Festspielhaus attracts a steady stream of tourist buses, both in the Festival season and out of it. The building is a monument without being monumental. And Wagner had already begun to recognise his remarkable achievement after the first Festival in 1876. 'In former times the artist used to dance attendance on emperors and princes; now for the first time the emperors and princes have come to the artist,' he said. (The Kaiser, as well as the besotted Ludwig, attended the first Festival.) By the 1890s Mark Twain was describing a visit to the Festival, with only gentle irony, as a pilgrimage of devotees coming from the very ends of the earth to worship the prophet in his own Mecca. (It was Twain who originated the saying: 'Wagner's music is not as bad as it sounds.') And before his death in 1883, Wagner had established that *his* festival for *his* music could only be operated with due reverence by people who were inheritors of his name. The line of succession was decreed, and to this day only a Wagner has ruled the Festival. Bayreuth is still a family business, and the basic product remains unchanged, apart from some variations in style. Only Wagner's operas are performed there, though they do not include *Rienzi* and *Das Liebesverbot*, which are not thought 'revolutionary' enough.

Richard was succeeded by his wife Cosima, the daughter of Franz Liszt, who was a Frenchwoman by birth and education, and imbued with enough of her second husband's arrogance to believe that no one but she was capable of executing his testament. Another legacy was Wagner's virulent anti-semitism, which prevailed in Bayreuth for fifty years after his death. Wagner stated that he did not wish to work on the same stage as Jews, whom he held largely responsible for his own ills as well as the world's. (Curiously, the first performances of *Parsifal* at the Festspielhaus in 1882 were conducted by a Jew called Hermann Levi, the reason being that King Ludwig made the presence of Levi and his Munich orchestra a condition of his generous subsidy.) The cause of Wagner's anti-semitism is obscure: Ernest Newman suggests that it was the outcome of Wagner's bitter rivalry with the German composer, Meyerbeer. I suspect it might also have grown out of a paranoid association of Jews with moneylenders who had the temerity to demand repayment of their loans to Wagner, with interest. Whatever the cause, Bayreuth and anti-semitism became inextricably linked – one reason why Wagner has been so hated.

Cosima's influence extended to ensuring that stage performances remained unalterable memorials to her dead husband. One of Wagner's original Rhinemaidens, Lilli Lehmann, returned two decades later to sing Brünnhilde, and reported: 'The ideals of individuality have given way to a tyranny that demands submission as a prime requisite. Even if a tyrant's rod is wielded with much amiability it remains just that – a tyrant's rod.' But it was Cosima's single-mindedness that properly established the Festival.

Although nominally out of office, Cosima dominated the Festival until 1930. Siegfried Wagner was a distinguished conductor, performing regularly at Bayreuth for thirty-five years, and a composer in his own right, though his reputation is overwhelmed by his father's. Siegfried fought to free Bayreuth from Cosima's domination, but he died only a few months after Cosima, before the transformation could begin. He was replaced by his wife, Winifred, a lady with some Welsh blood in her veins, born in the genteel English seaside town of Hastings, and Bayreuth was soon drawn into the maelstrom of Hitlerism. Hardly less stubborn, arrogant, and prejudiced than her mother-in-law, Winifred defended herself by claiming that Bayreuth's urgent need of state subsidy necessitated her alliance with the Third Reich. But her personal ardour for Hitler was undoubtedly genuine: she is even rumoured to have purchased the paper on which he wrote *Mein Kampf* in prison in the early 1920s. When Hitler became Chancellor in 1933, and Winifred was forced to choose between her political patron and some of the finest musicians of the day, she chose Hitler. Arturo Toscanini, among others, did not return. Hitler stayed each year in the family house, Wahnfried, on Richard Wagnerstrasse, and dandled her sons Wieland and Wolfgang on his knee. The Führer, who found Bayreuth's anti-semitism and Wagner's German nationalism entirely in tune with his own, planned to turn the Festspielhaus into a Wagnerian Acropolis. (Reading Wagner's life persuades me that the composer would, if he could have known him, soon have extended to Hitler the same contempt that he had for all politicians.)

Hitler ordered that the inspiration provided by the Festival should remain available to Germany during the War, and Winifred struggled on until 1944. A year later when the Festspielhaus was 'liberated' by a young American soldier called Joseph Wechsberg, the stage was still set for *Die Meistersinger von Nürnberg*, Wagner's hymn to Holy German Art, and Wechsberg (a fine writer, who recalled the scene in the *New Yorker*) suggests that the set had been left there as a symbol of continuity. Later in 1945 the American occupying troops commandeered the Festspielhaus for variety shows, and the nine Valkyries were replaced by nine Rockettes, chorus dancers from Radio City Music Hall in New York. Immediately after the War the shrine was regularly desecrated by works other than those of the Master; even the sound of comic opera was heard.

In 1947, when a de-Nazification court ruled that Winifred must relinquish her grasp, an agonised debate took place about the control of the Festival. One faction argued the case for its being taken away from the family entirely, while others pointed out that Richard's grandsons, Wieland and Wolfgang, had not been Nazis: being photographed sitting on Hitler's knee, as both boys were in 1936, was not a war crime.

Their sister, Friedelind, had exiled herself earlier, and spent the War in the United States. Wieland, the heir, had been exempted from military service so that he could assist his mother, and towards the end of hostilities had exiled himself to Lake Constance, where he mulled over the dramatic possibilities of his grandfather's work. There had been no exemption for Wolfgang though he was an aspiring conductor; conscripted in 1939, he had been wounded in both arms in Poland a few months later, which ended his career as a musician, and been sent home. When the Festspielhaus had closed, Wolfgang had been conscripted again, this time as a civilian in Bayreuth's public works department. As there was no political case against them, and they were capable artists, the brothers were allowed to inherit their grandpatrimony, and the Festival began once more in 1951, with Wieland as artistic director and Wolfgang as administrator.

Wieland's aim, at that period, was to strip Wagner's work of its nationalism and its naturalism: the German word which describes his method is *Entrümpelung*, which means 'clearing the attic'. And Wieland's passion for the abstract was not confined to the *Ring*. When he directed *Die Meistersinger* in 1956 he did not attempt to recreate medieval Nuremberg; since it had been bombed, he argued, why bother to reconstruct it on the stage at Bayreuth? According to the Festspielhaus's dramaturge, Dr Oswald Bauer, the boos and catcalls that were to become a feature of the Festival were first heard that summer. But it was Wieland's *Ring* that restored Bayreuth's reputation. Influenced by classical Greece and by Freud, Wieland chose an abstract set that became the model for Wagnerian productions throughout the operatic world. His *Ring* was in the repertoire for seven years, until he tired of it in 1958 and suggested that Wolfgang should direct a new production the following year. Wolfgang, who had been directing other works since 1953, was taken aback by such an abrupt proposal, but still managed to mount his first *Ring* two years later, a more architectural version of Wieland's, but conforming strictly to the new Bayreuth style. Wieland had time to direct his second *Ring* before he died in 1966; Wolfgang's second version appeared in 1970, by which time he had taken sole charge of Richard Wagner's legacy.

Wahnfried having been turned into a museum (one that contains hardly a hint of Bayreuth's Nazi period), Wolfgang Wagner moved out, and now lives just across the broad road that sweeps up Siegfried Wagner Allee through Richard Wagner Park and alongside the Festspielhaus, only fifty yards from the door leading to the brick office-block built below the stage house. A visitor can watch him trudging between the Festspielhaus and his new home, deep in thought, walking with a stoop so that his thick, straight, white hair falls over his forehead. Normally, he wears a tweed coat, slacks and a poloneck sweater, revealing a paunch. Wolfgang carries more weight than his grandfather, but the resemblance is there, particularly in profile when the prominent nose and the pugnacious Wagner jaw are unmistakable. When Wolfgang speaks, however, it is with a Franconian accent so thick that even Bavarians from Munich miss a phrase here and there. Sentences issue from Wolfgang in a torrent; his spoken paragraphs are remarkably long, and brief conversations with him are rare.

Wolfgang is usually the first person to arrive at the Festspielhaus in the morning and he is often also the last to leave, carefully locking the door himself. No obscure passage inside the theatre is unknown to him, and few rehearsals do not attract his proprietorial presence. In the darkened auditorium his voice is instantly recognisable, and sometimes it quickens and rises when he is displeased. Wagner is self-conscious about these explosions of temperament, and explained to me ingenuously that they are a trait inherited from his Welsh mother. (Apparently Winifred, though born in England, had a fiery Celtic temper.) A successful director himself, Wolfgang has personal experience of the problems confronting a director in Bayreuth, and he is anxious to help. But he is, he says, known as a tolerant person who does not interfere. Wolfgang told me this one afternoon as we talked in the conference room behind his office, a small bright room with a wooden table and cane chairs. The light slanted in and caught the blueness of his expressive eyes, which are never still, and seldom direct. I asked him whether the twin roles of administrator and director did not cause him discomfort. Not at all, he replied; this kind of schizophrenia was characteristic of the family – after all, his grandfather had been both artist and administrator. In fact, said Wolfgang: 'Everybody has a split personality; that's the tragedy of Wotan.'

It was Wolfgang, in his capacity as administrator, who decided that the family's post-war monopoly of *Ring* productions should be broken. One significant consequence of this decision was to make the role of the conductor more influential. As directors, he and Wieland had always chosen the conductor they preferred to work with, but Wolfgang reversed this process in 1976 by asking the distinguished French musician, Pierre Boulez, to conduct the cycle and then letting him choose his own director. Boulez's first choice was the Swedish film-maker Ingmar Bergman, but he turned out to detest Wagner. Boulez then talked to Peter Brook, who was not keen; finally a choice had to be made between Peter Stein, a fashionable German theatre director, and a young Frenchman, Patrice Chéreau. Since Stein announced that he wished to cut the *Ring* so that it could be played in two nights instead of four (a heresy in Bayreuth, where the *Ring*, of course, is never cut), and to rebuild the auditorium so that the *Ring* could be played in the round, Chéreau became the director. His production in 1976 – the 'dam *Ring*' – was so controversial that Boulez's part in it was largely overlooked. As we have seen, Chéreau's 'dam *Ring*' finally became a considerable critical success. Nonetheless, in the summer of 1978, Wolfgang decided that another new production ought to be planned to mark the 100th anniversary of Richard Wagner's death in 1983, preferably conducted and directed by people who had never worked in Bayreuth. Once again Wolfgang started by choosing the conductor first and then letting him find his own director. In the modern Bayreuth Festival, as Wolfgang sees it, the conductor holds 51 per cent of the shares in a production, leaving the director and designer with a 49 per cent minority holding.

In principle, the choice in 1978 was not difficult to make since there were then only two Wagner conductors considered both great and experienced, Herbert von Karajan and Georg Solti, and only the latter had not yet worked in Bayreuth. (Von Karajan had conducted there in the 1950s; Sir Reginald Goodall was never listed.)

Georg Solti had been approached in 1952, but nothing had come of it. Then Wolfgang had made a firmer offer to him in 1968, asking him to conduct *Tristan und Isolde* in 1973, but negotiations had broken down because Solti did not approve of the rehearsal schedule, and Wolfgang had refused to alter it. Then, in the summer of 1978, Wolfgang says he noticed an interview with Solti in the opera magazine, *Orpheus*, in which Solti expressed a wish to do the *Ring* in Bayreuth. The timing was coincidental, but perfect. 'I

16

interpreted it as a signal that our earlier conflicts might be resolved,' says Wolfgang. He did not approach Solti directly, however, perhaps fearing another rebuff. That summer in Bayreuth, Wolfgang sought out Hans Ulrich Schmid, German agent for the Chicago Symphony Orchestra, and asked Schmid to find out whether Solti was genuinely interested. During the orchestra's autumn tour Solti confirmed that indeed he was, and Wagner and Solti arranged to meet in Berlin on 28 February 1978. It was there that Solti agreed, in principle, to conduct the 1983 *Ring*.

Wolfgang Wagner and Solti discuss a problem in staging the new production, at Solti's London home, December 1981.

3

Georg Solti: jumping all hurdles

Georg Solti is not his real name. It was manufactured in the mid-1930s as a consequence of the obsessive anti-semitism of Admiral Horthy's Fascist regime in Hungary. Solti is really Gyuri Stern, who was born in Budapest in 1913, his parents having migrated to the capital from the countryside in search of a comfortable living which they never quite achieved. Solti began to learn the piano when he was seven, and by the age of twelve he was talented enough to win a place in the Franz Liszt Academy, a school that boasted Béla Bartók, Zoltán Kodály, and Ernö von Dohnányi among its teachers. Solti decided what kind of musician he wanted to be when he was fourteen, at a concert in the Hall of the Academy which was conducted by Erich Kleiber. Arriving home, he informed his mother that he simply had to become a conductor; she patiently told him to pass his piano exams first, and so he did, becoming a first-class pianist, good enough, when he was seventeen, to obtain a job as a *répétiteur*, playing for singers and at rehearsals, at the Hungarian Royal Opera House. An ambitious young man, he went to Germany to broaden his experience, but, as a Jew, was hounded out of Karlsruhe and Mannheim. However, his luck was not all bad. He was in Salzburg when one of Arturo Toscanini's *répétiteurs* fell ill, and he got the job, though that was no passport to a position in Budapest. Solti had to wait until 1938 before the Hungarian musical authorities consented to his conducting a couple of orchestras, and during the second of these performances, his operatic debut with *The Marriage of Figaro*, most of the audience left before the end of the third act on hearing the news of Hitler's Anschluss in Austria. (A good review the next morning did, however, identify Solti's 'strong rhythmic grasp'.) That Solti's career would not prosper in Hungary

Facing page: Solti rehearsing in the orchestra pit, Bayreuth, July 1983.

was confirmed in 1939 when the Horthy regime passed a law debarring Jews from holding jobs in state organisations, which included the opera house. Fortunately, he was in Switzerland trying to persuade Toscanini to give him work in America when war broke out in September 1939. His mother cabled, 'Don't come back.' Solti stayed in Switzerland for five years; he never saw his father again.

Wagner's music had hardly impinged on Solti's musical consciousness in Hungary. During a long conversation in which I took notes for a musical biography of Solti, he said, 'I was at that point absolutely, totally absorbed by Mozart, Verdi and Puccini. Wagner did not belong to the daily life of the Budapest opera house. Even in the 1930s, Wagner operas were very difficult to cast. But *Tannhäuser* and *Meistersinger* were played frequently, and I loved *Meistersinger* as a young musician. I did hear the *Ring* because we had a highly talented amateur Italian conductor who knew the whole of the *Ring*, even though he could not speak German. He did not have much idea of the style of Wagner, but that is how I first heard it, in Hungarian, with an Italian conductor. It didn't mean much to me then.' Without that limited knowledge of Wagner, Solti would have found his first years of the War in Switzerland even more painful than he did. 'I knew only one person in Switzerland, a *Heldentenor* called Max Hirzel. When I telephoned him he said: "Why don't you

come to my house for a couple of weeks? I'm working on *Tristan* and you could work with me." I was always a very good coach and piano player; those two weeks became one and a half years. In that time I learned *Tristan* very well. *He* never did. That is my beginning with Wagner.'

As a middle-European Jew in his early thirties, Solti was lucky to have survived the War, but he felt musically frustrated in Switzerland. He won a prestigious piano competition in Geneva, and scratched a living teaching and giving recitals, but the opportunity to conduct was confined to three performances of Massenet's *Werther* in Geneva. Solti had to wait until the chaos and misery of the aftermath of the War in Germany finally brought him the opportunity he so impatiently sought, and when it came it was better than he could ever have imagined. The great German conductors, Karl Böhm, Herbert von Karajan, and Hans Knappertsbusch, were forbidden to work until their relationship with the Third Reich had been thoroughly investigated. Conducting vacancies existed all over Germany, and the power to fill the position at the Munich Opera rested with a young American soldier who was a contemporary of Solti's from Budapest. Solti's first proper job, in 1946, was as music director of one of Europe's most famous opera houses.

Die Walküre was the first Wagner opera Solti conducted, in Munich in 1947. 'I had a miraculous cast. The young Hans Hotter was Wotan, and I learned a great deal from him about the tremendous dynamic range of the music, and the phrasing. I did four Wagner operas in six years, all for the first time, and I began to understand that you must have a sense of architecture. You're not making bars, you're making scenes. The other essential is a feeling for the drama boiling over in the music. I did not know all this in 1947, though. I conducted in contours, big lines, but people said the dramatic verve was very good. Furtwängler saw my *Tristan*, and he told my secretary: "Watch out for this young man. He will be something." I grew to like Wagner very much in Munich, though it was strange, because there were no young people in the audiences because of Wagner's anti-semitism. Wagner was a dirty word to them. But I was a Jew, playing Wagner, no one could accuse me of being a Nazi.'

By the time he left Munich, a casualty of internal Bavarian politics, Solti had added *Das Rheingold* to his *Ring* repertoire, and when he went to Frankfurt as music director that repertoire was extended to include *Götterdämmerung*. In the mid-1950s, he made his first Wagner record, the third act of *Die Walküre*, produced for Decca by a young Englishman, John Culshaw, which was a great success. By the end of the 1950s, Culshaw realised that long-playing records made a recording of the whole *Ring* feasible and he gambled on the existence of a market for a set of nineteen discs. For his conductor Culshaw returned to the little-known Hungarian Solti, who had so impressed him when he had heard his first *Walküre* in Munich in 1947. By the time the cycle was completed in 1965, Solti had an international reputation and Culshaw's gamble had succeeded brilliantly. The recording is still considered by many critics – the authors of the Penguin *Stereo Guide*, for example – as the finest of all, in competition with Karajan's and Boulez's versions, produced later. (Solti himself thought that his recordings gave too much emphasis to the orchestral sound, to the singers' detriment.)

By the mid-1960s Solti had been music director at Covent Garden for five years. His turbulent start there was typified by a disastrous production of *Die Walküre*, but by 1965 that production had been revised, the cycle was complete, and Solti had become an experienced Wagner conductor. 'Once you move from a recording studio to an opera house, it's entirely different, because it's much more difficult to forge Siegfried's sword, for instance, on stage than in front of a microphone. So the conductor must be flexible. I wasn't, as a young conductor, no one is. But I learned that when you want a singer to perform at certain speeds or with a particular expression, you must be flexible. If a singer can't produce enough *legato* or *diminuendo* then you say: "All right, let's do it differently." If a singer's voice is not as big as it should be, then you fade the orchestra downwards and you ask him to sing as low as possible, so when you go upwards again, he's still got something.'

Solti's Covent Garden *Ring* was designed by Gunter Schneider-Siemssen, and was an influential success among the students of design in the 1960s. 'When it started, I liked it,' Solti recalls, 'but it soon became boring, very unromantic, very unpicturesque. When we finished, everyone liked it, and I hated it.' Solti regarded the staging of his first full *Ring* as a failure, but he had learned the awesome demands of a cycle conducted in a single week. 'It is a monster, because you have no time to collect your strength. If you add together the *Ring* score pages, they come to well over 2,000, compared to 100 pages in a major symphony, so conducting the *Ring* cycle is equivalent to doing twenty concerts. When you step on to the rostrum for *Rheingold* you look at your hand, knowing that hand will not stop for two and a half hours. You wonder: can I sustain it? What shape will I be in? Will I want to go to the toilet? You get to Scene Three, the Nibelung scene, and when you finish that, you are totally exhausted, but you still have another forty-five

From the orchestra pit Solti checks the balance of sound of the orchestra with his assistants in the auditorium, David Syrus and Ed Spanjaard.

minutes to do. The same worries occur in the first act of *Götterdämmerung*, which lasts two hours. You have to say to yourself: watch out, there are two more scenes coming, take it easy, take it easy. But it is always the same: utter physical exhaustion.'

Having completed a decade at Covent Garden, and been knighted for his services to British music, Solti, then in his mid-fifties, decided to concentrate on mastering symphonic music. While retaining his home in London, where he lives with his second wife, Valerie, and two young daughters on whom he dotes, Solti became director of the Chicago Symphony Orchestra. He says he grew up as a musician during his years in Chicago. (This is not false modesty, for Solti is disarmingly frank about his own abilities. Speaking of a conductor who had doubted whether Solti could really conduct *Tristan* for the first time in such an imposing house as Munich, he says: 'He forgot there are some exceptionally talented people who can jump over all hurdles.') Solti believes that a chemical reaction between himself and the Chicago Symphony Orchestra inspired both, and the audiences concurred, rating the orchestra among the best three or four in the world.

But Solti did not wish to desert opera entirely. In 1968 he was initially tempted by Wolfgang Wagner's proposal that he conduct *Tristan und Isolde* at Bayreuth in 1973. However, that was before he had discovered that the orchestral players would change between performances, unacceptable to so precise and disciplined a conductor, so a meeting with the orchestra's director was arranged and a compromise agreed. Then Solti learned about the rehearsal schedule. 'We were going to have rehearsals, and then for a week nothing, then stage and technical rehearsals, and then for another week nothing. I said: "Look, I can't do that. Can't we change it?" Wagner was very upset that I should ask for such a thing, and the answer came back: "No, take it or leave it." No, in actual fact it was worse than that: "Leave it," he said.' Solti did.

He was then tempted by an old friend, Rolf Liebermann, to go to Paris to conduct a *Ring* cycle directed by Peter Stein. It was a most unhappy experience. 'Only after *Die Walküre* in the second year – 1977 – did I say I couldn't take it any more. I suffered a great deal, I thought I'd done my last *Ring*.' Valerie Solti recalled that one of the items in this production which so upset her husband had been the covering of the stage with sandbags in the first act of *Die Walküre* so that sand got up the singers' nostrils when they breathed. Then, when the sandbags were dampened to combat the dust, Siegmund and Sieglinde had to lie on a wet surface. 'Not the best health cure for singers. Paris really was a disaster,' she notes. The failure rankled so badly that within a year of quitting Paris, Solti had accepted Wolfgang Wagner's offer to come to Bayreuth.

For Solti, 'The *Ring* is one of the greatest human deeds in the history of mankind. I am a musician. I hear it.' Solti does not admire the philosophy or the personality of Richard Wagner but does believe the music is a work of genius. Solti was sixty-six when Wagner asked him to conduct the *Ring* and he would be seventy when he actually made his debut at Bayreuth. This did not worry Wagner, who had seen plenty of evidence of conductors being exempt from the normal ageing process, but Solti himself was not so sanguine. Valerie recalls that his initial reaction to the invitation was surprise, then delight, followed by caution.

For twenty years his annual schedule had been organised around a two-month break, taken in the summer at his house in Italy, which is on the Mediterranean 220 kilometres north of Rome in a village called Roccamare. Half of Solti's time there was for rest; half for studying the scores he would conduct in the following year. Conducting summer cycles of the *Ring* for at least three years – the engagement Wagner offered – would spoil that pattern, and that was only one of many factors counselling caution. Solti had never worked in the pit in Bayreuth; he did not know who was to direct the production; he thought it foolish to produce a complete new *Ring* cycle in one summer; he remained suspicious of the Festival's rehearsal schedules and of an orchestra that was put together only for the summer festival, whereas he was accustomed to the mighty professionalism of the Chicago Symphony Orchestra; and he wanted a completely new cast of Wagnerian singers at a time when they were rare commodities. On the other hand, although he had recorded the *Ring* and conducted it many times, he had never been satisfied with his performances. Solti cherishes his reputation, and he remained anxious to achieve a satisfactory *Ring*, to fulfil his ambition to be a complete conductor, whatever hazards had to be overcome.

When Solti talks to Wagner, he speaks fluent Hungarische-Deutsch. His English, on the other hand, is heavily accented and bears the marks of another grammar, so his reaction to Wagner's offer, written exactly as it was spoken, is: 'Of course I vas pleased. I hated that, so to speak, "Solti out Bayreuth". Because I felt very hurted. Vanted to do as good as possible. So I vas very pleased. First reaction.' The phrases are delivered staccato, and the expressive hands appear to conduct the animated conversation. When he listens, Solti inclines his bald head, with its fringe of grey hair, as if to concentrate on the sound rather than the appearance of his companion. He thinks quickly and laterally.

When I got to know Solti better, it occurred to me that he was a fundamentally shy man; and he confirmed this. 'But conductors have a reputation for being extroverts,' I said. 'That's false,' he replied, 'I'm a Libra man, very easy to depress, up and down. I love balances and never find them.'

This discontent about his failure to find the proper balance is one of Solti's characteristics as a musician. After his recorded *Ring*, he need never have changed his interpretation; had he conducted the same thing all round the world, there would have been few complaints. But as Solti pores over scores in Roccamare, the sounds he hears change and develop. This is a solitary process, uninfluenced by the work of other conductors, though he does play their records, and, over the years, has listened attentively to the work of an earlier generation of Wagnerian conductors – Böhm, Knappertsbusch and Furtwängler. Although he never went to Salzburg to hear Karajan's *Ring*, he listened to the records and found them good. 'He is basically looking for lyricism and I am looking for the dynamic. It is a German tradition not to conduct with a rhythmical sense; they

26

The evolution of the set for *Götterdämmerung* Act II.

A very rough trial of the essentials, to measure spacings and dimensions, February 1983. In the top picture the stage gauze is partly lowered.

The finished set at a performance, July 1983. Act II Scene 3, Hagen summons the vassals to the Gibichungs' Hall.

Solti and the full Festival orchestra,
in the covered pit at Bayreuth
Festspielhaus, July 1983.

Overleaf: Die Walküre Act III Scene 1.
Brünnhilde pleads with the eight Valkyries
to protect the exhausted Sieglinde:
'Hört Mich Eile:
Sieglinde ist es,
Siegmunds Schwester und Braut'

Götterdämmerung. Act II Scene 3. Hagen, surrounded by the vassals, encourages them to drink to the arrival of Gunther's bride.

Wolfgang Wagner and Hall; an early rehearsal, on Rehearsal Stage No 3. The inclined ramp behind them is in position to test whether Brünnhilde's horse can climb the gradient.

Lady Solti with Wolfgang Wagner in a break from the meeting at the Soltis' London home, December 1981.

say that I over-emphasise it compared to Karajan, who under-emphasises it. He loves to make the music flower, while I like to have some sharper bits. We are basically poles apart.'

Solti told me that the *Ring* would sound different in Bayreuth, less passionate and more reflective than his recording twenty years earlier. I asked whether he was hearing different sounds in his head, and he replied that he was, though he found them difficult to define, partly because he seldom listens to his old recordings; he hears mistakes and they irritate him: 'You must go always ahead, not looking back.' When I pressed him to be more specific, Solti explained that he was looking for more colour and more internal expression in the voices, adding up to a greater dynamic range. 'I can do it bigger now, because I dare. When you are a young conductor and you are working with a good orchestra, they will tell you what is not possible. Now I know it is possible; I just tell them to try it. I love to open up Wagner as a sound; all the details glittering. Now it is slower too, and the extremes are bigger. And from the singers I want *legato* and *piano* phrases, and a sense of rhythm, not barking or shouting.'

The style of the 1983 production was effectively to be dictated by these sounds in Solti's head; abstractions would not fit. Solti wanted

27

to see the changes in the seasons, the peaks, the thunder, the fire, and the water that he heard in the music. Being a musician rather than a writer, his word for this was 'romantic', which was what he had hoped for in Paris. He made it clear to Wagner that if he was not convinced that Bayreuth really intended to do what he asked and not just promise it, he did not wish to conduct the cycle. Wagner, agreeing, suggested Rudolph Noelte as a German director who might qualify. As far as Solti was concerned, he didn't. Like Boulez, Solti toyed with the idea of Peter Brook, though why he should think that Brook would necessarily succumb to the appeal of naturalism is not clear; anyway, Brook was still not interested. Another name Solti mentioned to Wagner was that of Peter Hall. He and Solti had worked together ten years earlier at Covent Garden on a famous *Tristan* and a spectacularly controversial *Moses and Aaron* by Arnold Schoenberg. But Solti assumed that Hall would be too busy at the National Theatre to think of doing the *Ring*, and in the back of his mind there was the memory of a *Magic Flute* in Hamburg from which Hall had withdrawn, causing Solti to declare: 'That was finish.'

Sixteen months went by after the Berlin meeting and Solti, still without a suitable director, began to consider abdication. Before committing himself, however, he decided to see whether he was right about Hall being unavailable. One summer's day – it was 27 June 1980 – Solti demanded to see Hall immediately as he wished to put a question to him that could not be asked on the telephone. Hall was intrigued enough to rearrange his day's schedule and they met in Hall's office at the National Theatre, a narrow, unprepossessing room, with concrete walls and a glass-topped desk, relieved by a few pictures, cartoons, books, and a fine view of Somerset House across the Thames. Solti came straight to the point. Hall recalled the moment well: 'Georg told me that I had always said I wanted to do a romantic *Ring*, and, if that were still the case, he would like to do it with me in Bayreuth in 1983. I thought: "Oh fuck; the *Ring*'s an impossible thing to do."' But it took him only twenty-four hours to telephone Solti and announce that he too was in principle prepared to try to do the impossible. By the summer of 1980, with three years to go, Wagner had enticed Solti, and Solti had lured Hall.

Facing page: Solti and Hall in Hall's office, the National Theatre, May 1982.

4

Peter Hall: trusting the tale

Peter Hall was born in 1930 in the agreeable Suffolk market town of Bury St Edmunds, the son of Reg Hall, a conscientious railwayman. During the Depression a job on the railways had the virtue of security, and although the pay was not generous, the Halls lived frugally and saved hard to lavish money on their one luxury – their only son, Peter. Hall was precocious, passing exams with facility, and winning places at excellent private schools, on which some of the family savings were spent. From the Perse School in Cambridge (Reg Hall was then the station master at Shelford, eight miles down the main line to London), Hall won two scholarships to St Catharine's College, and by the time he left Cambridge University in 1953 he was a particularly well educated young man.

Music and the theatre had taken a grip early in his life. When he was given a fretwork set at the age of six, Hall built a stage for his puppets. But his most intense childhood passion was for music. He graduated from the piccolo to the flute and soon after his parents bought a piano, when he was nine, Hall was able to accompany his father, who sang in local amateur productions of Gilbert and Sullivan. A year later Hall saw his first Mozart opera, *The Marriage of Figaro*, in Cambridge. As the teenage son of a railwayman he could travel free, and during the War he went to London regularly to listen to Verdi and Rossini; at the Perse School, he was introduced to the work of the young English composers, Michael Tippett and Benjamin Britten. When his parents discussed what their son would do when he grew up, they feared that he would be a musician, an occupation they regarded as being much too precarious for their boy. Reg Hall entertained the hope that his son would be sensible and become a management trainee on the railways after he left university, but any such prospect disappeared when Hall dis-

Facing page: An early rehearsal of *Das Rheingold*; Hall and Doris Soffel.

covered how seductive it was to direct plays. During his last year in Cambridge two of his productions were well reviewed in national newspapers, and Hall left the university for London, where the streets were full of theatres.

Hall very nearly started his career in opera. Carl Ebert, Glyndebourne's director of production, asked whether he was interested in becoming his assistant, but by the time the job was confirmed, Hall had been asked to direct at the small London Arts Theatre. He had several successes, including the London premiere of Samuel Beckett's *Waiting for Godot*. By the time he was twenty-five he was still learning his trade, but his apprenticeship was undertaken in the best theatrical company, and habits were formed then that never altered.

In 1957, directing *Cymbeline*, his first Shakespeare at Stratford-upon-Avon, for example, Hall began to deploy the methods of play-directing customary at the time: carefully working out moves beforehand, using toy soldiers on a stage model. In one scene he had planned that Peggy Ashcroft should move right across the stage, but when she had completed the move she said: 'Peter, I don't feel comfortable doing that; couldn't I stay still?' At that moment, says Hall, he had to decide what sort of director he would be: a dictator with toy soldiers, or a collaborator with real actors. He chose the latter, and since then has never prepared a detailed plot from which to direct, preferring to arrive with an outline of what he wishes to achieve, and then thinking on his feet – not always agreeing with what the actors propose, but always listening. 'The way I work is wasteful of effort and it can be very irritating, because if I don't find a solution, I just go on nagging at it, and people have to stand around and wait. No matter how well you prepare, things don't begin to take shape until you have people on the stage.'

Hall directed his first opera in 1958, an obscure English work based on Somerset Maugham's *The Moon and Sixpence*, at Sadler's Wells. 'It was a revelation. Singers are so easy to direct. They want to learn and are very eager, perhaps because they are used to the discipline of the conductor and the music staff. I realised, too, that the whole basis of operatic drama, as in most acting, is the release of physical tension. The music sounds better if you can get the body well placed and centred, because the singer feels better.' Hall also began to appreciate the role of the conductor; at Sadler's Wells this was the equally young and ambitious Alex Gibson (now Sir Alexander, conductor of the Scottish National Orchestra). 'Alex and I discussed the set beforehand; he came to rehearsals, and I realised that it would be an absolute waste of time working with a conductor

32

who was not involved in the production. If he just comes and plays the music when the audience appears, he will normally ruin all the work we've done in rehearsals by not understanding what we are trying to achieve. If you have decided that a phrase has a particular psychological or emotional meaning, and the conductor then comes along and plays the music faster, even half a second faster – the singer can't feel it, or can't do it, and the drama's gone.' Since 1958 Hall has consistently declined to work with conductors who do not appreciate the theatre. Consequently, he has worked with very few – Gibson, John Pritchard, Raymond Leppard, Bernard Haitink, James Levine, and Georg Solti: not a bad hand. The reverse, he thinks, is also true: all opera directors who are any good are musical.

Hall met Solti for the first time in 1961, when he rejected his offer to direct Verdi's *Macbeth*. 'Solti screamed and raged, and said that if people like me and Peter Brook refused to work at Covent Garden, how could he do the job?' But Hall had just recently been appointed director of the Royal Shakespeare Company, and during the hectic 1960s he could fit in only one opera: *Moses and Aaron*, which was done with Solti. (Hall's customary devotion to the text led him to insist that a camel appear on stage in this opera. Covent Garden obliged and provided a camel. In rehearsal, the camel panicked. 'Cut the camel,' said Hall.)

His remarkable cycle of Shakespeare's history plays, *The Wars of the Roses*, at Stratford in 1963 was the most widely acclaimed of many productions and reflected the influence of Wieland Wagner. Hall had been to Bayreuth in the late 1950s and had admired the way in which light was used instead of elaborate sets and costumes. Later Hall was to tire of this style in which less was supposed to mean more; his work became increasingly naturalistic, and his passion for the true text, inspired by the teaching of F. R. Leavis at Cambridge, became almost obsessive.

When Hall left the Royal Shakespeare Company in 1968, exhausted after organising its expansion into the Aldwych Theatre in London, he diversified, making films and taking opera seriously for the first time. He worked with Solti again on a number of new productions at Covent Garden: *Eugene Onegin*, *The Magic Flute* and *Tristan und Isolde*, though the experience did not endear him to the ways of great metropolitan opera houses. For instance, Birgit Nilsson had been engaged to sing two performances, and Hall was responsible for acquainting her with the production. He had rather less time in which to do this than Nilsson took to sing the part: 'She didn't want to hear about motive, just to know where she stood. It was neither creative nor interesting, though it was efficient.' After

Following page: Solti and Hall; amicable discussion masks the tension after a stage rehearsal of *Siegfried*, Act II.

producing Michael Tippett's *The Knot Garden* at Covent Garden in 1970, Hall decided to concentrate on festival work, and in the following decade he directed seven operas at Glyndebourne (including Mozart's three operas with libretti by Da Ponte, and Beethoven's *Fidelio*). These productions were notable for their scrupulous loyalty to the text and the uncommonly high quality of the acting. Moreover, singers were cast only if they looked the part and were willing to rehearse for a great deal longer than four hours. But Hall was aware that outside Glyndebourne those standards would rarely be applied. 'Everyone who administers a theatre is concerned for efficiency, budget controls and the quiet life. That is the law of theatre production, whether they are conscious of it or not. The job of the director and designer, on the other hand, is to push towards the limits of the possible, especially in an opera house. If you actually listen, from day one of a production, to everything everybody tells you about the effect of the budget on the cast, the set and the technical possibilities, you will end up with a third-rate cast, sitting in a straight line on a bare stage with no costumes, no wigs, and no lights.' His own experience as an administrator made him, if anything, even more demanding as a director.

Hall's love-hate relationship with Wagner began when he saw the first post-war *Ring* cycle at Covent Garden in the late 1940s. Though Hall found the music intriguing, he decided that the man was intolerable. 'When I read about Wagner on Judaism, I found the anti-semitism pitiful, repulsive, crazy. I realised that all Wagner's critical writing was simplistic and over-inflated; it contained none of the contradictions and ambiguities that appear in his creative work. But today when I get really uneasy with Wagner, I remember D. H. Lawrence's dictum: never trust the artist, trust the tale.'

Directing *Tristan* in 1970, Hall awoke to Wagner's musical brilliance. 'I began to understand what that highly emotional, illustrative style was about. Previously I had thought it debased, because Wagner, without knowing it, fathered all those middle-Europeans who wrote incidental music for Hollywood. Listen to *Gone with the Wind* – all the illustrative music, the rain on the window or the blowing wind, is derived from Wagner. I also began to think that post-war productions that exposed the dialectic and told us that the *Ring* was about human beings rather than gods had lost a lot of the musical energy in Wagner.'

Hall had known instinctively that he would do the *Ring* one day. He and Solti had talked about this during his Covent Garden years, when they discovered a mutual yearning for a production that would dispense with abstract sets. When Hall became director of production at Covent Garden in 1970, his name was confidently written into the planning schedule for the new *Ring* that Sir Colin Davis was to conduct in the mid-1970s. But the relationship between Hall and the Royal Opera House did not flourish, so Goetz Friedrich took his place and Hall went off to direct the National Theatre. Hall was later asked to direct the *Ring* in Berlin, but pleaded overwork. He gave the same excuse when Wolfgang Wagner asked him if he would like to direct *Parsifal* at Bayreuth, despite the offer to work in a festival environment like Glyndebourne's, where committed singers, musicians and stage staff work intensively in surroundings that offer no distractions, which Hall believes to be the only satisfying way of directing opera.

Hall saw Colin Davis's Covent Garden *Ring* and heard a couple of parts of the cycle conducted by Karajan at the Metropolitan Opera in New York. He also heard a great deal about Chéreau's Bayreuth production, and he began to reconsider his own view of the *Ring*. 'I decided it is unnecessary to tell the audience that the Rhinegold is the means of production; or to make it obvious that Wotan is destroyed by his lust for power; that's evident. There is a tendency to perversity in opera, which is natural enough because there are only about forty works that are played regularly, and in order to make their mark directors tend to become extreme. I despise extremism for its own sake. Admittedly, if I'd done the *Ring* in the late 1960s I would have been more interested in Wotan as a study in the corruption of power, because I don't think I would have trusted then what I realised later: that I would like a twelve-year-old to understand what is happening. Most twelve-year-olds watching the *Ring*s I've seen wouldn't have the slightest idea.

'Wieland and Wolfgang directed abstract *Ring*s to make people understand the basic psychology of Wagner's work, and Chéreau's political *Ring* was a reaction to that. The *Ring* I began to visualise was a corrective to fashion and history – a reaction to Chéreau. I wanted to see a *Ring* based on nature, about the weather, about rain, and clouds, water and mountain tops, and fire. Of course, I am still interested in the political side of the *Ring*, but it's been so over-emphasised that we've forgotten the sensual and sexual side of the work. Siegmund and Sieglinde, for example; they're so erotic that I've often wondered what the Victorians made of the behaviour of brother and sister; if he'd written it in England Wagner would probably have been sent to prison. And when I read the *Ring* I discovered again that the craggy naïveté of the language is all at one with the period in which he wrote it: it is a child's fairy story elevated into an adult myth.'

1980 saw Hall emerging from a difficult period at the National Theatre. The long-delayed move to the new building had been emotionally tiresome and tormented by internal dissensions; the critics had been ungenerous for the first couple of years; and Hall was sniped at continually, inside and outside the theatre, because of his high earnings. (Hall earns a great deal of money by English standards, and he spends an equally large sum. Since the comparative austerity of his childhood, he has indulged a taste for fast and flamboyant cars and expensive homes, but the main financial burden has been an extended family. In 1980 he had four children of two marriages – the first was to the French actress, Leslie Caron – who were being expensively educated; he was responsible for his parents and an ageing aunt who lived at his house in the country; and in 1981, when his second marriage broke up, the alimony payments to Jacky Hall were formidably large. By 1982 he had a third wife, the American opera singer, Maria Ewing, and a fifth child.)

In the 1970s, many members of the theatrical profession and some London newspapers were critical of people like Hall who have an appetite for creative power. Some were content to make a living from, or guardedly to appreciate, the organisations he had played a major part in developing: the Royal Shakespeare Company and the National Theatre. But when Hall was knighted for his services to the theatre in 1977, the honour was regarded by his opponents as confirmation that he had joined the establishment. The mask of stoic unconcern that Hall wears for his public performances rarely slipped, but the fierceness of the criticism upset him.

By 1980 he was actually beginning to look his age. For years he had retained the boyish features of his youth, but by then his hair was thinning, his beard was grizzled, and he was finally putting on weight, a fact often revealed by his preference for poloneck sweaters. Though Hall still had a proprietorial commitment to the National Theatre, he was anxious for a change, and the *Ring* would certainly provide that. Within two months of accepting Solti's offer he was beginning to wonder whether it was the kind of change he wanted. Late in August 1980 Hall went to Bayreuth to watch the last performance of Chéreau's *Ring*. He did not wait until the end of the ninety-minute ovation after *Götterdämmerung*, but left at once, appalled by the scale of his undertaking. He was shortly to direct the *Oresteia* at the National, the company's most ambitious production ever, and the *Ring* was three times as long.

From Bayreuth, Hall went directly to Roccamare, where he and Solti were to outline to Wolfgang Wagner their conception of the

1983 production and discuss terms and conditions for their work. Valerie Solti remembers Hall picking at his croissant at breakfast and announcing that they must both be quite mad. Solti and Hall agreed that the only method that would make their working lives tolerable was to produce *Das Rheingold* and *Die Walküre* in the first year; followed by *Siegfried* and *Götterdämmerung* in the second year. 'We thought we might just force Wagner to do it that way,' Hall recalls. But Wagner adamantly refused to compromise one of Bayreuth's inflexible traditions: three cycles of all four works had to be done in one summer, he insisted. 'We tried a stand off, and said we would not do it, but then Georg said we must, so we did,' Hall says. Despite the flurry, the meeting with Wagner was amiable enough, and, mad or not, they were finally committed. Hall described the occasion as the Treaty of Roccamare – surely one of the first treaties signed before hostilities commenced.

The two teams at the Soltis' home; l. to r. Solti and Hall, Wolfgang Wagner and Frau Gudrun Wagner, who interprets and takes notes.

An early meeting at the National Theatre, London. Hall, Solti and Dudley refer to a recording of an earlier production.

There was one more position to fill: they wanted a designer capable of realising on stage their naturalistic *Ring* with real water, real fire, real trees, a horse that looked like a horse, and a carriage drawn by two splendid rams. Normally Hall gave no thought to his designer; he had worked with John Bury since his Stratford days, and virtually every production he had done at the National or at Glyndebourne had been done with Bury. They understand each other perfectly; Hall says that he can do more with Bury in thirty seconds as they pass each other in a corridor, than he can with other designers in half a day. Their work together had a distinctive style, spare, dark and architectural. No one ever described it as romantic.

Solti had told Hall in June that he did not want a production distinguished by shades of black, and it was clear to Hall that Solti did not feel Bury was the man to design the *Ring*. This caused Hall acute embarrassment, because he had always assumed that he would be collaborating with Bury and the scale of the *Ring* made an intimate understanding with his designer vital. Hall turned to Bury himself for advice. 'John said to me: "I think I've got a *Ring* in me, but it's a 1960s *Ring*. I can't seem to think of anything after that. If you've got a really strong lead you can give me, then I could do it. But you know what you're going to get from me, and I don't think it's what you want." And I knew it wasn't.'

40

Repertory work at the National Theatre and the Royal Shakespeare Company had spawned a new generation of British designers whose work was realistic, colourful and ingenious. William Dudley was one of them. Though Hall had never worked with him, he had encouraged Dudley at the National, where his designs for a series of mystery plays, entitled *The Passion*, were an international success. Dudley was familiar with the inside of opera houses too: by 1980, when he was thirty-three, he had already worked at Covent Garden, the Metropolitan in New York, Hamburg, and Glyndebourne, where his director was Peter Wood, who gave Dudley an excellent reference when Hall asked for one. Moreover, the *Ring* was not unknown to Dudley: in 1978, he had been asked by Peter Hemmings, the new administrator of the Sydney Opera in Australia, to design their new *Ring*. Dudley's work for Sydney had been influenced by the English illustrator, Arthur Rackham, whose drawings tell the story of the *Ring* simply and clearly. But shortly after Dudley's arrival in Sydney, Hemmings was unceremoniously sacked, and Dudley, as he puts it, 'was thrown out with the bathwater'.

Hall alerted Solti, who saw Dudley's designs for *The Undiscovered Country*, a play by Arthur Schnitzler at the National, and for a stunning production of *The Tales of Hoffman* at Covent Garden, and was entirely satisfied by what he saw. In mid-August 1980 Dudley was working at the National on a float that the National Theatre was taking to the Edinburgh Festival as a piece of self-advertisement; the vehicle was to look like a funfair, with places for a band in which Dudley would play the accordion and Hall, disguised by a moustache, was to be the piano player. 'Peter came out to see it in front of the National and said to me: "Have you got a minute? I've got a little project on."' Hall's little project was the Bayreuth *Ring*; he wondered whether the idea appealed to Dudley. 'My knees literally trembled,' Dudley recalls. He blurted out that of course, yes, he was interested, but there was an obstacle. After the débâcle in Australia, Dudley had agreed to design a new *Ring* at the English National Opera which was also scheduled for 1983. Dudley went to David Pountney, the director, and asked what he should do. 'You don't have any choice do you?' replied Pountney. Dudley was the second member of the team who took the job because he felt Bayreuth's reputation gave him no choice but to say yes.

5

Bill Dudley: designing a thinking man's pantomime

His programme credit reads 'William Dudley', but he is a Bill, not a William. It might not be possible to hear the sound of Bow Bells in Islington, where Dudley was born in 1947, but he is nevertheless Cockney, ebullient, witty, disorganised and casual with the English language. His eyes are blue, his expression cheerful, and his most remarkable feature is thick, black eyebrows that meet in the middle. His father is now a plumber, who occasionally asks modestly of well-heeled clients whether they have heard of his son, William. When Dudley was a child, his father had been a jack-of-all-trades, and the one that most intrigued him had been his father's spell as a stagehand at the Finsbury Park Empire, a music-hall theatre that did not survive the 1960s. That first spark of interest in the theatre flared when Dudley saw Gilbert and Sullivan at Sadler's Wells, but the truly formative influence on him was Lionel Bart's *Oliver*. Aged eleven, Dudley took the 19 bus into the West End five times to queue for a gallery seat. He would have liked to audition for a part as one of the Cockney urchins, but he was too chubby to be a convincing waif, and eventually it was the *Oliver* sets that left the greatest impression. Designed by Sean Kenny, an Irishman who had studied architecture briefly with Frank Lloyd Wright, they revealed unsuspected visual possibilities in the theatre, both to Kenny's contemporaries and to impressionable young theatregoers like Dudley.

He started to build his own stage models at home, and tolerated his local comprehensive school only as the means through which he could get a place in art school. But Dudley found himself out of

Facing page: Dudley in the design studio at Bayreuth, August 1982.

sympathy with the St Martin's School of Art, which was trapped by the prevailing passion for abstraction and where his hero, J. M. W. Turner, was insufficiently appreciated. Academic theorising about painting made him impatient; he thought it should be a popular art form. He supplemented his own student income by painting realistic portraits and landscapes from photographs. Later he went on to study stage design at the Slade as a postgraduate.

As a boy, working in the local Canonbury Bookshop, he had been steered towards the Tower Theatre, an excellent amateur repertory company that was then an important part of the small fringe of London theatre. At the Tower he began to act, and to help with painting and building the scenery. Much of the time when he should have been at St Martin's he spent working on sets for Tower Theatre productions, for he found theatrical design an agreeable fusion of sculpture, painting and literature. Dudley's generation was the first to be completely liberated from the box sets of traditional West End designers. Their painting was what is called post-modernist – colourful, related to what people see, and influenced by artists like David Hockney; their stage models were meticulously sculpted, with the latest technological and engineering devices enthusiastically adopted.

The stage-design course at the Slade ends with an exhibition of student work, and Dudley wrote to forty directors suggesting that they might like to come to see his exhibits. Of the three who did, one was Anthony Page who was sufficiently impressed by Dudley's student work to ask him to design *Hamlet* at the Nottingham Playhouse. When the production was seen in London's West End, Dudley was hired by the Royal Court, where he designed three productions before going to the National Theatre to work with the designer Jocelyn Herbert and the director John Dexter. Before long, Dexter asked Dudley to design Britten's *Billy Budd* in Hamburg.

One of Dudley's many childhood ambitions was to be a marine artist; he loved the grace of ships and the folklore of the sea, so he was acquainted with the story of *Billy Budd*. But he did not know the music. He played it the night before he left for Hamburg. 'I'd hardly heard of Britten; I didn't even know whether he was still alive. I had an absolute hatred of opera. I believed Ken Tynan's assertion that it was a dead nineteenth-century art form in which great fat ladies bellowed at each other.' His conversion took place in Hamburg. 'Dexter kept me there for six weeks, and I'd stand in the wings every night and watch. There were lots of productions passing through, including Wieland Wagner's *Flying Dutchman*, and Wolfgang's *Siegfried*. I found I loved it when the full force hit, though it

Dudley in the studio of his London home. November 1982; experiments with designs for the movements of Brünnhilde's horse.

took me a lot of time to get into Wagner. I found during his operas that there would come a point when I couldn't take the human voice any more, particularly when the soprano had been too high for too long.'

Dudley's conversion to Wagner was gradual, and never quite complete. He saw the *Ring* at the English National Opera in 1977, before flying to Australia to work on the abortive production. 'The thing that makes Wagner at all interesting to me is the musical expression of nature. People who know about music say that Wagner is the father of modern music, but I find him locked into mid-nineteenth-century romanticism. People call him a fluke, but I find it peculiar how many British poets and painters, particularly Turner, express what I feel is the essence of the *Ring*. Beyond that, I don't mind admitting I'm not bothered to read Wagner's writings or many commentaries on the *Ring*, apart from Ernest Newman's *Wagner Nights*. I started reading Donington [Robert Donington's psychoanalytic account of the *Ring* entitled *Wagner's Ring and its Symbols*], but it meant little to me.

'The things that trigger me in the *Ring* are the first scene of *Rheingold*, where you've got to put your cards on the table, as Chéreau did. That's the best set of his whole *Ring*, his strongest, clearest statement. Then the end of *Götterdämmerung* with the immolation of the gods in Valhalla. Very few directors attempt to do the ending properly, but you've got to make that one of your priorities; whatever you do early on, you've got to top it at the end. And the Ride of the Valkyries is a big moment. I suspect it is the big moments that capture the audience, not the endless analyses of the motives of the characters. I've listened to people talking about the choices open to Wotan, and it doesn't interest me. I think Jonathan Miller was clever when he called the *Ring* a Teutonic version of the Archers.'

I reminded Dudley that one day in Bayreuth, when he had been looking at models of the designs, he had called the *Ring* 'the thinking man's panto', which definition I liked better than Miller's. 'I stand by that, assuming you think pantomime is to delight and inspire awe in children. I think too many productions intellectualise the *Ring*, making it into a three-dimensional chess game where you find political, religious or absurdist equivalents. If Ken Russell were to set the *Ring* in Angel Tube Station, nobody would ask "why?", because they'd be afraid of missing the point and being thought reactionary.'

When Solti grasped that this was Dudley's approach to the Bayreuth *Ring*, he was confident that Hall had made the right choice. But before Solti met Dudley, he asked Charles Kaye, a lean, long devotee of the maestro who works as his assistant and lives near Dudley in Greenwich, to pop round to Dudley's house to obtain some specimens of his work. 'Charles Kaye was very grand, and I was in awe of Solti,' Dudley said, 'but I'd taken a decision a year earlier, after showing my drawings to John Schlesinger, director of *The Tales of Hoffman*, that nobody needed to see my work any more. My *curriculum vitae* is the shows I've done at Covent Garden, Glyndebourne, the National and the RSC.' This is not a mark of Dudley's vanity, for he has none, but he is decidedly stubborn. Solti therefore asked Dudley to join him for supper in his substantial late-Victorian house in St John's Wood. Hall wrote to Dudley before the meeting: 'Solti is a deeply instinctive fellow. All you have to do is to be yourself.' Solti then surprised Dudley by hardly talking about the *Ring* at all; he wanted to know instead about the work Dudley had done, his background, his parents.

The next time Dudley went to St John's Wood, it was with Peter Hall and Solti was in exuberant form, leaping from the sofa to the piano to illustrate musical themes in the *Ring*. Dudley was enchanted, for the conductors of most of the productions he had done had either been too busy (at Covent Garden, Colin Davis spoke his first words to Dudley as they went to take their bows on the first night), or had lived abroad. Discussing the quality of realism he hoped for, Dudley said he would design trees that look like trees; but Hall topped that. He stated that in Scene One of *Das Rheingold* the Rhinemaidens must swim in real water; that would be putting their cards on the table, all right. Solti was delighted; the idea had been in his mind too. None of them questioned whether real water was possible, whether it would make too much noise, or how they would get rid of it: designers are expected to overcome such problems. And none of them realised that such a simple extravagance would dictate the style of the whole production.

It was all very well to say 'real water', but Richard Wagner did not envisage anything so straightforward as Rhinemaidens gambolling on the surface. They had to be seen to be swimming *in* it, as the introduction to *Das Rheingold* made clear. Dudley first flirted with the idea of a very large glass tank in which the Rhinemaidens would swim underwater, surfacing only for air and an aria. It was never necessary, however, to put the singers to any such test, since, from a quick calculation of the weight of glass and water, it was obvious that the stage would not bear it. The next idea was more promising. He would have to create the illusion of a stage full of water, and brooding on this he recalled a Victorian stage trick called Pepper's

Ghost, which was used to give the impression that a man was seated in a chair that had been vacant a moment before. Dudley's instinct, plus a memory of schoolboy optics, told him that a solution might lie in a reflecting mirror, rather like the one used in Pepper's Ghost. Flown in at an angle of 45 degrees above the stage, the mirror ought to create the illusion that people on the stage floor, who in fact were moving backwards and forwards, were moving up and down. If those people were Rhinemaidens in a shallow tank of water, they ought to look as though they were swimming from the bottom to the surface, and the audience would have the impression that they were looking at a vertical wall of water.

Dudley tested the idea in a model tank with a sloping mirror, and Hall tinkered delightedly with it as though it were a Christmas present. But the illusion would have to be subjected to a more rigorous test, and Hall suggested I might like to come along to the Comedy Theatre in London early one morning in October 1981 to see the idea tried out. The play at the Comedy, called *Steaming*, had a small pool on stage suitable for a practical test of Dudley's concept for swimming Rhinemaidens.

An Australian singer called Robyn Archer, hired for the occasion, was waiting on stage in a black costume, and Bill Dudley had rigged a wooden frame containing a piece of stretched perspex at an angle of 45 degrees above the pool. Hall settled himself in the first row of the stalls and called out to Robyn Archer: 'Will you swim around on your back and sing something?' Then he sat back and said to no one in particular: 'This really is the crunch.' Shortly after she began to sing 'You're so Sagacious Solomon', Robyn Archer swallowed a mouthful of water, but the effect was already clear. As she swam back and forth, she appeared in the mirror to be diving to the bottom of the pool and rising to the top. Having been lit, the water shimmered as she moved, making Dudley cry out with pleasure at an unexpected bonus.

Solti, arriving after an hour, declared that the Pepper's Ghost idea was 'really spooky', but his own preoccupations were not entirely visual. He wanted to listen to changes in sound level; retiring to the back of the stalls and closing his eyes, he detected a change in the voice level, but it was so marginal that no one else could hear it. That was no problem, he announced. Now he wanted to know how he would see the swimming Rhinemaidens from the conductor's podium. Hall replied that the singers would have to follow him by watching television monitors. 'You are saying they would have to sing to television screens? It is not without dangers. For a whole act I would be worried,' said Solti. The two briefly discussed the

Facing page: The concept of swimming Rhinemaidens seen in a mirror is tested for the first time. Robyn Archer in the pool of *Steaming*, Comedy Theatre, London, October 1982.

possibilities of using doubles: having swimmers in the tank while the actual singers stood offstage with a clear view of Solti. But Hall preferred not to discuss doubles; they were a concession he would rather not make. And Solti did not argue. He left the theatre announcing: 'The visual effect is very, very good. I would give anything if we could get this effect.' As we trailed out after Solti, I asked Hall what Wolfgang Wagner thought of the idea. 'I don't think they believe it yet. They think we're mad.' Hall added casually that this feeling might be reinforced when he told Wagner that he wanted Rhinemaidens who would not only swim, but swim naked too.

Realisation of the swimming Rhinemaidens concept. Diana Montague and Agnes Habereder, Bayreuth, July 1983.

There was a more substantial problem than any incredulity on Wolfgang Wagner's part, however. Richard Wagner's stage directions indicated that the transition from the bottom of the Rhine (Scene One of *Das Rheingold*) to the mountain heights (Scene Two) should be made during an orchestral interlude lasting two minutes and forty-five seconds. Moreover, the Bayreuth tradition is that the curtain should not come down during the scene change; the theatrical term for this is 'changing in view'. Dudley had calculated that the weight of the water in the tank covering the Bayreuth forestage would be thirty tons: clearly there was no way the tank could be emptied and the scene set for a mountain top in less than three minutes. Hall made a virtue out of the difficulty, telling Dudley that changing in view had a purpose, as had most of Wagner's stage directions: it was intended to create the impression of a dynamic journey upwards through the elements.

The theory was fine, but Dudley found a practical solution hard to come by. He normally works fast. 'With other directors I get the concept over dinner, or in two quick sessions when the ideas go bang, bang, bang, like a game of tennis. But I was floundering. I thought: "So this is what the *Ring* does to you."' Dudley showed Hall some sketches in which the water was covered by a flat surface, and Hall's reaction was that nature is round. 'Think of curves,' he said. He was preaching to the converted. Dudley loves air travel, because of the view of the clouds, the mountain peaks, and, best of all, the curvature of the earth seen from a height of 30,000 feet. He admired the sense of space created in science-fiction film-fantasies like *Star Wars* ('the best pantomime I've ever seen,' he says). Walking through the backlot of Pinewood Studios one summer day in 1981 he saw how film-makers create a distant view of the planet. Instead of a whole sphere, they build only part of one, curved like part of a sausage, and cut square at each end. When filmed, it looks like a very distant horizon of the earth. Dudley toyed with the idea, and out of Meccano made a scale model, powered by a primitive engine, of a platform that curved softly on two planes. Such a mobile platform could settle over the water tank and give the impression that the gods bestrode the world. It was a neat solution.

Dudley was concerned that a platform might be reminiscent of the abstract *Ring*s of the 1950s; after all, Wieland and Wolfgang had each used a mobile platform. But he decided he could contradict any sense of abstraction by using scenery that looked real, like his trees. Solti did not complain when Dudley demonstrated his creaky model, and Hall was entirely persuaded. He had always said that the *Ring* was about two people talking to each other for thirty

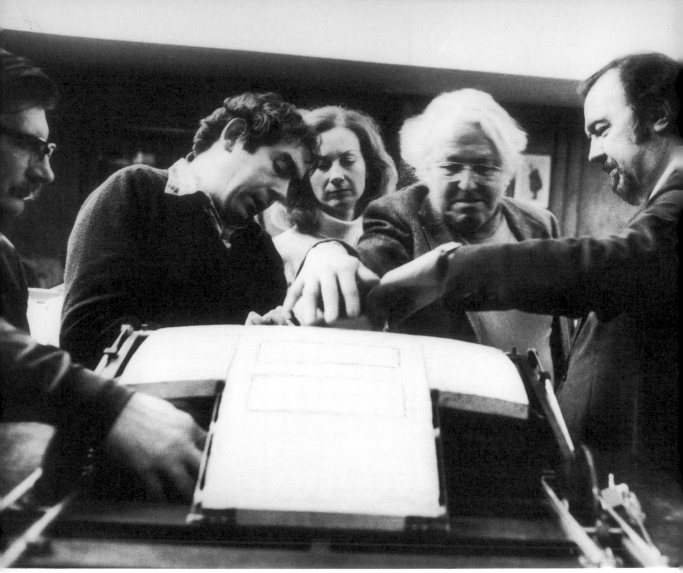

Dudley and Hall demonstrate the first working model of the platform, with a sliding centre section, to Wagner and Frau Wagner, December 1981.

minutes and then turning the world upside down; the platform might be a means of illustrating that idea visually. But the platform meant engineering work, and before committing themselves to it they had to find out whether it was technically feasible.

One man in England could answer that question: Mike Barnett, a hydraulic engineer, a member of the Institute of Mechanical Engineers, and author of a thesis entitled *Current Practices and Some Recent Developments in the Design of Theatrical Stage Machinery*. Barnett, a small, talkative, busy man, foresaw no fundamental engineering problems in making Dudley's platform work. It would be raised and lowered by a scissor-like mechanism driven by hydraulic power. Hydraulics are an old and well-tried idea in the

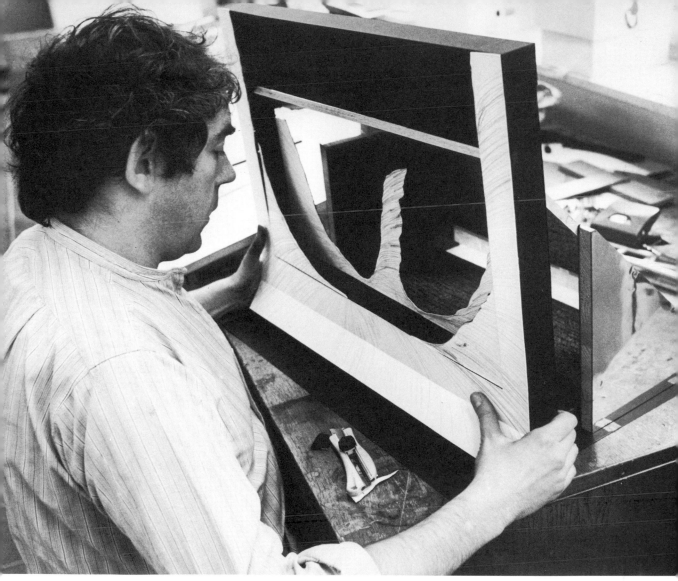

Dudley makes the model of an early design for *Das Rheingold*, Scene 1; design studio Bayreuth, August 1982.

theatre, having first been used for moving scenery in Booth's Theatre in New York in 1876, the same year as Richard Wagner's Bayreuth *Ring* premiere. Indeed, the basic technique was so simple that Dudley asked Barnett to incorporate more complex movements in the design, enabling the platform to move backwards and forwards as well as up and down. Barnett told Dudley of an artful device much used in the streets of London for hauling skips of rubble on to trucks; a version of that would do the job. Encouraged, Dudley next asked Barnett to design a platform that would turn the world upside down by rotating through 270 degrees. This was more ambitious, Barnett replied, but he would try and incorporate Dudley's ideas in a detailed working model.

The platform in use in its convex form, seen backstage during the setting of a stage cloth.

So Dudley's simple platform, first intended only to cover the tank of water in *Das Rheingold*, became a machine that could be used in all four parts of the cycle; on forestage or backstage; high up towards the flytower; in its convex form as the top of the earth where Wotan rules; when concave, as the inside of the earth where characters like Alberich, Mime and Hunding struggle for power. Furthermore, Barnett promised that the platform would be slim, like the wing of an aircraft; strong enough to bear the weight of some of the chorus as well as just the soloists; and lifted by two graceful hydraulic arms. For Dudley, the platform had two other virtues. He believed it would look like a mobile sculpture, especially under lights; and it would help him overcome problems with the backstage facilities in Bayreuth, which have great depth but little space in the wings, and a limited number of lifts in the stage floor. 'The Festspielhaus is basically ill-equipped to stage Wagner,' says Dudley, blithely uttering a heresy. The platform would be expensive, but that didn't worry Dudley; it would be worth whatever it cost.

Having settled on the water tank and the platform, Hall wrote to Wolfgang Wagner in the autumn of 1981 to suggest a meeting in London early in December. 'The designs will not be finished, but at least you will be able to see the direction in which we are moving. I'm very excited by it, though I think it poses enormous technical problems.' Dudley ought to have been elated, but was, on the contrary, very unhappy. Solti did not like his design for Covent Garden's new production of *Don Giovanni*, which opened in July 1981. He asked Dudley to call on him the day after he had seen it, and the occasion remains vivid in Dudley's memory: 'He floored me. He said that my *Don Giovanni* was the worst design he'd seen anywhere in the world. I thought "I really don't need this, it's a waste of time. I should be getting on with the *Ring*." But Solti didn't know what a bad way I was in that summer. It shattered the relationship we'd developed during our meetings. I was so depressed I had to go to the doctor and get some pills.'

By December Dudley's basic models of the stage and some of the sets, of the platform and the water tank, were ready for inspection. Wagner, accompanied by his wife, Gudrun, and Bayreuth's technical director, Walter Huneke, travelled to Solti's house to see them mounted in the conductor's studio. Lights fused; the models were not easy to manoeuvre; everyone seemed on edge; Solti, Hall and Dudley were evidently tired. Wagner was affable, though he did not say whether he liked the models. Instead he peppered Dudley with questions. How would the tank be filled with water? How would it be emptied silently? How much would it weigh? The inference was that the tank would be too heavy and the water too noisy. When they turned to the platform model, a strange Heath-Robinson device of wood and wires that needed two men to operate it, his questions began again. Might the platform slope too much for the performers to be able to stand and sing comfortably? What impact would it have on Bayreuth's delicate acoustic? Huneke's question seemed the one asked most feelingly, however: how much was it all going to cost? The model alone – paid for by Dudley – had come to £3,500: the real thing was obviously not going to be cheap. Barnett said he thought it could be built in England for approximately £100,000.

All the previous questions and arguments had been delivered by Wolfgang in German and answered by Dudley and Hall in English, which added to the confusion. Hall had had every intention of learning German, as he had told Wagner he would when they had first met in 1980, and he had begun to take lessons, but they were overwhelmed by his crowded schedule and were dropped. Consequently, though Hall could understand much of the German that was spoken to him, he did not speak it. Or rather he would not speak it, for he dreaded making a fool of himself by misusing a language he did not fully understand. Dudley knew even less German. However, they were both able to catch the tone of the barrage of questions which created a perceptible raising of tension. Solti tried to break it by saying to Wagner: 'When the audience see this, they won't even listen to the music,' and went on, jovially, to suggest that if Wolfgang was worried about the cost, he should cut the orchestra. Neither Wagner nor Dudley seemed notably more relaxed by this. Dudley, often intense, confessed later that he was surprised he did not have a breakdown that day. As the meeting ended, Hall said Wagner should take the plans away and decide whether Bayreuth could afford it: if they couldn't, he and Dudley would have to start all over again. But Hall told me after that meeting that he thought it was too late to ditch the tank and the platform. I wondered whether he wasn't, perhaps, being too sanguine.

An early stage rehearsal for *Das Rheingold*, Scene 1. Hermann Becht (Alberich) and Birgitta Svendén (Flosshilde).

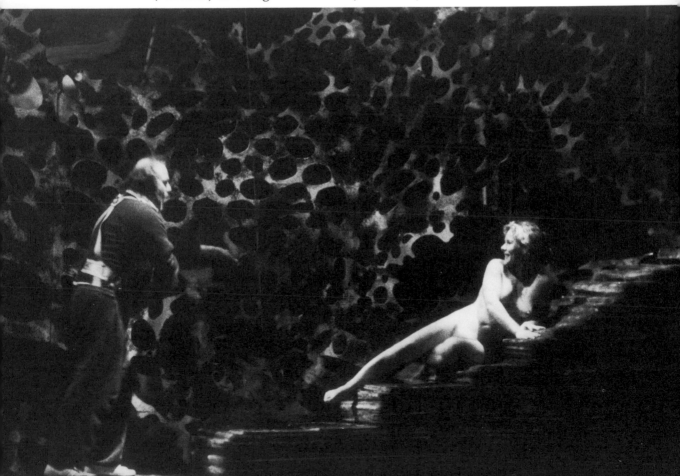

6

Casting: taking tremendous risks

The task of casting the *Ring* is a formidable one, though Richard Wagner knew exactly what performers of the *Ring* should be like: they should have a beautiful tone, perfect vocal technique, sensitivity to language, and the ability to act. Not content just with singers who reached this peak of professional achievement, Wagner wanted them to have cultured minds as well. One of the innumerable frustrations that beset him, not surprisingly, was his inability to find enough singers to do justice to his work. His music actually created a new category of operatic performer, the Wagnerian singer so beloved of cartoonists. The substantial soprano whose torso is covered by breastplates, and the tenor with horned helmet, are both figures from the *Ring*.

When Wolfgang Wagner met his 1983 *Ring* team at Solti's house in December 1981, many parts were still uncast. Some thirty soloists are called on during a complete cycle, and balancing the voices correctly is a complicated business. Wolfgang Wagner was beginning to fret as Christmas 1981 approached, and might well have recalled a dictum of his grandfather: 'Really good singers are so scarce, and so much sought after, that only a quick decision can secure them.' Solti and Hall had deliberately narrowed the field of choice by deciding not to use singers who had worked in the Boulez–Chéreau *Ring*. 'I fervently believe, and so does Wagner, that you must create constant new singing generations, but that is easier said than done,' says Solti. Solti and Hall had agreed in Roccamare in September 1980 not only to seek new voices but to choose performers who would look the parts they were singing – which narrowed the field even more. Hall's notes taken during auditions define what was unacceptable: one singer was 'a fat Edward Woodward'; a second 'a warthog'; the beautiful voice of a third was

The production teams meet in the Conference Room at Bayreuth, chaired by Wolfgang Wagner with Frau Wagner. l. Mostart, Hall, Dudley; r. Kottke, Huneke and McCaffery.

ruined by her being 'physically knotted up'. Solti's own comments reflect Hall's preoccupation: 'First class voice, but the figure – PH wouldn't have it.'

The part that troubled them most was Siegfried. Again, the composer would have sympathised. 'I am likely to be driven to despair by the, as yet, irremediable reason for the impossibility of giving my work – the lack of a *Heldentenor*,' Richard Wagner wrote. The heroic, bell-like voices for which Wagner wrote his leading tenor parts were no more common a century later. Indeed, Herbert von Karajan had announced magisterially that there existed no decent *Heldentenors* at all, since if there were any, he would know of them. Intense physical demands are made on the singer who has to play Siegfried in both *Siegfried* and *Götterdämmerung* within three days, and one way of easing the strain is to cast two singers in the role, each singing one of the operas. Some potential candidates, like the popular German tenors René Kollo, who did not sing *Götterdämmerung*, and Peter Hofmann, who did not sing *Siegfried* at all, were out.

Solti appreciated the musical argument for splitting the role, but he agreed with Hall's feeling that it was dramatic nonsense to have two men sharing the same part.

By comparison, casting Wotan and Brünnhilde is straightforward, and Solti already had a candidate for Brünnhilde before Hall joined him. Hildegard Behrens had demonstrated that she could act as well as sing in parts like Richard Strauss's Salome and Leonora in *Fidelio*; Solti had then heard that she was beginning to include heavier dramatic soprano parts in her repertoire, such as Isolde in Wagner's *Tristan*. By asking Behrens to sing Brünnhilde, Solti was taking a remarkable liberty: most sopranos begin gently with *Die Walküre* one year, add *Siegfried* the next, and complete the process in three years with *Götterdämmerung*. At Bayreuth, Behrens would have to make her debut in all three in one week. Being a bold woman – exactly as Brünnhilde ought to be – Behrens told Solti that she was perfectly happy to try it.

Casting singers is not merely a matter of artistic choice, however. They are booked to sing years in advance, and Behrens was scheduled to sing in Puccini's *Turandot* in Vienna in the summer of 1983. Though rehearsal schedules in Vienna and Bayreuth did not completely overlap, Hall calculated that if Behrens were to sing in Vienna he would not have enough time to work with her in Bayreuth. Solti was surprised by Hall's intransigence in saying that he would not want Behrens if she did not work exclusively in Bayreuth. But Hall explained: 'It's not going to say in the programme: "I'm sorry this production is no good because I didn't have enough time to work with Brünnhilde."' Solti knew of other possible candidates (he thought, for instance, Eva Marton would be excellent, and Jeannine Altmeyer, who sang Sieglinde for Boulez, was about to play the role in San Francisco), but he was still anxious to cast Behrens. He appealed to Lorin Maazel, the music director of the Vienna Staatsoper, to release Behrens from his *Turandot*, and, as a favour to an old friend, Maazel obliged. But the role over which Solti and Hall had had the least doubt had, nonetheless, taken more than a year to cast.

As for Wotan, there is no shortage of good bass-baritones, only of actors capable of achieving the delicate quality of neurotic authority which the role requires. Solti and Wagner both felt that Hans Sotin could sing Wotan, but Hall wanted to see other candidates as well, and Sotin's full schedule for 1983 did not enable him to wait patiently to be chosen. He committed himself elsewhere. By September 1981 the field had narrowed to two candidates: Simon Estes, a commanding black American with a precise baritone voice,

Hubert Kopp, Stage Manager, Wolfgang Wagner and Solti.

and Siegmund Nimsgern, a German singer whom Solti had heard at an audition for *Lohengrin*. Solti and Hall heard them both in one evening in London, and Hall, not greatly impressed by Estes, whose voice, he said, he found 'one-dimensional and dull', was intrigued by the somewhat insecure and narcissistic quality he sensed in Nimsgern. Solti found the voice interesting and strong, a desirable quality in a singer who has to survive three performances in four days.

Hall's friend, John Schlesinger, had worked with Nimsgern in *The Tales of Hoffman* at Covent Garden, as had Bill Dudley. Each had cautionary tales to tell about Nimsgern as a performer. Wagner added to them, suggesting that Nimsgern's concentration would be found wanting in rehearsal. Hall thought these qualifications made Nimsgern sound pretty much like a Wotan, and Solti was confident that he could handle Nimsgern. Having asked him to sing in Haydn's *The Creation* with the Chicago Symphony

Orchestra later in the year, Solti interrogated him at supper afterwards and was persuaded by Nimsgern's spirited self-defence. (Estes took his failure badly, and claimed publicly that he did not get the part because he was black, despite regular denials by Hall and Solti who insisted that they had found the voice insufficiently pleasing. Hall might indeed have been troubled by the idea of a black Wotan surrounded by a large family of white singers; he did not object in principle to a black Wotan, as long as there were black singers among his daughters, but he felt Estes's audition had relieved him of the need to make such a choice.)

Solti had always had a sinking feeling about Siegfried. As the search began, he was pessimistic and philosophical: 'I was quite certain that we wouldn't find anybody, and the project would collapse anyway.' He and Hall clutched briefly at a straw when they heard that the great star of modern opera, the Spanish tenor Placido Domingo, might be about to shift from the Italian to the German repertoire. There was a rumour that Domingo was to sing *Parsifal*, a decision that would have been curious since Domingo's lyric tenor voice, so suited to Verdi and Puccini, would inevitably have had to broaden to the demands of a Wagnerian tenor role. In fact, Domingo had merely been talking about the idea; he did not intend to carry it out. Solti and Hall had to look elsewhere, and the names pencilled in the notes made at Roccamare were unpromising: this one was too old, that one too young, a third was a slow learner, and a fourth had too light a voice to cope with *Götterdämmerung*.

Later, in the summer of 1981, a friend of Solti's suggested he should listen to an East German who was just beginning to sing in the West. This was Reiner Goldberg, aged thirty-eight, who had been discovered while he was still working in a welding shop at Crostau. He had served a long musical apprenticeship in Dresden and East Berlin, and his repertory included Wagnerian *Heldentenor* parts like Walther in *Die Meistersinger*, Siegmund in *Die Walküre* and Tannhäuser. Wagner was unenthusiastic when Solti mentioned Goldberg, but with Siegfrieds so scarce it seemed churlish not to listen to him, and an audition was arranged in Bayreuth in August 1981. Singers are heard late at night, when the performance is finished, and Solti was already yawning as he sat with Hall and Wagner in the darkened auditorium. When Goldberg appeared under stage lights none of them recognised a Siegfried: he was balding, had glasses, and wore an old tweed jacket. Hall thought he looked like a bank clerk; Solti was reminded of a civil servant. Then

Goldberg sang, and Bill Dudley, sitting there too, says he has rarely seen such excitement in the theatre. Solti reported later: 'When he opened his mouth, I sat up. I said to Wagner: "That's it. I take risk." I didn't, at that point, know what a tremendous risk.' Hall admired the voice too, though he realised that it would take a great deal of skill to transform a bank clerk into Siegfried, the boy who knows no fear. He rationalised his acceptance of Goldberg with the thought that his evident naïveté might not be unlike the young Siegfried's. And he asked for more time to rehearse Goldberg than the other principals. Goldberg was nearly scratched from the cast because of an engagement to sing in Japan with the Berlin Staatsoper during the first week of rehearsals in Bayreuth. Only by juggling with both their schedules did Hall manage to obtain the minimum length of rehearsal time he believed was necessary.

By the end of 1981 only three more roles had been cast. Solti and Hall had broken their self-imposed rule by asking Hermann Becht, a most capable Alberich (the Nibelung who steals the Rhinemaiden's gold) in the Boulez–Chéreau *Ring*, to repeat his performance for them; excluding Becht would have been cutting off their noses to spite their faces. In the Bayreuth auditions they had heard Peter Haage, a good tenor who acted well and who was pencilled in as Mime, Alberich's hapless brother. Hall had hankered after an English singer, Robert Tear, as Mime because he found the part unsympathetic and thought it would be easier to direct a singer who spoke the same language as he did, but by the time Tear had extricated himself from his engagements for the summer of 1983, Wagner had confirmed to Haage that the part was his. It was a misunderstanding Hall had no cause to regret. One more German tenor was enlisted that summer. A few years before, Siegfried Jerusalem had been a bassoonist in the Stuttgart Radio Symphony Orchestra; then he discovered that he had a fine tenor voice and could act, and whoever heard of a bassoon player who regularly earns a few thousand dollars a performance? Jerusalem was keen to sing Siegmund, but Solti said he would rather have him as the god of fire, Loge, a lighter tenor part in *Das Rheingold*. 'You'll be wonderful,' Solti said, using the sole adjective he deploys for singers he likes.

But, with so little of the *Ring* cast by January 1982, the pressure was growing from Bayreuth. For instance, Wolfgang Wagner insisted that they must hurry if they wanted Brigitte Fassbaender to sing Waltraute in the long scene with her sister Brünnhilde in *Götterdämmerung*. So they hurried. Wagner could probably have cast the entire 1983 *Ring* from his unique files of Wagnerian singers in no time at all, but Solti still counselled patience. He believed that if he waited until he heard the right voice for a role, the fact that *he* was the conductor would be a sufficient incentive for singers to reorganise their plans. Generally, he was quite correct. He heard dozens of singers in 1982 between January and October; many were politely discarded. I thought this process should be described by explaining why singers were or were not chosen. I suggested to Solti that the fact that they had been considered worth listening to at an audition would surely have helped rather than hurt their careers. But Solti is reticent about his decisions. 'It is my unfortunate experience,' he wrote in reply, 'especially with singers, that there are very few who are pleased to have it known that they were considered but not selected for a part.' But clues to the way in which Hall and Solti made decisions can be found by looking at the names of those singers they considered but who were *not* available to sing in Bayreuth, even with Sir Georg.

Take, for instance, the case of Siegmund and Sieglinde, the brother and sister whose incestuous relationship in *Die Walküre* tips the gods towards destruction. Solti was intrigued by the idea of pairing René Kollo, a Bayreuth veteran, and Kiri Te Kanawa, the New Zealander who had been a superb Countess in Hall's production of *Figaro* at Glyndebourne. Both are well-established performers in the biggest opera houses, so it was not surprising to discover, in December 1981, that neither would be available. The alternative, therefore, was to find less well-known singers who would make their debuts in Bayreuth. Hall had admired the robust sensuality of an American singer called Dennis Bailey at Glyndebourne the previous summer, and Solti agreed he should be Siegmund. But the problem of Sieglinde was intractable. Solti toyed with the idea of Eva Marton, whom he had thought capable of singing Brünnhilde, but she had been cast by Lorin Maazel in Behrens's place in the Vienna *Turandot*; to poach from him yet again would be adding insult to injury. By the time Solti and Hall had again agreed to relax their rule about not duplicating the Boulez–Chéreau cast and had asked Jeannine Altmeyer to sing Sieglinde, she had accepted the part of Brünnhilde elsewhere in the summer of 1983. Only generous adjustments to the rehearsal schedules in Bavaria and California made her Sieglinde in Bayreuth possible.

Solti waited even longer before casting Gutrune. This is not a big part – she appears only in *Götterdämmerung* – but it is important to Solti who sees Gutrune as the sex symbol of the *Ring* and wanted to hear a suitably sexy voice. Hall said, a little diffidently, that the sexiest voice he knew belonged to his wife-to-be, Maria Ewing, and

in September 1981, when Solti heard her sing, he agreed. Hall was
delighted, since it meant that Maria would be able to spend much of
the summer with him in Bayreuth instead of their being separated
by an engagement Maria had been offered at the Salzburg Festival.

The business of casting the smaller parts is not only complicated
by the dense schedules of international singers, most of whom can
tell you exactly where they will be on a particular day in two or three
years' time; there is also the matter of the correct balance in an
ensemble of voices – among the Rhinemaidens, for instance.
'Because you have to find heavier voices for the second and third
Rhinemaidens, you want a light scintillating voice for the first, and I
got one – Agnes Habereder, a leading dramatic soprano with a
lovely vocal colour scheme. But finding similar, lower voices was
difficult,' says Solti. The second Rhinemaiden, an English singer
called Diana Montague, presented herself in the summer, but the
third proved elusive until Solti heard a young Swedish contralto,

Birgitta Svendén, in October – the last singer to be cast. Normally a conductor's job is to listen to the voices and select the best ensemble; it hardly matters if one Rhinemaiden is fat, another squat, and the third tall – sometimes they are hardly seen at all. But Solti had to choose Rhinemaidens for their looks too. Hall occasionally fretted that Solti was not taking his insistence that the Rhinemaidens swim naked literally. He need not have worried. Solti not only chose slim singers, he conscientiously asked each if she would swim naked. When Diana Montague went to an audition accompanied by her husband, Solti asked him too. And Solti found that his Rhinemaidens were not only willing, but seemed positively to be looking forward to it.

Solti was pleased with his final choice of singers: 'Few flops, *very* few,' he announced during rehearsals. Indeed, whenever he became depressed about this *Ring* and felt like giving up, he would revive his flagging spirits with the thoughts: 'At least they'll have a good cast.' It looked good enough to ensure that Solti was never serious about quitting.

There were crises, of course, between autumn of 1982 and the beginning of rehearsals in the spring of 1983, and the greatest of these was caused by Solti's choice for Siegfried. Reiner Goldberg was cast to sing Tannhäuser in Vienna in October at Lorin Maazel's debut as the new music director at the Staatsoper, a great Viennese occasion. Solti watched the dress rehearsal: 'I went to see my boy, and it was beautiful singing. I came away very pleased saying, "No, I did not make any mistake."' Then disaster struck. On the opening night Goldberg appeared on stage only to disappear again after about five minutes. Later he explained this by saying that he had a virus infection and had agreed to sing against his better judgement. The disaster was widely reported in the European press and caused great anxiety to Solti and Hall. At the same time Bernard Haitink, a friend of Hall's, murmured that he had heard that Goldberg had recently given a poor performance in a recording session.

An understudy had been chosen for Goldberg, Manfred Jung, the tenor who had sung Siegfried in the last cycles of the Boulez–Chéreau *Ring*. The safest course would have been to give the part of Siegfried to Jung then and there, the moment they'd heard about Goldberg's problems in Vienna, but Solti was insistent. 'It was terrible. I talked with Wagner three times on the telephone because, as you can imagine, he was out of his mind with worry. He tried to persuade me to take Jung as Siegfried, and I refused to do that. Then I said to Goldberg he must come and work with me now. He came, two days to London in January. I thought he really seemed to know the part of Siegfried and I came away with a good feeling because for the first time in my life I had heard a singing Siegfried.' They decided to stick with Reiner Goldberg.

Hall knew about the next crisis intimately, since it flowed through his drawing-room. Maria Ewing had been busy in New York and Geneva during the winter, and had a commitment in Paris in the spring. Deciding that she was not spending enough time with their child Rebecca and that singing Gutrune would make things worse, she cancelled. Wagner, not unreasonably, was very angry indeed. Not caring who Maria Ewing was married to, he fired off a telegram to her agent: 'Since no replacement approved of can be found by Georg Solti and Peter Hall relative to the rehearsal schedule I cannot release her from her contract.' Three weeks later, however, the English soprano, Josephine Barstow – who had been looking

Siegfried Jerusalem at a coaching session for *Die Walküre* with Solti; David Syrus at the piano.

forward to an idle summer among the horses on her Sussex farm – was tempted by the idea of singing Wagner in Bayreuth with Solti, and signed on as Gutrune.

The tremors caused by Maria Ewing's departure were offset by Solti's news from the United States in April 1983. He had shrewdly arranged that the Chicago Symphony Orchestra should give three concert performances of *Das Rheingold*, and he reported that Nimsgern as Wotan had been 'wonderful', as had Jerusalem as Loge. But then disaster struck again. A growth had been diagnosed on one of Dennis Bailey's vocal chords; his doctor had ordered him not to sing for nine months and so he would not be able to play Siegmund. The pack would have to be reshuffled. Jerusalem became Siegmund and Manfred Jung, who was Goldberg's understudy and so free for much of the summer, was thrust into the role of Loge. It seemed that, finally, the cast was settled.

7

A tale of three resignations

Just as problems were inevitable while the *Ring* was being cast, there were obviously likely to be difficulties during the simultaneous process of deciding how the production would look. But what Hall and Dudley in London, and Wagner in Bayreuth, experienced cannot accurately be described as tremors. Between December 1981 and April 1983, relations were regularly strained to breaking point.

Moran Caplat, an old friend of Hall's from Glyndebourne where he had been general administrator for a generation, observed: 'Peter doesn't like grand opera. He doesn't like the people who run it, or the dramas they make.' Hall, who is accustomed to running his own theatre his way, is capable of making a fair bit of drama himself. Even so, his clashes with Wolfgang Wagner, and the Welsh temperament Wagner claims to have inherited from his mother, were more combustible than either had expected. The story of that relationship is, perhaps, best characterised by Hall's three threats of resignation.

The first was a shot fired mainly to establish the working conditions Hall required. Bayreuth is more generous with rehearsal time than any other opera house, but then, since a whole new *Ring* cycle is produced in one summer and then performed three times, it has to be. Traditionally rehearsals for a new *Ring* begin on 15 May, ten weeks before the opening night. At Solti's house in December 1981 Hall's assistant director and translator, Guus Mostart, told Gudrun Wagner, Wolfgang's wife, that Hall's method of working dictated a start on 1 May. Mostart is a Dutchman, fluently trilingual in Dutch, English and German. He is in his early thirties, born in The Hague, tall, fair, and casually dressed – I think I saw him wear a tie twice. Having been seduced by a Monteverdi season in The

Hague, Mostart gave up his medical studies to learn operatic stage management and direction. He was brought to Glyndebourne by the director John Cox, and then acted as Hall's assistant in his last three productions at Glyndebourne. So when Gudrun Wagner protested that the existing rehearsal time was a Bayreuth custom Mostart replied, 'I know the way Peter works and I know it's not long enough.'

Hall decided that the issue should be clarified with Wagner; if he could not have his way on a relatively small point, it would augur badly for the more substantial battles later on. He wrote to Wagner on 14 January 1982: 'This letter is the result of a good deal of thought and study. I am not trying to make difficulties or unreasonable demands, but I do not have time to do the *Ring* unless I can start on 1st May . . . Much as I want to work in Bayreuth, I would not wish to do such a major undertaking with a schedule which I believe cannot achieve results. I do hope we can work something out.' When Hall and Wagner met again six weeks later in Berlin, Wagner merely said that he could have more rehearsal time but not all the singers would

Walter Huneke, Technical Director, left, discusses points of the proposed platform's construction with its designer Michael Barnett; Frau Wagner interprets.

be available; he clearly did not intend to make an issue of it. When the rehearsal schedule was finally completed, with work beginning on 24 April, Hall discovered, to his mild chagrin, that Wagner had taken him at his word: during the thirteen weeks of rehearsal he had been given only two days off.

The first indication of a more serious conflict arrived in a letter from Wagner to Hall in February 1982, before the first technical rehearsal – known in Germany as a *Bauprobe* – took place on stage in March. It came at a moment when Hall and Dudley were feeling more cheerful; after an arid autumn they had worked well together in the New Year, and Hall reported to Solti: 'I think we have a major design developing. It is very beautiful and very workable. It is also much, much simpler.' Dudley was no less enthusiastic, as he told me later: 'Peter's mind was focused on it; he applied himself to the text with great care, and he had an absolutely clear line what the thing was about.'

First trial for the feasibility of a tank on stage; Bayreuth, August 1982.

But Wagner and Walter Huneke, the technical director, did not regard Dudley's sets as either workable or simple enough. Wagner's letter seemed to prejudge the *Bauprobe*: he hoped that Hall could persuade him of the relevance of the tank, both technically and artistically. 'I am convinced Dudley's fantasy has to find another solution,' he wrote, and then went on to express doubts about the platform: whether it could be built to conform to stringent German security regulations, and whether it might not make so much noise that it would ruin any live recording of the performance. Hall was unmoved. When I asked him what he would do if Wagner announced that Bayreuth could afford neither the tank nor the platform, he replied that since the first scene of *Das Rheingold* established the whole style of the production, he could hardly agree to cutting them. 'There are some things a director has to insist on, and if he doesn't get them, he has to resign,' he added emphatically.

Wagner, who had not welcomed my presence at the meeting in Solti's house, feeling that it inhibited his freedom to comment, asked that I should not be present at the *Bauprobe*, and I have relied on Mostart's notes of this. As I was to discover later, the Festspielhaus in March is inhospitable; because of the fear of fire, the auditorium has no heating system, and the only warmth is provided by three two-bar electric fires at the back of a small three-sided hut placed in the centre of the auditorium. It was much too cold, Wagner said that March, for a swimmer to test the tank and the mirror. Instead, the local sex shop had provided a blown-up dummy of a naked lady: 'A rather bizarre joke,' Mostart recorded. But the stage staff had suspended a section of mirror at the correct angle above a large tank of water, and as the dummy floated into view, the mirror, even with visible joins in the material, did not substantially distort the image. The audience would indeed see a vertical wall of water, as Dudley had intended. Both he and Hall were well satisfied by the demonstration, though Mostart sensed that Wagner was not so pleased. 'The last thing he expected was for Peter to say it was fine.' Over lunch, Wagner commented that while Hall might be satisfied technically, the music did not really suggest swimming. The text did, Hall replied, cheerfully adamant.

After lunch, a full-scale model of the platform was suspended above the stage, and pivoted by hand. The movement was imperfect, naturally, but the shape and the vastness of the platform were impressive. Mostart reported: 'The moment he saw the platform on stage I knew Peter was sold. He said to Bill, "That's it, then." And I thought it was quite stunning.' When they had completed the viewing in the auditorium, everyone adjourned to

71

Wagner's office to discuss details, such as the coloured floor cloths that would cover the platform, changing from act to act to illustrate changes in the natural environment, and the film projections that were planned to accompany the Ride of the Valkyries. It was a hard-working session; only as it neared its end, when he was sure that Hall had no intention of shifting his ground, did Wagner play his wild card. He announced that the Bavarian organisation responsible for the safety of industrial machinery, known as the TUV, imposed conditions that would make the platform theatrically unworkable. With mounting emotion, Wagner listed the demands they would make: no one could be on the platform while it was moving, which would make changing scenes in view of the audience quite impossible; there would have to be a railing to prevent singers falling off the platform; traps in the platform, allowing singers to make entrances and exits, would not be permissible; and no one would be allowed under the platform when it was suspended in the air. These conditions would clearly nullify virtually every reason for designing the platform in the first place.

Hall, furious at Wagner's ultimatum, nonetheless controlled his temper and asked calmly whether he and Dudley could see the TUV officials in Munich. By talking directly to bureaucrats, Hall had often discovered that regulations were less inflexible than they seemed on paper. But Wagner did not think that was a good idea. Hall asked whether Wagner would not go to Munich himself. No, that would take too long. Eventually, Hall summed up: he and Dudley believed they had designed something spectacular and workable; he admitted the designs had arrived later than promised, but having seen the platform he was sure it was the only way they could do the production. If the platform was unacceptable to German safety officers, it looked as though he and Dudley were wasting their time. That being the case, he thought it only fair that the two of them resign immediately and allow Wagner time to replace them.

That had never been Wagner's intention, and he was clearly appalled by the prospect. Gudrun Wagner, who shared the burden of translation with Mostart, intervened to keep the conversation moving, and at the end of the seven-hour conference Wagner had agreed to go to Munich, armed with Mike Barnett's finished drawings, and argue the case with the TUV. 'We thought we'd won,' says Mostart.

A letter from Wagner to Hall (each wrote to the other in his native language) a few days later appeared to confirm their victory. The translation said: 'Concerning the problems that arose during the negotiations I would ask you to attribute those to the sometimes slightly difficult means of communication – and to a certain extent to my personality which takes some getting used to – and let's now consider the matter closed.' The letter ended by asking Hall 'to bear in mind the realities of Bayreuth'. But the only reality Wagner referred to specifically was money: this *Ring* would be the most expensive Bayreuth production ever, despite threats of a smaller subsidy from both Bavarian and Bonn governments in 1983.

But the matter of the platform was *not* closed, and the argument broke out again within a month. Visiting London in April, Wagner and Huneke brought with them a completely different design for the platform. 'It was a real facer,' says Dudley. The Bayreuth version was much heavier than Mike Barnett's, and to distribute the weight Huneke had calculated that the pivoting centre of the platform would need to be two metres thick, instead of the one metre specified by Barnett which gave it an elegant, aerodynamic shape. Barnett arrived at the meeting after it had begun and found himself subjected to a cross-examination. The implication of the case against him was that his design was irresponsible, because someone might actually be killed working on a platform that conformed to it. 'It's lucky Mike's such a mild man,' Dudley commented, describing the scene. By the end of the day, Barnett had agreed to redesign some aspects of the platform, though he refused to compromise on the shape.

Barnett's new drawings for the platform arrived late enough in Bayreuth to allow Wagner – who wanted the platform constructed and working in the theatre by November – to redeploy his case in favour of the German design, and this provoked another angry response from Hall. 'The problems of the set are causing me great concern, and I think once more we are near to breaking point on the project,' he wrote on 7 June. 'If you believe Mike Barnett must be dispensed with because he has been incompetent, then I must disagree with you. If you believe his advanced technological knowledge can be replaced by other people, from the evidence I have so far, I must disagree with you. If you believe that Bill Dudley will continue to work without Mike Barnett, I have to tell you you are wrong. I dislike confrontations in the theatre because I believe they achieve very little. However, I think we have an extremely serious situation. . . . Please help me save it.'

Wagner replied that his position had been misinterpreted. But Hall was becoming despondent. When it was arranged that Dudley, Barnett and Mostart should go to Bayreuth at the end of June to settle the argument about the platform once and for all, Hall told Mostart: 'If we can't have Mike Barnett, fuck it.'

Having become accustomed to friendly collaboration with fellow engineers, Barnett was also rather sick of the affair now. 'I wasn't saying it was easy – I was saying it could be done, it wouldn't fall down, and it was safe.' A German engineer who had been invited to Bayreuth to check Barnett's calculations agreed that they appeared feasible but suggested that a computer in a local university engineering department should act as a final arbiter. The result, which only came out after Barnett had returned to London, vindicated him entirely. But this did not make him any more acceptable in Bayreuth. The contract to build the platform did not go to an English company, as Barnett had hoped ('it is an English *Ring*, after all'), and when a German company, Treffel AG of Wiesbaden, got the job, that was a pretext for paying Barnett off. Dudley was upset at the departure of an ally, and Barnett would have liked to complete the job he had begun. 'But I did prove that Bill's concept could be realised; I proved that the essential slimness was possible, and I proved that the platform could be built for a sensible price,' Barnett concludes. Wagner appealed to Hall and Dudley to trust the Germans to build the platform, and Hall told Dudley that since the principle had been accepted, they should behave generously. Anyway, they needed to conserve their ammunition; there was another battle to fight, over the water.

A *Bauprobe* for the water tank had been arranged for the beginning of August 1982. Since Wagner raised no objection, I went to Bayreuth with Hall, and we arrived in mid-afternoon, walking up the tree-lined hill to the Festspielhaus in the wake of the dinner-jacketed audience attending a performance of *Tristan und Isolde*. Mostart met Hall on the way and reported Wagner's assertion that singers could not possibly work in water. He had also asked Mostart who was to pay the premium for insurance, should a leak in the tanks cause a performance to be cancelled. Relations did not improve when, towards midnight, the *Tristan* set had been struck, and both the tank and the reflecting mirror were in place. A plump stagehand perched on a ladder in the tank with his trousers rolled, and the reflection was so poor that he was barely distinguishable in the mirror from the water. Plainly, the effect was not working, and Hall and Dudley – who had arrived a couple of days earlier – sat gloomily in the darkened auditorium. 'This proves nothing,' Hall observed; then, changing his mind, 'or rather it proves it doesn't work.' Dudley pointed out that the mirror material was not correct. 'Why did you ask for it then?' snapped Wagner. Dudley retorted that the material they had seen the previous March had been quite different from the mirror now on stage. Where was the original?

After much shouting on stage, during which Wagner's voice rose above all the others, another variety of reflecting glass was produced, but it was only a little better. Not until 2.30 a.m. was the silvery mirror Dudley remembered from March brought out, and the patient stagehand could instantly be seen clearly in the shimmering water. 'That's beautiful, terrific,' shouted Dudley. 'That's the right stuff,' he added when Huneke returned to the auditorium.

'You can't have it,' Huneke replied abruptly.

'But it's in the catalogue.'

'It's too expensive, costs more than crystal; they use it in your Concorde,' said Huneke. Wagner chipped in with the opinion that a singer would appear to be on the surface of the water, not in it, but everyone was tired now, except Wagner. He wanted a meeting with Hall and Mostart, who translated steadily until 4.30 a.m. Hall and I drove back to Nuremberg Airport together as the sun rose, and Hall remarked on Wagner's remarkable 'split personality'. Normally he behaved like a worried administrator, full of doubt about the ability of his theatre to transform a conception into a stage production less than a year later. But during the night, in his office, Wagner had momentarily been transformed into the artist who had directed two productions of the *Ring* in Bayreuth. 'It was extraordinary,' Hall reported. 'He said we might be the first people ever to pull off the first scene of *Rheingold*.'

Wagner continued to raise objections, but no longer to the principle of tank and mirror, though he was reluctant to provide a mirror of the quality Dudley wanted. The water would have to be heated to an exact temperature, at great cost, he announced. He thought it absolutely necessary to hire doubles for the singers since he was sure they would not be capable of singing while swimming on their backs; he had asked some of the singers from the chorus to experiment in Bayreuth's public swimming pool, and they had found doing both simultaneously extremely difficult. Moreover, Wagner argued, not even the doubles would be able to swim naked, since they would be local girls with reputations to preserve.

That August Hall's greatest concern was not the tank, which had actually been made, or Wolfgang Wagner. It was Bill Dudley, who had appeared drawn and weary at the Festspielhaus when he demonstrated his stage models in sequence to Wagner and Huneke. They clearly admired much that they saw, but when Dudley reached the second act of *Götterdämmerung*, Huneke asked: 'Have you ever thought about money?'

'I haven't got any,' replied Dudley.

'I don't mean your own.'

75

'I've responded to the text,' said Dudley defiantly. (Later his temper finally snapped when Wagner used one of the carefully made models of a platform covering as a tray for some cakes.) The models were striking works of a vivid visual imagination, and Hall, looking at one of them, turned to me and said: 'He has the simplicity of genius.' He reflected for a moment before adding: 'And the inefficiency.'

The trouble with Bill Dudley was that he was both overworked and demoralised. He had designed two plays at the National that summer, one opening in June, the other in September, and he was thinking about a new production of *Der Rosenkavalier* at Covent Garden, although that was not due to open until 1984. Perhaps he should have been concentrating on the *Ring*, but he was hard up. The models had cost him £6,500 and Wagner was contesting responsibility for the bills. Hall and Solti had visited Dudley at his home in Greenwich earlier in the summer, and he had poured out a comprehensive list of sorrows: he was broke; Bayreuth seemed intent only on ruining the platform; and he had too much to do. 'Something's got to give,' he said, 'and at the moment, I think it's going to be me.' Solti was instinctively generous, but Hall was less sympathetic, having severe views about working in the theatre: it is a job, so do it. Dudley's memory of the conversation is that it went something like this: 'Peter said, "You've given up on this, haven't you?" and I said that in a way I had, so Peter said, "Well, I think we'd better jack it in." The *Ring* was attacking the very core of who I was, and what I was able to do. It was the first real setback I'd ever had. I told Peter I'd been quite a good designer before this, but that I kept waking up in the middle of the night and wondering if I'd done my best. I still needed pills to sleep.'

They did not jack it in, of course, and the models kept on coming, and when they arrived they looked good. But another problem was looming. Dudley's contract with Bayreuth specified that the costumes should be ready by 15 May 1982, and by August 1982 they had hardly been begun. Predictably, Wagner was furious. It was Hall who had insisted that a single mind should work on the total design of the *Ring*, including the costumes. 'I didn't particularly want to do them,' said Dudley, 'because I know many people are doing it better than me, which isn't something I feel about sets. It's partly because I've never been stuck on clothes myself. There are so many more interesting things to buy, like books. I'd have liked a costume designer as an ally too. I've never been so alone on a show.' Wagner extended the deadline for the costumes to mid-September and then to 5 October. As the weeks of August slipped by, Hall toyed with the idea of co-opting John Bury to design the costumes, but nothing came of that. Instead, Hall and Dudley lurched towards the third resignation.

Notes taken at a series of meetings between Hall and Dudley during September give the surface impression when first read of solid design work being accomplished, even though it was six months late. Although some scenes were being redesigned, the broad concept was complete, and decisions were being made about such details as Brünnhilde's horse, the toad into which Alberich transforms himself, the bear that Siegfried chases, hunting dogs and real blood for the dragon. A hundred minutiae were discussed, but the dominant theme underlying all the meetings was what had *not* been done.

In mid-September Dudley was told by Hall that he would not go to Bayreuth on 5 October as scheduled unless the costume designs were finished. 'He said he felt he could no longer defend Bill,' Mostart recorded. 'There was a long silence. It was awful.' Hall thought that Dudley seemed to be waiting for the axe to fall. When, on 24 September, Dudley confessed that he still had not been able to do any more work, Hall's confidence in their professional ability to do the *Ring* ebbed; he felt there was no ground on which they could defend themselves. He said to Dudley: 'Sorry, Bill, I'll call Bayreuth and tell them there's no *Ring*,' and he walked out of the room.

Left together, Mostart and Dudley began to talk. Mostart's notes record Dudley's misery. 'Bill said he didn't think he had a creative partnership with Peter because when he met him he got an enormous guilt complex. He added that Wolfgang Wagner had had a devastating effect on him, especially in their first meetings.' Mostart repeated Dudley's explanation to Hall on the telephone the following morning, but Hall was so depressed that he spoke only of the form of his resignation. Later he dictated a message to Wagner. It read: 'Dear Wolfgang, I personally guaranteed the delivery of the *Ring* costumes and set from Bill Dudley at the beginning of October. It is now clear to me that I am going to fail. I feel that I must, regretfully, offer my resignation, not because I have lost enthusiasm for the project but because it is the only honourable way to give you the opportunity to salvage the desperate situation. I am very sorry. Yours sincerely, Peter Hall.'

This resignation was serious. The other two were tactical, and Hall would have been disappointed and surprised if they had been accepted. The third was clearly the fault of Hall and Dudley and Hall felt personally responsible, but Wagner behaved as decently as he had done before. Instead of debating the issue, he immediately proposed a further extension of the deadline, to mid-October. Offered the compromise, the circumstances dictated that Hall accept; Dudley now had a deadline that seemed realistic to him, which spurred him on. In the last week of September he produced a remarkable volume of work, and on 30 September Hall, seeing it, announced that he thought it was stunning. Solti joined them that day. He knew of the ructions of the previous week, and had spoken to Wagner who had told him how much he admired Dudley's designs – though he worried about whether he could afford all of them. Solti himself liked the first costume designs. Dudley had made them deliberately artless: 'An awful lot of costumes could have worked on that set, but what I try to do is design wearable clothes. If the singers feel good in them, they'll move better. You shouldn't make a singer look absurd on stage. I don't for instance like the patterns and motifs that turn singers into toy soldiers.'

The shattering episode of the late costume designs was one the principals preferred to forget. It was hardly spoken of among themselves, let alone to others, until months later when Hall and Dudley were more cheerful and confident. Goetz Friedrich's *Ring* was being performed at Covent Garden the week after Hall had despaired of doing the Bayreuth production. Mostart saw all four parts of the cycle, and Hall a couple, but neither betrayed the least hint of the passions of that week when I met them during the intervals. One evening Hall leant on the bar and sketched his idea of Siegfried's death scene from *Götterdämmerung*, explaining how marvellous it would look as the platform moved away from the audience. He turned to me, and grinned like a naughty schoolboy. 'This is going to be the most expensive production in operatic history,' he said.

8

Ascension Day: they have lift-off

Since Wolfgang Wagner had to meet the cost of the 1983 *Ring*, he was not as amused as Hall about its record budget-breaking potential. His original production budget – excluding the cost of the singers and musicians – was DM 1,200,000, already the highest in the history of the Festspielhaus; Hall's blithely exaggerated estimate was that this sum might cover one-third of his costs. Certainly, the budget was already overspent by DM 300,000 in October 1982. By the New Year the budget figure had risen to DM 1,818,000, of which the platform consumed 30 per cent. In spite of the increased budget Dudley was being asked for more cuts to his designs. In October, when he took the costume drawings to Bayreuth, he telephoned Hall to say that the cuts requested were so drastic that he was going to be left with a bare stage if he did not fight back.

With the major battles over, Wagner had begun to attend to detail: having been involved in so many *Ring* cycles, he was keen that his experience should be drawn on. I was in the room one day that winter when Wagner began to reminisce about the way a scene from *Die Walküre* could be played. He described Chéreau's version; then his and Wieland's (*'mein Bruder'*); next Emil Pretorius's before the War; then that of *'mein Vater'*, and eventually that of *'mein Grossvater'*. Everyone in the room shared glances as Wolfgang talked unselfconsciously about Richard Wagner himself. There were things about the 1983 *Ring* which Wagner clearly did not like, such as Hall's scenario for the end of *Götterdämmerung*, which he thought insufficiently accepted that Siegfried and Brünnhilde are redeemed by love. Eventually Hall understood why, and changed his plan – though he did not do that in every case.

Dudley was not unsympathetic to Wagner's suggestions either. Used to working in opera houses where administrators are

79

The platform:
Top and middle: Creating the steel structure and the concave surface.

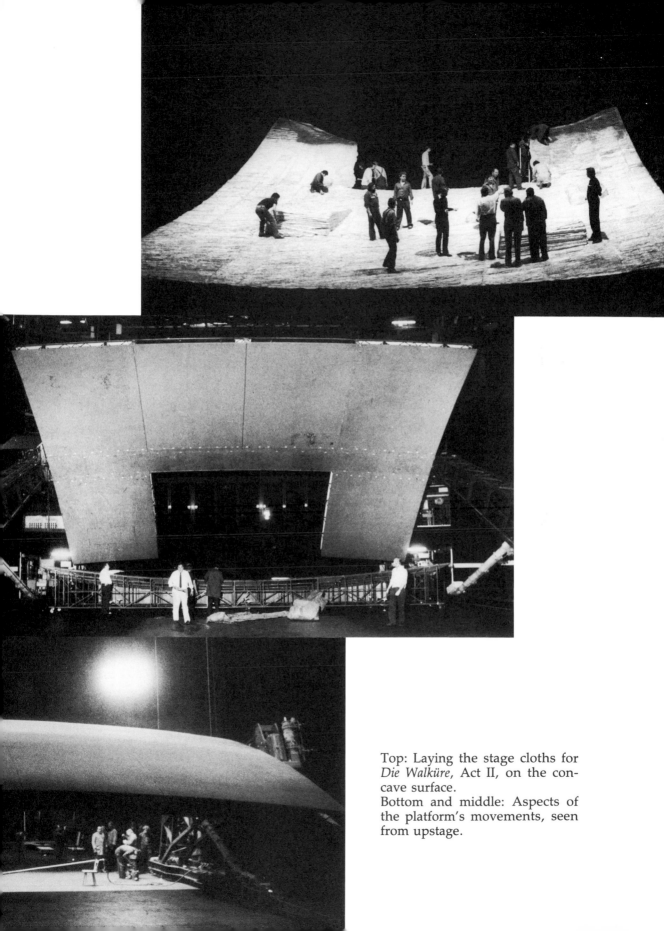

Top: Laying the stage cloths for
Die Walküre, Act II, on the concave surface.
Bottom and middle: Aspects of
the platform's movements, seen
from upstage.

preoccupied with singers or trade unions rather than designers, he welcomed advice on points of detail. 'He's very astute,' says Dudley, who had been particularly impressed by Wagner's criticism of a scene in which he accused Dudley of failing to find an aesthetically pleasing position for the platform. 'They're great at schematicising art, to give it order, function, and theory. The British are much looser. That autumn they started calling the platform "the Floor of Destiny". I wondered what Christmas cracker they'd got that from.'

Next Wagner discovered a scene in *Siegfried* in which the platform seemed to perform no function at all.

'What does the floor do here?' he asked.

'Nothing,' replied Dudley.

'Nothing?' said Wagner ironically.

'Well, I'm sorry, I've done my best,' said Dudley. 'There are no aisles, they can't get out for an ice-cream. They're just going to have to sit there and listen to the music.' Wagner never quite came to terms with Dudley's personality. Noticing one day that Dudley was listening intently to tapes on his Sony Walkman, Wagner commented: 'There is the first designer to work from the original score.' Dudley thought it would be cruel to tell him he was listening to an Irish rock band.

Good humour tended to evaporate easily. Dudley felt he had been cheated of two metres in the backward movement of the platform because of over-fussy fire regulations, and when he saw the first painted cloths he found them of a poorer quality than he had expected. Consequently, he began imagining more projected photographs, especially as Hall had decided to play the *Ring* behind a front gauze. Old-fashioned though that had become in the theatre, it seemed necessary to mask the mechanical arms that moved the platform. The decision about the projections and the gauze were taken just before Christmas 1982, when Wagner took Hall, Dudley and Mostart out to lunch and recounted gory details of the momentous first performance of Chéreau's *Ring*. Fights had broken out; the police had had to be called. Two ladies in the audience had battled so bitterly that when one had pulled at the other's earring she had wrenched the whole earlobe away. Gudrun Wagner had had her dress torn, and Wolfgang himself had decided that it would be indiscreet to go into town after the performances. 'Whatever you do on the first night, Peter, don't wear earrings,' Wagner advised. Hall was not really amused, and became increasingly worried as Wagner went on to describe the passionate and reactionary nature of the Wagner Societies throughout Germany and Austria, which had spearheaded attacks on Chéreau's Shavian interpretation of the master's work. Wagner revealed that these Societies had heard about Hall's much-criticised production of Verdi's *Macbeth* at the Metropolitan, New York, that November, which had also caused a small riot. Reviews had been reprinted in Austrian newspapers, and the Societies were asking: 'Will this happen in Bayreuth this summer?' Of course, Wagner went on, Hall should not worry. Bayreuth was like that; he was certain to be attacked by *some* part of the audience. But the conversation made Hall dread a hostile reception such as Chéreau had had. He began to dream that he was being booed off the stage. Overwork was weakening his natural resilience.

Hall's schedule that autumn and winter was unusually punishing. He had directed productions of plays by Oscar Wilde and Harold Pinter at the National Theatre in London, and had then gone to New York for the Metropolitan's *Macbeth*. *Amadeus* had had to be recast for a national tour in the United States. In the New Year Hall was rehearsing a new production of *The Marriage of Figaro* in Geneva, and taking studio rehearsals, in London at the National, of a new Marvin Hamlisch musical based on the life of the American actress Jean Seberg, which was to open in the autumn of 1983. There was not much time to think about the *Ring*. No wonder German lessons were abandoned.

Hall's next visit to Bayreuth was at the end of February 1983; he flew there straight from Geneva after the first night of *Figaro*. We travelled on the aircraft together and Hall commented: 'This is the weekend when we find out whether it all works.'

Dudley and Mostart had joined us in Frankfurt, and as we walked up to the Festspielhaus we saw children skating on the pond in the park, for the weather was icy. Inside the auditorium everyone wore a thick coat. The scene was already set when we arrived and it disguised the platform. Half an hour passed before Huneke ordered that the scene be changed. Hall and Dudley walked on to the forestage as the floor covering was stripped off, and the platform began, without warning, to move up and level out, before floating down so that it rested on the stage. Dudley watched quite rapt, eventually turning to Hall to ask if he had noticed how the light-patterns changed shape as the platform moved. Though not quite silent, the slight whine of the hydraulic machinery was not obtrusive; the platform appeared to be stable. The framework of thin tubular steel was one metre thick in the middle, as Barnett had specified, and the first impression, despite the bulkiness of the arms, was that the platform was superb.

While the platform was being set with new scenery, Wagner took Hall and Dudley on a conducted tour of the area beneath the stage, showing how the stage floor had been strengthened by a series of steel columns so as to bear the weight of the platform and the water tank. Plastic pipes trailed down to the basement where a new concrete floor had been laid, and a large new machine, humming quietly, had been installed to provide hydraulic power for the platform. Wagner's pride in these new toys was so evident that he might have designed them himself.

Reassembling the platform, section by section, Walter Huneke, left, directing. *Siegfried*, Act III, tree seen lowered downstage.

Despite the striking beauty of the moving platform, however, there was a sense of unease in the auditorium. Mostart was concerned because so many of the sets were still incomplete, the more so, because the fault – the designs being late – was theirs. Dudley fretted at any mention of budgets. 'We'll have to get rid of the tap dancing,' he joked, but that was putting a brave face on his dread of being asked for more cuts. Hall was unhappy with some of the completed sets. Looking at the second act of *Die Walküre*, he said to Dudley: 'This act's a total mess.' All three agreed that the painted cloths they had been shown looked tatty and unconvincing, even when lit.

Reassembling the platform, the drive motor to the right; the control panels in the foreground.

At the end of the day, they conferred in the bar of the Bayerische Hof, the hotel by the railway station where they stayed during brief trips to Bayreuth. Hall announced: 'What works is the platform, which is taking over and looks marvellous. The rest doesn't, so we'll have to get rid of the rest.' Even allowing for Hall's hyperbole, many designers might have been upset and argumentative, but Dudley did not fundamentally disagree. He asked for a piece of paper and began to sketch a second platform, the same shape as the one that was already there, but much lighter because it would not have to bear any weight. This second platform would be hung in the fly tower; its movements would complement those of the stage platform; and it would be used as a screen on to which filmed images could be projected, replacing the painted cloths. Dudley's improvised inspiration was quickly named the projection platform. I was intrigued by their eagerness to introduce, at such a late stage, so basic a change in the design – one that would certainly cause chaos in the workshops. Hall said: 'All the best directors – Peter Brook, John Dexter, Peter Wood – have given me, as a theatre administrator, the same sort of trouble.' Cheerfully he added that all the best administrators respond positively during such crises.

Wagner proved to be no exception. The following morning the plan was put to Wagner, Huneke, and Manfred Voss, who was in charge of the lighting, and a rough model was ordered for inspection later that day – all this in spite of Wagner's revelation that the cloths that would have to be replaced had already been paid for. In the afternoon, they all trooped to the studio where Dudley worked, in the block beyond the workshops. The model had been prepared and sprayed with white paint; hand-held in the stage model, it moved and pivoted. 'It's beautiful,' judged Hall. In the absence of any opposition to the new idea, Wagner said ruefully: 'I should have kept my mouth shut. This should have come in the second year of the production, not the first.' (The tradition of Bayreuth as a theatre workshop, developed after the War by Wieland and Wolfgang, means that the cash available for a new production is spread over two years, allowing the director to make expensive adjustments once he has seen the first year's stage performances.)

The good temper did not survive the day. Wagner's Welsh temperament made an appearance when Dudley asked to be repaid for money he had spent on films for the projector. Wagner's outburst suggested that Dudley had overlooked his good fortune at being able to work in Bayreuth at all. Mostart was too embarrassed to continue his translation, and the edgy atmosphere helped

Previous page: The mirror for *Das Rheingold* laid, face downwards, has lighting equipment attached to the top. Stage lighting gantries, with TV monitors l. and r. at 1st and 2nd levels.

obscure a remark by Manfred Voss about the difficulties of lighting the set from above the stage – top lighting – if the projection platform were to hang in the tower. When the three discussed Wagner's anger over dinner, Hall said that if he were Wolfgang, he would be just as exasperated. They were learning to roll with Wagner's temperament now, and Hall seemed to think that it had become a less significant factor in their work. 'I know it's unlucky,' he added, 'but after this weekend I feel confident.' Dudley shared the feeling: it was the first trip to Bayreuth he had really enjoyed. When everyone else left for London the next day, Dudley stayed on, and had another brush with Wagner. 'It was like dying embers of a fire, quite operatic,' he observed. But that fire had bigger fuel supplies than Dudley knew of.

When they returned to Bayreuth shortly after Easter 1983, Hall and Dudley took a companion along with them, an actor from the National Theatre called Jim Carter who distinguished himself offstage as a teacher of acrobatics. He was in Bayreuth to demonstrate stilt walking, and not as an incidental entertainment. A problem that had tormented Hall and Dudley for two years was how to make the giants in *Das Rheingold*, Fafner and Fasolt, look like giants. Originally, they had imagined filming them live, and projecting their magnified image on to a screen, but that was unsatisfactory because they would appear in only two dimensions. Chéreau had placed his two bass singers on the shoulders of strong men, which had been effective, but neither Hall nor Dudley wanted to copy Chéreau. Inspiration did not strike Dudley until August 1982, and then it seemed so obvious that he failed to understand why he had not thought of it earlier. One of the shows he was designing at the National Theatre that summer was Bertolt Brecht's *Schweik and the Second World War*, and in it he had made the actor playing Hitler look like an intimidating giant by placing him on stilts. These were not like ordinary stilts; they had been invented in the United States to enable house painters to paint ceilings comfortably without ladders. Hall knew the idea would make Wagner nervous, and had written to him explaining why he wanted Jim Carter to demonstrate the stilts: 'Otherwise I know what will happen. One of the stage staff will get on the stilts, fall down and break his leg – and you'll tell me we cannot have stilts because they are dangerous, and singers will not wear them.'

Carter's demonstration showed that he could stand, walk, run and even fall safely to his death, as Fasolt must, on stilts and on the platform. But Carter's presence on stage revealed a further difficulty: how were the giants, on their stilts, going to make their

89

Stilts for the giants –

Top: the first tests on the platform's convex surface by Jim Carter. The projection screen, later discarded, is in position. April 1983. Photo by Stephen Fay.

Bottom: an early rehearsal for *Das Rheingold*. Schenk (left) and Schweikart on stilts.

Constructing Erda's tree roots for
Siegfried Act III, Scene 1.

Peter Holowka, in charge of properties,
and an assistant welds the basic structure
of wire, to be covered later with
papier-mâché and painted.

The music staff, Solti (*centre*) conducting,
rehearse Reiner Goldberg and Hildegard
Behrens in *Siegfried*, Act III.
The production team (Hall and Mostart, l.)
are also in attendance with Frau Wagner
(*in green*); Rehearsal Stage No 3.

Das Rheingold, Scene 1: Alberich (*centre*) climbs towards the Rhinegold, taunted by the Rhinemaidens; l. to r. Flosshilde, Woglinde and Wellgunde.

Das Rheingold, Scene 2: The argument amongst the gods over payment to the giants Fafner & Fasolt (*at rear*). l. to r. Fricka, Wotan, Donner, Freia and Froh.

Das Rheingold, **Scene 4: The gods admire the Rainbow bridge and Valhalla beyond.**
Wotan (*centre*), Donner and Froh, with the prostrate Fasolt, and (*bottom* r.) Loge.

Die Walküre Act I Scene 3: Siegmund withdraws the sword Nothung from the tree, watched by the enraptured Sieglinde.

    'Nothung! Nothung!
    So nenn ich dich, Schwert'

(*on previous page*): Siegmund is visited by Sieglinde, while her drugged husband Hunding sleeps. Brother and sister embrace passionately.

entrances and exits on a platform whose edge is some four feet above the stage floor? Carter admitted that even he found it difficult to walk up steps, and Huneke patiently discussed how a gently sloping ramp might be built, but meanwhile, Wagner stalked the stage in fury. He thought, he thundered, that the whole point of the platform was that everything would be simple. *'Auf Wiedersehen!'* he roared, stumping out of the auditorium, only to return a few minutes later to continue where he had left off. Later he declared that Dudley would *have* to find an alternative to the stilts. But Dudley did not have an alternative, and did not want one. Anyway, he was at the time more concerned about the projection platform.

The new platform was not as Dudley had ordered it: it had not proved possible to make it turn through a full 360 degrees, and only the convex side had been covered with plywood, since to cover both would make it too heavy. Nevertheless, when a slide was projected on to the moving platform the effect was amazing, since it looked, inexplicably, three-dimensional. 'It's wonderful, a hell of a bonus,' shouted Dudley. Hall turned to me, and said: 'I think Bill has actually done it now.' But test-film that was projected on to the screen – German Air Force film of clouds over Bavaria – dampened their enthusiasm: the picture was dull and the definition poor, though both improved a little when some black gauze, which had hung forgotten in front of the projection platform, was raised.

At the end of the day, the stage was set for the last act of *Götterdämmerung*, the climax of the *Ring* in which the mirror and the water tank were to reappear to create the illusion of the mighty wave in which Hagen drowns. The effect promised to be stupendous, if it worked, and Dudley was confident that it would, but Hall was worrying about what image, exactly, he wished to leave in the mind of the audience at the end of the *Ring*. He was still mulling it over in the car to Nuremberg airport at 6.00 a.m. the following morning. It was by no means the only question left unanswered, and rehearsals were due to begin in less than three weeks' time.

Hall had been deliberately evading decisions about the fine detail of the production, such as entrances and exits, an exact log of the platform changes, and the singers' moves. Mostart had told him weeks earlier that Wagner was expecting these, and they had begun work on a list of scene changes, defining not just the page, but the exact bar in the score at which the change ought to be made. Hall had worked diligently for half an hour or so, only to burst out laughing when he realised how long it would take. 'Leave it for the rehearsals,' he told Mostart. Nonetheless, Hall had no intention of deviating from his normal standards, for as a theatre director he believes that a show must by ready when the first-night audience arrives. When the *Ring* was performed at the end of July, he wanted it to look as it would during the ensuing years. He had no desire to use the Festspielhaus as a workshop, thinking that a little hard on those who had purchased expensive tickets the first year. Solti felt the same way about the pit; he wanted to experiment with the sound balance during rehearsals, not performances. Neither really questioned whether their laudable ambition could be achieved in Bayreuth.

The trees in Richard Wagner Park were still in bud when Hall arrived to begin rehearsals on 24 April 1983. Because Reiner Goldberg was due in Japan early in May, Hall started with the first scene of *Siegfried* which involves Mime but makes minimal use of the platform. Not until the end of the week, when Hildegard Behrens arrived to work on scenes from *Siegfried* and *Götterdämmerung*, did the platform start moving while singers were performing on it, and immediately Hall began to use it more freely, tilting, turning and lifting it. Walter Kottke, who operated the levers on the control panel just offstage, was asked to exaggerate movements they had discussed. The singers were not in danger, but the platform was becoming not just the top of a mountain, but the steep sides as well. Behrens was excited by the platform; Goldberg seemed to have no opinion about it at all.

When I arrived in Bayreuth in the second week of May, Hall had gone back to the beginning of the *Ring*, the first scene of *Das Rheingold*, with the Rhinemaidens in the water tank. It was my fourth trip to the Festspielhaus but the first time I had heard the sound of music in the auditorium. The sound of the first chord, the E flat major, on the *répétiteur*'s piano was a delightful reminder that, eventually, Wagner's *Ring* is not all about technical difficulties on the stage. The tank was masked by a perforated plastic screen in different shades of watery green, looking like weed-covered coral, which rose to a slender point in the brighter area of the water, where the gold would shine and Alberich would climb to steal it.

The Rhinemaidens slipped into the water splashing and giggling, wearing their own swimming costumes. When they had first tried the tank a couple of days earlier, Wagner had thoughtfully provided them with outfits like wet suits to cover them entirely and keep them warm during rehearsals. To a woman, the singers had found them cumbersome and discarded them: it was warmer in the water than out of it, they said. As for the doubles – local girls looking forward, no doubt, to their debut at the Festspielhaus – they had been informed that they would not be needed. The Rhinemaidens

The mirror –
Top: an early trial surface.
Bottom: the final mirror is raised
from its storage trolleys.

announced that they could swim on their backs and sing clearly and comfortably, watching the conductor through television screens in the wings.

After three days' rehearsal the Rhinemaidens were swimming in a formation that would not have displeased Busby Berkeley, and, apart from their wigs, which they found awkward, they looked completely relaxed, tempting Alberich to draw closer, a development Hermann Becht clearly relished. The following morning Hall was demanding more intricate work, explaining to the singers that he wanted the Rhinemaidens to be like children, first grave, then animated, and innocently erotic, like Lewis Carroll's Alice. At the end of the session, Hall congratulated them and said he was looking forward to the swim-through scheduled for the late afternoon. The Rhinemaidens retired for a long lunch.

It was Ascension Day, and the stage staff had a holiday, so there were only a few people in the theatre that afternoon, nine of us in all. Shortly after the musical introduction ended, the Rhinemaidens appeared in the water, and it was evident that something had changed; all looked whiter than before. It suddenly dawned on us: they were swimming and singing, and they were naked – unselfconsciously innocent, and, indeed, erotic. The performance was absorbing, and as the scene ended with the three Rhinemaidens forming a tableau that might have been painted by Alma-Tadema, I realised that no one had spoken or even shifted during the twenty-minute run-through. The first scene was a *coup de théâtre*, even under working lights.

There was a problem, of course. For two days the singers appeared in the mirror looking more like *calamari* than Rhinemaidens. The image of their limbs was distorted because sections of the reflecting glass in the mirror had buckled in the humid atmosphere of the auditorium. Huneke said he understood what had happened; his men had made insufficient allowance for expansion in the material. He promised that the mirror would be fixed. But the pleasure Hall and Dudley took in the boldness of the Rhinemaidens was spoilt by this frustration. Dudley commented: 'The things you thought were going to be a problem, like the Rhinemaidens, aren't, and what you didn't worry about turns out to be trouble, like the mirror.'

Whatever the obstacles presented by Richard Wagner's work, Wolfgang Wagner's Bayreuth and their own personalities, Solti, Hall and Dudley now thought that at last, after more than two years of struggle, it might be possible to see their vision of the *Ring* realised on the stage. They now might just be capable of scaling the 'biggest great work of art ever created'.

Facing page: Das Rheingold; the Rhinegold and the Rhinemaidens.

9

A balancing act in the pit

The Rhinemaidens had already sung and swum when Solti arrived on 15 May. This particular visit was to enable him to establish the correct balance between the sound of voices on the stage and the orchestra in the pit. We must recall here that Richard Wagner had designed the Festspielhaus so that words were not drowned by music. That is why he placed the conductor and the orchestra out of sight, in a sunken pit. This pit was not tailored to suit the convenience of the conductor, nor his ego, since he is hidden by the cowl.

A conventional orchestra pit, such as that at Covent Garden, is visible from the auditorium, to which the pit is connected by a gate that remains open during rehearsals. Balance is not easy to achieve anywhere but, working under normal conditions, Solti signals to one of his assistants, who comes to stand beside him, and when Solti puts his finger on the score, the assistant takes over while Solti prowls around the auditorium, listening for balance. Most conductors do the same, but it had become something of an obsession with Solti since his meeting, as a young conductor in Munich after the War, with the composer Richard Strauss, who considered a proper balance between the voices and the orchestra to be the essence of good operatic conducting.

In the Festspielhaus, the conductor cannot slip out into the auditorium. Because of the cowl, he is visible to the music staff sitting in the auditorium only on internal television monitors; and he can communicate with them only by direct telephone line. When Solti picked up the receiver behind his podium, the telephone on the music staff's desk buzzed like an angry wasp, and one of his assistants, picking it up, would tell him whether or not the balance was correct.

Solti heard about the problems of the Bayreuth pit from his old friend Pierre Boulez, who had conducted the *Ring* in Bayreuth for the last five successive summers, when they met at the Ritz in Paris in 1981. Valerie Solti was there too, and remembers Boulez saying that he had sometimes felt as though he was conducting under water in a swimming pool, he could hear so little of what was being sung on stage. Boulez advised great care, and infinite patience.

Solti had, of course, already made every effort to ensure success: he had asked for the best available players, and arranged enough time for rehearsal. As early as 1980, when Wolfgang Wagner visited him at Roccamare, he stipulated that there should be fourteen two and a half hour sessions with the orchestra before they even began to work with the singers on the stage. For that, Solti wanted a further sixteen sessions. This was more than Wagner had previously allocated to any conductor in Bayreuth, but he did not argue. The only disagreement between the two occurred when Solti asked Wagner to hire a couple of soloists he knew well from the Chicago Symphony Orchestra. The request conflicted with a Bayreuth tradition that the players should be drawn from German orchestras (a custom that is entirely agreeable to the German musicians' union), and Wagner refused to alter it. Solti would have no soloists from Chicago, but Wagner did promise that the personnel in his orchestra would remain as unchanged as possible – though horn players cannot blast out Wagner's music night after night, so some replacements are inevitable. Furthermore, Wagner agreed that the players allocated to Solti would arrive in Bayreuth earlier than usual, on 17 June. This gave Solti a month to work with the singers before he tackled the problem of balancing their voices and the orchestra.

He could not do this entirely by himself; he was aided by a multinational force of musical assistants, most of whom were aspiring young conductors. Solti's chief assistant was David Syrus, a cheerful, fastidious coach from Covent Garden, who was assisted in his turn by a Dutchman, Ed Spanjaard, who had his own orchestra in Holland; a Scot named Donald Runnicles, who was learning the conductor's trade in Mannheim; and a German, Helmut Weese, who had had years of experience coaching in Bayreuth. In May I asked Syrus to guide me through the complexities of vocal and orchestral techniques, which he readily agreed to do (though any errors which follow are my responsibility, and not his). An obliging figure, with a military moustache and a fondness for shorts and a sweatshirt, Syrus loved Wagner's music – his first job at Covent Garden had been prompting for its *Ring* cycle.

The final music-and-movement rehearsal for the Valkyries (foreground) on Rehearsal Stage No. 3. It is the same size and has the same rake as the theatre stage; the cloth for *Die Walküre* has already been laid.

Moreover he shared Solti's passion for rhythmical orchestral playing, and his admiration for singers who didn't try to produce more sound than they were capable of achieving.

The music staff arrived before Solti and checked that the singers knew their parts; that they were breathing correctly, since the emphasis of a line changes according to the word on which a breath is taken; and that they appreciated the rhythms Solti would insist upon. This coaching took place intensively in the rehearsal rooms scattered around the Festspielhaus, and more casually during stage rehearsals when the singers were working with the director, discovering where they would move and why. Syrus had learned some of the tempi Solti proposed using, when they went over the score together the previous winter, and he applied them strictly, though not always without receiving comment. Siegmund Nimsgern, who had sung Wotan in Solti's American concert performances of *Das Rheingold* in April, would lean over to the pit from the edge of the stage to claim that the tempo had been different in Chicago, and Syrus would acknowledge the advice politely.

Syrus placed great emphasis on the grammar of the text, insisting, for example, that singers get the word endings grammatically correct. But when Solti arrived, the emphasis shifted slightly: he wanted the singers to make a beautiful sound wherever it was possible, and asked them for more variety from their voices, more *piano* phrases and *legato* lines. (*Legato* means singing a whole line smoothly, making the sound more lyrical.) Solti told me that his object was to make the singers understand the musical character of the part they were playing. 'That's not easy: they're not used to being asked for colour and *legato*. Nobody else asks. So some of them say: "Why is he such a sadist, Solti?" But, no, he's not a sadist, he's just precise. He wants to do what's written. I ask them to stretch themselves, and you will find that 85 per cent like to be stretched. Only the bad ones don't.' Many of the singers had auditioned for their parts at Bayreuth simply so that they could work with Solti.

Solti rehearses Hildegard Behrens, with David Syrus, left.

'The music staff want to hear all the words,' said Birgitta Svendén, one of the Rhinemaidens, 'but Solti says the audience can pick up the words from the text they can buy at the bookshop. He wants to hear the *legato*.' Doris Soffel, the German mezzo-soprano who sang Wotan's wife, Fricka, explained to me that it is psychologically important to a singer when a conductor like Solti insists on more vocal variety: 'Many conductors are satisfied when they realise you know your part; they don't ask for more because they don't know the piece or what they want.' (Soffel also outlined the difference between Bayreuth and other great opera houses. 'Singing Wagner in big opera houses, you first find out how to survive. Here I feel more comfortable; it's like singing a heavy Verdi role, and you never feel you have to press your voice. You can make Wagner sound as beautiful as Berlioz.')

A session with the Rhinemaidens was scheduled one afternoon in May, and since I knew their part of the *Ring* as well as any other, I asked Solti if I could sit in and listen. 'Of course,' he replied; 'we have no secrets, just hard work.' Solti was followed by members of the music staff into a brightly-lit rehearsal room, furnished only with a grand piano and a number of chairs against two walls. Syrus sat at the piano and Solti stood beside it, his score in front of him. Across the piano from Solti was Hermann Becht, the burly, good-natured German bass who sang Alberich, with the three Rhinemaidens standing on his left. The personalities of the Rhinemaidens complemented each other, as did their voices. Agnes Habereder, an energetic, inquiring extrovert from Stuttgart, was the dramatic soprano, Woglinde; since she had already sung a Brünnhilde, in Barcelona, she assumed leadership of the trio. Diana Montague, the mezzo-soprano singing Wellgunde, was from Covent Garden; coltish, evidently shy, and more intense than her colleagues. The contralto, Flosshilde, was Birgitta Svendén from Stockholm; small and blonde, patient and secure.

Solti started with a line-by-line commentary on what he wanted to hear. The pianist played the music of the Rhinemaidens' entry and as they sang he shouted: 'You're not having a coffee break, you're having fun.' While Agnes Habereder was singing, Solti skipped across the room, put his face just six inches from her own, and said: '*Piano, piano*, Agnes.' Throughout the rehearsal he insisted on greater variation of vocal colour – soft from the Rhinemaidens, sharp from Alberich. To make a particular point to Becht, Solti moved around to the keyboard and played himself: 'Spot the half *staccato* here, I want to hear every word.' He distinguished which phrases he wanted sung short, which long, which with *vibrato*, which with *legato*. When he heard what he liked, Solti banged his score with his palm or made a salute with his open hand as part of his conducting motion.

The Rhinemaidens should compete with each other, he suggested; each should try harder to seduce Alberich. But always with pure sound: 'Diana, you're a coquette, could you colour it a bit more, like a pop singer? A bit more *vibrato*, less Bach and more Wagner.... Birgitta, you're too loud to start with. I want this really *piano* to drive him crazy. If you could make that *piano* I would be very glad.... Agnes, when you first mention the gold, don't be so dark. It must be more mysterious. Alberich doesn't know what you're talking about.'

When Agnes Habereder sang the lines explaining that before he can steal the gold and make the ring, the thief must pronounce a curse on love, Solti exclaimed: 'That's the *Ring* story; if you don't know that you can go home. If I close my eyes and listen, I have to know that's the secret. *Piano, piano*, Agnes.... Birgitta, more length.... Diana, give a little more concern or we don't understand.... Three good musicians such as you are, could you sing pup-pup-pah, not pah-pah-pah?'

The Rhinemaidens; *Das Rheingold*. l. to r. Birgitta Svendén (Flosshilde), Agnes Habereder (Woglinde), and Diana Montague (Wellgunde).

They finished the scene and Solti was pleased, but not extravagantly so. 'Very good. We need a little time, it will come, but we have time. I've been concentrating on him,' Solti said, indicating Reiner Goldberg, his Siegfried, who had just come into the rehearsal room to sing his scene with the Rhinemaidens in *Götterdämmerung*. The mood changed with Goldberg's entrance. There was more tension, less laughter. When the Rhinemaidens see Siegfried's ring and sing *'Den gib uns'* (Give it to us), Solti ordered that each word be heard. 'Don't rush, keep to *piano*. You're good here, but you're missing it on stage.' Goldberg, who sat to sing, provoked no banter at all, and there was an uncomfortable moment when he sang: *'Noch bin ich beutelos'* – I've nothing with me to give. Solti glanced up from his score and said *'Jawohl, mein Herr.'* Later I asked David Syrus whether the use of such a phrase was deliberate. He said he believed it was.

Solti concentrated on this kind of work in rehearsal rooms, rather than conducting from the podium during the stage rehearsals. His occasional appearances in the pit were signalled to those of us watching in the auditorium (who could not see who was conducting) by the high whistle with which Solti always accompanied the singers – one of the most distinctive sounds in modern music. Solti did try once to test the general balance before the whole orchestra arrived in Bayreuth by asking Doris Soffel to sing from the stage while he conducted a single oboe in the pit. In the pit, the oboe sounded terribly loud to Solti, but when he went out to listen in the auditorium, Soffel's voice covered the oboe. The experiment confirmed what he had already been told.

Wagner had agreed to reschedule a stage rehearsal so that the orchestra could use the pit late on the first day that they played together in the Festspielhaus, 17 June. That morning Solti had introduced himself to the orchestral players, who had arrived from a wide variety of orchestras in Germany, at a rehearsal in the restaurant alongside the Festspielhaus (it has a better acoustic than any other restaurant in the world, naturally), and Valerie Solti was delighted by the way they had responded to each other. The players, who can drive inexperienced conductors to the verge of a nervous breakdown by wilfully misunderstanding them, had worked hard from the first.

That evening the orchestra was tuning up in the pit ten minutes before Solti arrived. The players are so cramped that it is not possible to shift them around to alter the sound balance, as Solti often likes to do. The first violins are on his right, second violins on the left – unlike most other pits where the violins sit together on the

Facing page: Explanatory words from Solti to Reiner Goldberg (Siegfried); after a Siegfried rehearsal.

Solti shares a joke with the stage staff at a piano dress rehearsal; Ed Spanjaard, one of his assistants, on his left.

conductor's left. This is how Richard Wagner said it should be, and so it still is. One step down from the violins, the violas are ranged in a line across the pit, and below them are the cellos, flanked on each side by the basses. They stand in front of the harps, who are raised above the woodwind players on platforms. At the bottom of the pit, right underneath the stage, are the brass players and the percussionists.

Solti let the orchestra play for fifteen minutes, and the auditorium filled with orchestral sound for the first time that summer. It was as if the Festspielhaus had taken a deep breath after a long winter hibernation, even though the stage was bare, and no human voice was to be heard – apart from Solti's whistle. The clarity of sound was immediately apparent, but David Syrus confirmed what I thought I heard: that the brass and woodwind were distinctly fainter than they would be in a concert hall.

When the orchestra stopped, Solti talked rather more than he would, say, with his orchestra in Chicago, where he knows the capabilities of the musicians, and they are familiar with his intentions.' He spoke German, breaking into English only when he picked up the telephone to ask Syrus if he thought, for example, the trombones were loud enough. Later Syrus went into the pit to draw the same sound from the orchestra, and Solti sat at the music desk, a towel round his neck, marking the score in front of him. Dramatic scrawls in thick red pencil indicated the tempi, and the entrances of various instruments. The red pencil became his baton as he conducted snatches of the music to himself, and on the first occasion, in the pit and out of it, he was not satisfied by what he heard. The loss of sound from the woodwinds and the horns seemed to him to remove 'blossom' and vitality from the music; and he detected a further imperfection in the balance between the cellos and the basses. He would have liked an extra bass player, but there was simply no room for one in the pit.

In the Bayreuth pit the musicians can hear only what their neighbours are playing; the rest of the orchestral sound is inaudible, which creates a tendency for individuals to play louder than they normally would. (A further consequence of this inaudibility is that the orchestra is very difficult to tune.) Solti's major difficulty, however, was how to produce the excitement he wanted to hear without making too much noise and spoiling what Bayreuth is famous for: the equal balance of sound between the singers and the orchestra. 'I have never been so confused in all my life,' he said later.

When Richard Wagner first produced *Parsifal* in Bayreuth in 1882, six years after the *Ring*, he altered the acoustical architecture of the pit by building a hardboard cover jutting out some three feet from the edge of the stage, confining the space between the stage and the cowl even further, and controlling the sound more rigorously. Underneath the cover is a perforated layer of hardboard through which the sound flows more freely. Syrus told Solti that Boulez had experimented by removing the hardboard cover. Solti tried this, but found, when he did so, why Richard Wagner had put on the cover in the first place: the sound was so loud that it blurred the distinction between the strings and the woodwind and horns. Solti then replaced the top layer of hardboard except in the central sector directly above the woodwind. This compromise, releasing the woodwind sound and giving the brass more chance to be heard, pleased him better. But his only rule-of-thumb for correct balance remained necessarily vague. 'When I can't hear anything on stage, I know I am too loud, and when I can hear easily I know I am too soft. When I can hear a little of the singers' voices above the orchestra, I think it must be right.'

Solti's objective now was to get the orchestra playing Wagner's music with intense rhythm and great colour – in contrast to Boulez who had looked for remarkable clarity of sound, and had worked hard to achieve the correct transition from one tempo to another. Boulez interpreted the score intellectually: although highly disciplined, Solti's approach was more overtly emotional. He wanted to hear from the orchestra the same dynamic range he had demanded of the singers; and asked for much more *piano* and *staccato* playing from the German musicians than they were used to. Some conductors, like Carlos Kleiber, are content to allow soloists freedom to express themselves. Not Solti, who insists that everyone conform to his overall pattern. (Solti had made another discovery in the pit which made discipline more difficult. He illustrated this for me one afternoon when I was sitting at the back of the pit where the brass section plays. I was thirty-five feet or so away from the podium, and when he stood up to conduct the singers, I could not see his face. 'You see,' he called out, 'I have to sit down to conduct the brass.')

With a first-class, permanent orchestra, there would have been little difference between the sound Solti heard in his head and the sound the orchestra produced. With an *ad hoc* collection of players, Syrus explained to me, a perfect relationship between conception and execution is very difficult to obtain straight away. Solti insisted on two rehearsal sessions each day that the orchestra was available – on other days it had to play for other conductors performing other parts of the repertory, for revivals of *Die Meistersinger*, *Parsifal*, and *Tristan* were also scheduled for the 1983 Festival. Two daily sessions were twice as many as Solti would have undertaken with the Covent Garden orchestra, and the intensity of this schedule began, by the beginning of July, to tire him.

Minor irritations were dealt with expeditiously. For instance, the desk on the podium was too small to take the enlarged scores that had been copied and bound for Solti in Chicago. The desk was rebuilt. The lightshade above the podium was so deep that Solti hit his hands and forearms when conducting. He asked if it could be remade 3 cm shallower, and Huneke said it was no problem. But these were just about the only things that were no problem.

As I sat below Solti during a piano rehearsal in the pit one day, he looked down and said: 'If anybody had told me when I was at music school that I would one day be in a pit where I couldn't hear anything or see all the players, I would have become a doctor.'

Facing page: Rehearsing *Götterdämmerung*. Josephine Barstow and Bent Norup, the chorus and, as the dead Siegfried, Christopher Thomas from the stage staff.

10

Das Rheingold: succumbing to the Wagner virus

One of the first entries in my notebook, made in the summer of 1981, records Peter Hall's reference to the reputation of the Festspielhaus in the post-war years under Wieland and Wolfgang Wagner. 'One wonderful thing about Bayreuth is that it's actually a very serious place as far as the director is concerned,' he said then. Although the conductor has become a more influential figure following Wieland's death (Wolfgang, as we have seen, feels that the conductor holds '51 per cent of the shares' in a production), Bayreuth retains its reputation as a director's theatre. Because the theatre is closed to the public for the best part of eleven months a year, a director has more time to work on stage than in metropolitan opera houses. The sprawling engineering and scenery workshops behind the auditorium have excellent facilities for building original scenery and props, and there is, besides, over 100 years' accumulated experience of producing Wagner's operas.

Of course, even a director's theatre has rules, and Hall and Dudley had already broken one of these: that the set and costume designs should be prepared a full year before a new production was scheduled to open. But they both assumed that once they began work in the Festspielhaus on 24 April 1983, the machine controlled by Wolfgang Wagner would move into top gear and the recriminations and delays of the previous eighteen months would be forgotten. Instead, they were about to undergo an education in what Wagner, a year or so earlier, had called 'the realities of Bayreuth'. Interested in what this 'reality' might be, I watched the rehearsals of *Das Rheingold* from early May, when they started so

108

The production team discusses a problem. l. to r. Guus Mostart, Michael McCaffery, Hall, Dorothea Glatt-Behr, Dudley, Christopher Thomas.

successfully with the discovery that the Rhinemaidens could sing and swim, until the dress rehearsal in July. I learned straight away that the emotional temperature inside a theatre rises and falls more quickly than in any other workplace I know.

Walter Huneke and his colleagues in the workshops had already achieved a great deal before Hall and Dudley arrived in Germany. The platform was installed; the tank and the mirror were ready; and the projection platform, that had been hurriedly conceived one day in February, had been built in two weeks, though at the considerable cost of suspending all other construction in the workshops during that time. Huneke was rightly proud, claiming that no other theatre in Germany, perhaps in the world, could have managed what his team in Bayreuth had done. But Hall and Dudley, feeling the management had been so grudging about the whole conception, regarded each stage as a battle to be won and gave insufficient credit to the achievement of actually installing tank and platform. The stage staff would have liked to hear a few compliments, but Hall and Dudley were too preoccupied with other production problems.

Nothing caused more anxiety, and few things more argument, than the stilts worn by Manfred Schenk and Dieter Schweikart, who played Fasolt and Fafner. Their stilts were quite unlike those worn by circus clowns. Plates at the bottom of each stilt, connected to the top by sprung steel tubes, could react sensitively to every muscle movement in the wearer's feet, and duplicated normal heel-and-toe actions in walking. This made them easier to balance on, in theory at least.

Aged fifty-three, Schenk was a grey-haired and portly bass, apparently rather too old for playing games, but he was nonetheless the first up on stilts one afternoon early in May. Both Schenk and Schweikart had gamely agreed to try the stilts, though Wagner had reserved exclusively to them the right to refuse if they found them too dangerous or difficult. Hall and Robert Ralph, another National Theatre actor brought over to demonstrate the stilts to the singers, shepherded both basses as they took their first steps, peering up at them from the stage floor because on 27-inch stilts they were over eight feet high. Schweikart, a neater and more compact figure, seemed the more nervous of the two, but within twenty minutes they were both striding along the flat surface of the stage floor. The next task was to get the giants on to the platform. A ramp had been constructed specially for the purpose, but when Ralph led the way up, even he found the grade of the ramp difficult: for the two singers it was impossibly steep. Huneke obligingly offered to prepare another ramp with a much gentler incline, to be ready for the following morning's rehearsal. When Schenk and Schweikart returned to their dressing-room after that first try-out they agreed that the stilts *were* both dangerous and difficult, but Schweikart told me later that they decided, because Hall had asked them so politely, to try again next day.

Hall was not much less nervous than the giants. 'They look wonderful,' he said, 'but it's only going to work if one of them doesn't fall over in the next couple of days.' Wagner hovered about the stage during these rehearsals, making Cassandra-like noises, but in fact neither did fall, although they discovered that because they were using their stomach muscles to help their balance, they could not breathe as easily as they would have wished when they sang. Nonetheless, at the end of the second day they agreed again to go on trying. On day three Schenk had to perform the trickiest feat of all, falling dead on the stage. Ralph showed him how to do it, crumpling at the knees and then toppling forward. Schenk fell, received the first bravos of the summer from the auditorium, and announced that he was unhurt. Though he was fearful every time he fell, Schenk never failed Hall.

110

'After Fasolt's fall, Peter was very clever,' observed Schweikart. 'At each rehearsal he would ask us to wear a new piece of costume: first the tunic that makes our shoulders so broad; then the mask which covers the whole of our heads; then the hands; then to carry our big axes, and finally the heavy sack I have to bring on stage.' Had they been asked to wear the whole costume at one rehearsal, it would have given the giants a perfectly reasonable pretext for declaring the rig impossible. Taking one at a time, they found they could cope, though not without difficulty. The masks were designed to give them even more height, and they looked out through the nostrils, with their mouths on a level with the mask's chin. Trying on the mask one day, I realised how greatly it distorted the sound of the orchestra. For a singer, that alone would have been sufficient reason for refusing to wear it, especially as Solti was demanding more delicate *piano* phrases than Fasolt and Fafner usually sing. Wagner made it clear to each of them that he would not mind at all if they refused to wear the stilts, but Schenk and Schweikart were among the boldest performers at Bayreuth in 1983. They did appear terrifying, and when they towered over Freia, the goddess of beauty whom they wanted to carry off as payment for building Valhalla, she looked like Fay Wray about to be snatched by King Kong – the image Hall had originally intended. Before the first night, Schweikart declared: 'By now I feel *almost* confident.'

Schenk and Schweikart were told early on by Wagner that they were the first Fafner and Fasolt at Bayreuth who actually *looked* like giants. (When Hall reported this to me, he added, 'The singers were amazed; Wagner usually praises no one.' I asked why and he replied: 'You don't praise people in church.') But Hall heard of Wagner's compliment only indirectly. From Wagner himself, he received a formal letter stating that he, Hall, must pay the premium to insure the giants against loss of earnings resulting from any injury incurred while they were on the stilts. Hall replied, equally formally, that as a theatre administrator himself he always understood that insurance was the responsibility of the house. Not so, Wagner replied informally, and there the matter rested, unresolved.

In fact the most serious threat to the giants' physical well-being came from the awesome expenditure of physical energy as they sang in their heavy costumes. After each act, Schenk and Schweikart literally wrung the sweat out of their shirts, and the resident Festspielhaus doctor calculated that they sweated three times as much during a performance as they would in a sauna. He gave them injections to offset the effects of dehydration, and made them consume copious quantities of a sweet drink given to athletes to help restore their energy. (Both found that beer helped too.) The outcome of this treatment was that neither of the substantial basses lost a single pound in weight during the summer.

The actual stage performances were a luxury compared to the hours the giants had to spend on their stilts, rehearsing entrances and exits. They were the best single example of a problem that dominated rehearsals: how to get people on and off the platform at the right time and in the right place. The ramp up which the giants walked met the platform at its lowest position, which was some four feet above the ground, but in the action that preceded their entrance the platform was steeply angled, to suggest that Wotan and Fricka were asleep (as Scene Two of *Das Rheingold* opened) just below the mountain peak, beyond which Wotan's great new castle, Valhalla, could be seen in the distance. (Valhalla was a painted cloth looking like a castle designed by a committee of Tibetan and Cambodian architects.) The platform was operated from the wings, and in the early weeks of rehearsal smooth movement was rarely achieved as

Gods and Giants – *Das Rheingold*. l. to r. Nimsgern (Wotan); Soldh (Freia) backview; Soffel (Fricka); Demitz (Donner); Davies (Froh) with Schenk and Schweikart (Fasolt and Fafner).

Walter Kottke, the operator, slowly mastered the technique of stopping the platform at the required position. Because there was only a skeleton stage staff in May and June, it was impossible to anchor the platform quickly when the correct position had been reached; consequently, the platform swayed as singers strode across it, thus adding a sense of physical insecurity to the aching thighs and calf muscles caused by walking on the steep slope. Once I watched the cast pale as the platform fell a foot or so without warning. None was exactly overjoyed at working on the platform, but none complained about the idea itself. What they found irritating were long delays while the platform movements necessary for their entrances and exits were synchronised with the music. Early in May Wagner insisted that Hall and Dudley should work out the entrances and exits before rehearsals began, which was only fair to the singers. The two did so, only to change them again when they actually saw the outcome of their draft plans on the stage.

Concentration: Peter Haage works out details of his interpretation of Mime with Hall.

A high access tower had to be built so that Wotan and Fricka could mount the platform before it settled down over the water tank at the beginning of the second scene; Donner, the god of thunder, and Froh, would hide behind some rocks placed upstage, which meant they had to be in position from the beginning of the scene; Freia, the goddess of love, climbed up a ladder at the back of the platform. At least Loge could walk up the ramp, since he, like the giants, was supposed to be walking up the mountain from the valley of the Rhine. Eventually, a solution to all the entrances and exits was found, but the time it took strained tempers in an atmosphere that was already charged with tension.

The uneasy mood was partly caused by the schedule, which might generously be described as arduous, but perhaps more realistically as ridiculous. A total of twenty days was allowed for rehearsing *Das Rheingold*, which would not have been generous for a new production that took place entirely on the stage floor and contained no such technical complexities as the tank and the platform. *Das Rheingold* may be the shortest piece in the *Ring* cycle, but it is no less difficult to stage than *Götterdämmerung*, which is twice as long, since its four scenes have to be played without interval, one set in the Rhine, the next on a mountain top, the third underground in Nibelheim, and the fourth back on the mountain top.

By mid-May I had begun to feel oppressed by the gargantuan size of Wagner's work, and decided that the only explanation for the foolhardiness of those who try to put the whole *Ring* on stage in a single season is that they have succumbed to a rare allergy. I named this the Wagner virus, and briefly thought it an original idea; shortly afterwards I read Bernard Levin on the subject of Wagner fever, a slightly different strain of the same bug. Others may well have thought of it too. The diagnosis of the Wagner virus is not merely that a sufferer has fallen under the spell of the music: a true victim is under the illusion that the theatrical and musical challenges of the *Ring* can actually be overcome, and its most virulent form is to be found in Bayreuth, naturally, where the four parts of the cycle have to be produced in a single summer.

After watching the technical and artistic havoc wrought by this requirement (for the *Rheingold* rehearsals stopped while the preliminary staging of the other three parts of the cycle began), I asked Wolfgang Wagner why the Festival imposed such a gruelling timetable on the director, designer and conductor of a new production. There was no crisp answer. He replied first that the Festspielhaus was the theatre designed specially for the *Ring* by

Richard Wagner; not an explanation in itself. Second, that it was the way Richard Wagner had done it in 1876. And third, that Richard Wagner had disapproved of separate performances of his work. 'We don't want to keep to prefixed tradition,' Wagner continued, but the main reason for insisting that a new production be done complete was that the *Ring* was a Festival work *par excellence*, best seen by an audience that did not have to fight through city traffic for a curtain-rise at 4 p.m., but by an audience that assembled for a week solely to see the entire work. There was a price to pay for this in the first year, Wagner admitted. 'I know perfectly well that when a director does a new conception of the *Ring* for the first time, it cannot be perfect in the detail. The second year is the important one.'

When Hall arrived in Bayreuth, he was reluctant to admit that the production would not be as he wanted it by the opening performance in the first year, and he offered me a further justification for doing the *Ring* in a single summer. It imposed on all parts of the cycle a stylistic unity that was often lacking when a *Ring* was produced over three years. But the burden on the director and designer of telling the story, complete, in a single week was almost intolerable, even if everything went smoothly. In Bayreuth, in the summer of 1983, it did not.

The greatest disaster was the projection platform that was suspended from the stage tower, and operated so that it complemented the movements of the main platform. Film projections on this second platform, to take the place of the cloths that Dudley found unsatisfactory, had already been a source of recrimination between Wagner and Dudley. The film Dudley wanted to commission would cost more than Wagner was willing to pay; for his budget was already overspent. Dudley now feared that there would be too little to show on the second screen. For his part, Hall, after watching the uncertain movements of the main platform, suspected that the movements of the two platforms could not be properly synchronised. But these were not the deficiencies that led to the abandonment of the projection platform.

The occasion of this disaster was the arrival in Bayreuth from his home in Bremen of the lighting director for the *Ring*, Manfred Voss, on 4 June. A reserved, handsome man of great authority, Voss pointed out that with the projection platform in the grid from which it would be hung, there would be no room for the rows of lamps needed to light the stage from above. Voss had mentioned the problem earlier, in February, but he had done so discreetly, rather than in a flamboyant Wagnerian manner. Both Hall and Dudley had

Facing page:
Top: Hildegard Behrens tests the rescue of Sieglinde while Hall and Dudley watch.
Bottom: Peter Holowka (left) from Vienna, in charge of properties, directs the men in the horse through a hole in the polystyrene body.

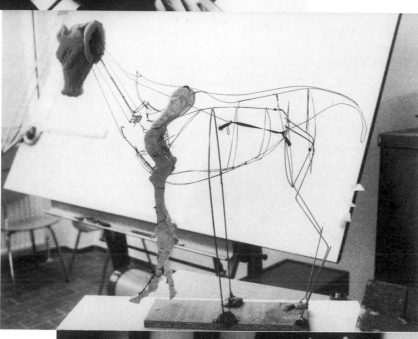

This page:
Brünnhilde's horse –
Top: Dudley makes trial designs.
Middle: a wire model in the design studio.
Bottom: the head sculpted in polystyrene.

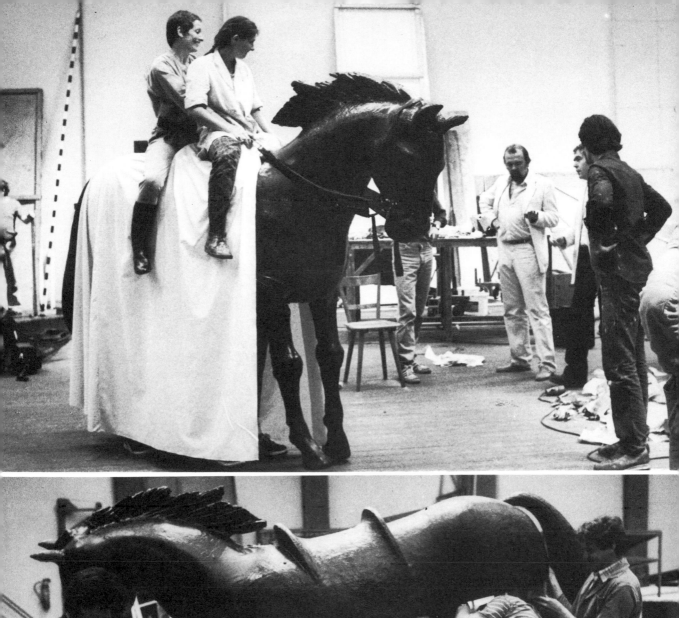

thought he was referring to a solvable problem. In fact, the only solution was a Hobson's choice: they could either have top lighting, or the projection platform. But top lighting was absolutely essential. The platform was scrapped, literally. It was laid to rest on a piece of ground by the canteen, and stayed there all summer, a permanent reminder of a costly failure.

Dudley was dejected by the decision, which was a token of the misunderstandings that had created such a gulf between the management and himself. He was already worried about the cuts in his designs, made either because the workshops could not produce finished material in time for the performances, or because of cost, or for artistic reasons. As we stood together one day in the auditorium, while Hall walked thoughtfully about the platform, Dudley said nervously: 'I've got a feeling Peter's going to cut something.' Hall joined us and said: 'Bill, I'm going to be provocative. I think this set is too cluttered, we've got to cut something.' There was a metal tree from which Freia's golden apples – the fruit that invests the gods with immortality – were to hang, whose branches made a distracting noise, like delicate cymbals, every time a singer moved on the platform; the tree went. So, eventually, did the bed of flowers on which Wotan and Fricka were sleeping at the beginning of Scene Two of *Das Rheingold*. But Dudley minded most about a cloth showing a prospect of the Rhine that was intended to hang below Valhalla. His passion for separate visual planes defining the exact location of the action was at its most intense in this scene: in the sky was a misty vision of Valhalla; the gods inhabited the mountain top (on the platform); down below was the Rhine, where the mortals lived. Dudley knew that the Rhine prospect was in danger of elimination early in May, and spoke of it as a resignation issue. When the moment of decision arrived, however, Dudley himself offered to cut the Rhine prospect, realising unhappily that it was inevitable: money was running out, and the workshops were still at full stretch, and behind schedule.

One evening early in June, as we walked through the woods behind the Festspielhaus, Dudley listed his frustrations: the set for some scenes was becoming too bare, too minimalist; he had had to fight uncommonly hard to retain the birch trees that framed the set for Siegfried's death; worse still, he sensed that the staff of the Festspielhaus had turned against Hall and himself, even in the costume department where he had thought he had good friends. Backstage, there was much talk about the virtues of the Chereau *Ring*, in comparison with which their own always seemed to fare badly. The only reassurance he had received had come from his local assistant, a sensitive and hard-working young man named Johann Taubenschuss, who told Dudley that his experience was not unique. Chéreau's designer, Richard Perduzzi, had also had a hard time with Wagner and Honeke, and the designer of the previous summer's *Parsifal* had quit under the strain of a similar barrage. 'Bad-mouthing artists seems to be a tradition of the place, but knowing that doesn't help me at the moment,' said Dudley, sadly.

The cuts caused the workshops almost as much pain as they did Dudley. Two weeks' solid work had already been wasted on the projection platform, but the case that best illustrated the workshops' growing dislike of the English way of making decisions was that of the craftsman who had voluntarily decided that he could not possibly go to a family wedding because he had to finish a rock for the *Walküre* set. A day after it was completed, the rock was cut.

As if by magic, Wolfgang Wagner appeared in the auditorium every time there was trouble. (It took Dudley weeks to work out how Wagner's timing could be so perfect; he finally remembered the television monitor in Wagner's office that shows what is happening on stage.) Wagner was free with his criticism because, he said, it was the product of his own experience and therefore would be helpful. But he was sparing with his praise. He mentioned to the giants that they looked uncommonly like giants, but the risk inherent in the use of stilts meant that he spoke to Hall only of their impracticality. He repeated the approving remark he had made to Hall the previous summer – that the use of water was the best artistic solution to the Rhinemaidens' scene he knew – but he made the comment to a visiting reporter, not to Hall or Dudley. For them he had no compliments at all. Though Hall intended to ask Wagner for advice, he stopped doing so when he found that he always got a historical lecture on the ways a scene had previously been played. He declared that he had never before worked in a theatre where the management seemed to be willing him to fail.

One day Georg Solti, in the pit waiting for a rehearsal to start, called out pleasantly to Wagner, on stage, that in a radio interview he had urged that Bayreuth should receive a more generous subsidy. Wagner's Welsh temperament surfaced as he shouted ferociously at Solti that Bayreuth did not need more money, just less incompetence from Hall and Dudley. Solti, who thought he knew how to keep the peace with Wagner, was shaken by the episode: it revealed just how deep the gulf between production team and management had become.

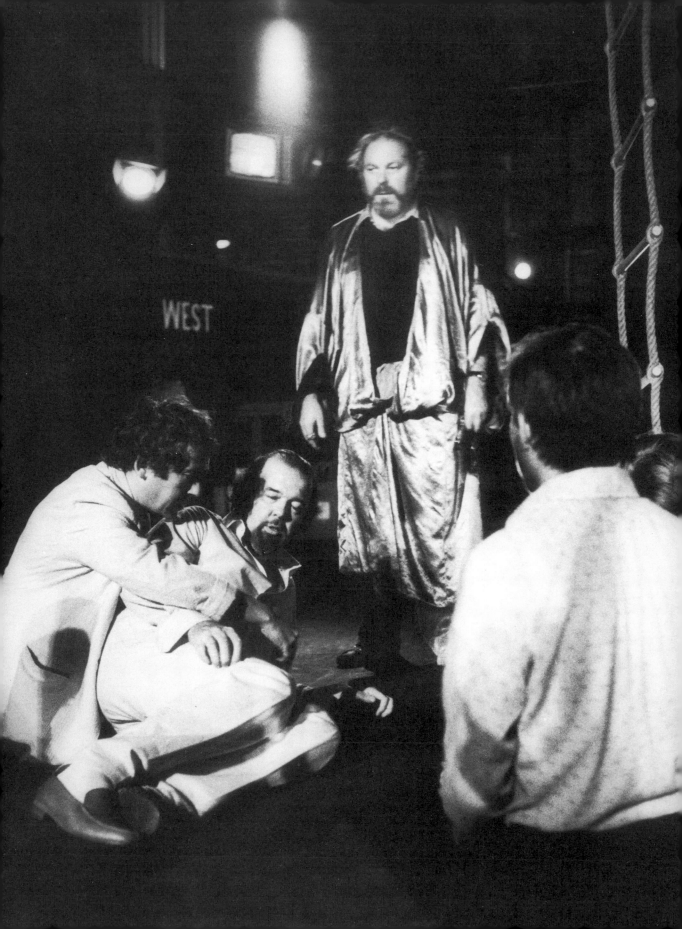

When Wagner bellowed, Hall never snapped back, and thus he broke one of the time-honoured traditions at Bayreuth: that Wagner and his directors (especially Goetz Friedrich) should indulge in quite astonishing shouting-matches. They were a characteristic of the house, and they had a purpose: release of tension, with neither side apparently harbouring ill-feeling. Hall's level voice and controlled demeanour seemed to unsettle Wagner, and the conversations between the two became increasingly one-sided, Hall's response being confined to 'yes' or 'no'. It was so controlled that it could easily be interpreted as British arrogance.

Hall and Dudley took responsibility for some of the production blunders, but the errors were not all on their side. The mirror continued to distort the image of the swimming Rhinemaidens until the dress rehearsal, and even then only two-thirds of the mirror contained the stretched glass Dudley had insisted upon a year earlier. Huneke had promised that the mirror would be corrected; it was in his power to do so and neither Hall nor Dudley doubted that it would be done; but they were unhappy at the length of time it took. A greater frustration confronted them daily, and that was the quality of the stage management. This is an unglamorous job that tends to be taken for granted in the theatre since it involves cueing singers and checking stage properties. But on innumerable occasions neither props nor singers were present on schedule. When the singers dribbled back from a break, or a prop had to be asked for, Hall would say wearily: 'Who's in charge here?' It was a rhetorical question, for although there was a stage manager he was evidently not in charge. Guus Mostart, whose job as Hall's assistant director should have been to help direct the performers, was forced to act as a substitute stage manager. This was Mostart's third role, since he was also Hall's interpreter.

Peter Hall's lack of knowledge of the German language caused considerable problems of which he was well aware. Since most of the singers spoke English ranging from excellent to passable, the obvious communications gap was between Hall and the stage staff, and Dudley also spoke little German. In *Das Rheingold* only Manfred Jung as Loge, Manfred Schenk, Heinz-Jürgen Demitz as Donner and Hermann Becht needed to have Hall's instructions translated, but some of the other singers – not all German either – were unhappy that they could not discuss the German text with Hall. Hall himself said: 'The trouble with Wagner's text is that I have to read the words in translation all the time, because I find the language so clotted and difficult. It does exert a hypnotic spell, but it's hard, terribly hard, and I'm very bad at languages.' Mostart's

Facing page: Das Rheingold, Nibelheim. Dudley tells Hall how the trap should work in order for Hermann Becht (Alberich) to disappear.

multiple occupations exhausted him. Unlike Hall, Mostart shouted regularly. He too was not finding Bayreuth much fun.

There is, of course, no rule that theatrical rehearsals should be fun, but this tension was sapping their enthusiasm. One evening I talked about the atmosphere to Hermann Schreiber, a German journalist also writing a book about Bayreuth, who was, like me, more accustomed to writing about the drama of politics than the opera. Before we left the theatre, Solti had been rehearsing, experimenting with various locations from which the Rhinemaidens could sing invisibly to Wotan as he was about to cross the rainbow bridge to Valhalla at the end of *Das Rheingold*, and Schreiber remarked that the rehearsal was characteristic of the communications breakdown between residents and visitors. Wolfgang Wagner had been visibly upset because Solti had not asked *him* where to place the Rhinemaidens; he knew exactly where they should go, and could have saved Solti time.

The scene changes that evening had been noisy and chaotic: Schreiber reported Wagner as saying that it would take six months for the staff to learn to do these complicated scene changes quietly and quickly. Hall's inability to communicate with the stagehands as Chéreau had done (he was known familiarly as 'Patrice' by the men in the workshops) made them unwilling to work any harder than they needed to. But the basic misconception, as Schreiber saw it, was Hall's belief that since Bayreuth was a director's theatre, he could have all he asked for, effortlessly. Wagner and Huneke, though they had not provided everything, *had* given him more than they ever thought was possible; and they felt their efforts were not appreciated. Schreiber concluded that Hall and Dudley had simply not understood the Bayreuth style, which treats the Festspielhaus as a workshop where problems are gradually ironed out from one year to the next: Hall was treating it like the National Theatre.

A few days later, talking with Hall over lunch, I outlined Schreiber's remarks, and Hall responded with his own view of Bayreuth, a little more than two months after his arrival. 'The first surprise was that Wagner's behaviour did not change. I thought that the disagreements of the previous year would be forgotten, and a united front created to produce a *Ring*. The second surprise was the depth of hostility towards us; and the third that their stage management is improvised instead of being scientific. I don't think that's the efficient way to do a job.' Hall concluded sadly that his high expectations of the Festspielhaus as a director's theatre had not been fulfilled.

Die Walküre, Act II, Scene 1: Wotan instructs Brünnhilde to guard Siegmund in his fight with Hunding. Later, after argument with Fricka, he reverses this order.

(*on previous page*): *Die Walküre* Act III, Scene 1. The 'Ride of the Valkyries'; Slain heroes brought by the Valkyries are laid out in the mists below.

Die Walküre, Act III, Scene 3: Wotan kindles the ring of magic fire to guard Brünnhilde, until she is awakened from sleep by the kiss of a fearless hero.
    'Loge! Loge! Hieher!'

Siegfried, Act I, Scene 3:
Siegfried (r.) fashions the
sword Nothung, to the delight
of Mime.

Siegfried, Act I, Scene 2:
In his forge Mime (r.) questions
Wotan, disguised as The
Wanderer, whom Mime
suspects is there to spy on him.

Siegfried, Act II, Scene 2:
Siegfried, having slain Fafner,
hears the voice of the woodbird
telling him of the Nibelung
hoard to be found within
the dragon's cave.

Siegfried, Act III, Scene 1: Wotan, disguised as The Wanderer, questions the earth goddess Erda in her cavern.

Next page:
Siegfried, Act III, Scene 3: Brünnhilde, rapturously greets Siegfried.
> *'O kindische Held!*
> *O herrlicher Knabe!'*

Siegfried, Act III, Scene 3: Brünnhilde, asleep on the mountain top, kissed by the fearless hero Siegfried, is awakened.
> *'Heil dir, Sonne*
> *Heil dir, Licht.'*

At the beginning of July, I heard Hall refer to 'next year' for the first time. This appeared to concede the impossibility of giving performances in 1983 that would sound and look exactly as he intended. Hall was reluctant to agree to this, but 'next year' was ever more frequently mentioned in his conversation. Of all Bayreuth's 'realities', that was the most difficult for Hall and Dudley to accept.

Meanwhile, back on stage an opera – one of four – was being rehearsed. *Das Rheingold* Scenes Two and Four are set on the green slope of the mountainside and mostly played within a circular green mound, which many spectators assumed was a symbol of the ring itself, though Dudley intended it as a reminder of the Avebury Circle in Wiltshire. Scene Three is in the depths of Nibelheim, where the platform becomes the rocky roof of Alberich's cave. Normally, when Hall directs an opera, he begins as he would in the theatre, discussing the work with the singers before setting foot on the stage. Hall's introductory talk was a popular tradition at Glyndebourne. Long before his arrival in Bayreuth, however, Hall had decided that he would be unable to start as he usually did. The operas were being rehearsed out of order, and he assumed that he would never have enough of the cast present at any one time to make the lecture worth while. And although most of the singers understood and worked in English, some might have had difficulties with a long talk. With the three Rhinemaidens it was different: they were delightfully willing, and Hall had an easy relationship with them, sitting down on the rehearsal stage for fifteen minutes and discussing, for instance, the motivation of their three cries of 'Siegfried' in *Götterdämmerung*. Nonetheless, some of the singers were disappointed when they did not hear Hall outline his conception of the *Ring* as a whole; it was the least, one commented, that he had expected from the Shakespeare director. Instead, on 15 May, when the cast assembled for the second scene of *Rheingold*, Hall put them straight to work.

Siegmund Nimsgern, the new Wotan, had arrived that afternoon, wearing a small beard, and with tightly curled ginger hair on the top of his head that made him look slightly taller than he is. Born in Saarland, Nimsgern is a man of strong opinions, one of which is that Wagner should be sung by Germans. He was the successor to a New Zealander, Donald McIntyre, who had sung Wotan throughout the Chéreau *Ring*, and he sounded as though he were restoring a birthright to his country. Off the stage, Nimsgern's manner was as commanding as Wotan's should be: he would tell Dudley what his costumes and wigs should look like, and the height of the lifts he

This page:
Top: Goldberg unconvincingly attacks the dragon Fafner in rehearsal.
Bottom: Further problems about the functioning of the dragon. Hall confronts the stage crew who were operating it.

Facing page:
Top: Peter Holowka and his assistants apply surfaces to trees for the *Siegfried* forest.
Bottom: With the stage gauze half-lowered, the tree for *Siegfried*, Act III, is lowered into place.

wanted in his shoes in order to appear more physically commanding. When we met, he would tell me where I should not eat and what I should drink. But Nimsgern is more sympathetic than he sounds. He was acutely aware that Wagner did not share Solti's and Hall's confidence that he would be a fine new Wotan. His nervousness showed when he first appeared on the stage to demonstrate to Hall the manner in which he thought his first moves should be played. They were clearly too emphatic, but Hall did not stop him, watching and listening patiently while Nimsgern went through his act. When the run-through of the first few pages was done, Hall sat on the stage with his cast, and tried to persuade them to play to each other. 'In this house you do not have to concentrate on reaching the back of the amphitheatre with a big voice; you can look at each other and still be heard. It's *true*,' he said. He took Nimsgern aside and told him to calm the gestures and forget the dramatic poses. 'But I'm a god,' Nimsgern argued. 'No,' Hall replied, 'you're Siegmund Nimsgern.'

When Manfred Jung arrived to play Loge (instead of Siegfried Jerusalem, who had taken over the part of Siegmund in the reshuffle that followed Dennis Bailey's illness), he announced casually that he had four Loges in his repertoire and wondered which one Hall would prefer? Hall wanted Loge to look like a matinée idol and be both passionate and ironic, but since none of Jung's options fitted that pattern, Hall decided to rely on Jung's professionalism rather than try to introduce him to a fifth Loge. He would allow Jung to give what he chose, and select what he wanted. Hall would not have been so permissive at Glyndebourne; he had already accepted that Bayreuth was going to be very different.

Hall had just six days during the first rehearsals of *Das Rheingold* for Scenes Two and Four. The last scene alone is as long as a whole act of *Don Giovanni*, and the amount of time devoted to it was no more than would be allocated to rehearsing one act of a play in a weekly repertory company in the English provinces. Besides worrying about the platform, and the entrances and exits, Hall had to block all the moves, a lengthy business of trial and error. The height of the platform above the stage floor meant that Hall either had to direct from the auditorium, where he could not speak to the singers, or stand on the platform itself, where he could talk but could not judge how the stage picture looked from the auditorium.

Working on stage, Hall crouched, making his arms look longer, and shuffled quickly across the surface of the platform, speaking softly and communicating with his hands as much as his voice. The hands pushed and pulled, pointed, showed where the eyes should be looking. The only thing this had in common with his working methods at Glyndebourne, which I had observed the previous summer, was his open shirt and beige slacks. In the smaller auditorium at Glyndebourne, Hall stood at the rail above the orchestra pit, with the conductor, Bernard Haitink, seated next to him, going through scenes line by line, pausing at the end of each significant moment in the libretto to discuss it with the singers: there, two and a half hours of opera (as *Das Rheingold* is) was allocated four weeks' intensive and consecutive stage and technical rehearsal. Bayreuth was more like Glyndebourne than a conventional opera house, in that Hall was able to call three rehearsal sessions in a day that lasted from 10 a.m. until 10 p.m. (Solti later intervened because he thought the third session imposed too great a strain on the singers' voices.) But the conditions did not allow for any intensive analysis of the characters the singers were playing. As early as 19 May I noted: 'There is really no time to explore motive, just to build up the stage picture; it's not old-fashioned opera in which a group of people who know the parts backwards walk through their moves a couple of days before a performance; but it's not full-blooded music-drama either.'

That was not intended as a criticism of the singers, all of whom worked hard between the first series of *Rheingold* rehearsals in May and the second series – five days early in June. By then it was clear that one of the singers would never learn to move correctly, and that the voice of another would be too light when it had to compete with the orchestra, even in Bayreuth. Judging from his behaviour during rehearsals, the reports of Siegmund Nimsgern's difficult manner were much exaggerated. Hermann Becht's performance as Alberich was growing visibly in dramatic strength, perhaps because he was the one singer who was determined to stop the music if he thought it was necessary, and talk through two or three pages of a scene with Hall and Nimsgern and Jung. And there were charming moments, like the transformation of forty remarkably well-behaved and disciplined children into hunchbacked Nibelungen carrying Alberich's gold – which had in turn been stolen by Wotan so that he could pay the giants for building Valhalla – on stage, and exiting with piercing screams. (Bringing the blocks of cardboard gold on to the stage was easier than getting them off after they had been built into a pile high enough to hide Freia from view; a man might have run a couple of marathons during the time that exit was debated.)

Concentration occasionally wavered. During a run-through of Scene Four, for example, moves planned the previous evening were forgotten; a platform cue was missed, and the rehearsal stopped.

Doris Soffel, playing Fricka, was not given a cue for her entrance; Donner, god of thunder, came on late; and in Froh's absence, Jung and Nimsgern sang his part in turn. Hall's sole response was a muttered 'Jesus Christ'. The run-through stopped again when the giants got their stilted feet tangled in the net finally used to carry off the gold; and as Fasolt fell dead, Manfred Schenk unaccountably began to laugh. When a rich bass voice like Schenk's bubbles with laughter, the sound might carry to Nuremberg on a still day. Donner's entrance was early; Nimsgern began to ignore other singers and sing directly to the auditorium; and the steps up the rainbow bridge were not yet built. When the misery was over, Hall commented: 'I don't get to go through this scene again until the stage and orchestra rehearsal, and by then it's all over for me.'

When the orchestra plays for a stage rehearsal, it forges ahead, stopping only when the conductor stops, not when the director would like to alter a move. At this stage of the *Rheingold* rehearsals, the front gauze was lowered, further divorcing the stage from the centre of the auditorium where Hall was sitting at the director's desk, following the score which was lit dimly by a desk lamp. He could react to events on the stage only after the scene had finished. His mood was not improved when Agnes Habereder, one of the Rhinemaidens, reported that she had cut her hand on a nail left lying on the floor of the tank, and complained to Wagner about improper stage management. Wagner's temperamental response was to tell her not to complain to him, but to suggest to Hall that the tank in Scene One should be cut. 'I really think I'm beginning to lose my temper,' Hall said when he heard of that exchange. By then it was probably too late.

Virtually everything was late. Dudley saw the costumes during an orchestral rehearsal, barely in time to order improvements. The wigs caused him still more anxiety. 'I was sitting in the canteen,' he reflected, 'and I thought, "Who's wearing that frightful wig over there?" and then I realised, "Crikey, she's in my show." The wigs were all too thick. I said to the wigmakers: "Don't think of Wagner; think of your own hair. Feel it in your hands, it's thinner than your wigs. I want you to be able to sit opposite me without me knowing you're in a wig."' (Fortunately, it was not too late for the wigmakers, whose work eventually met Dudley's exacting standards.)

Before the final run-through of *Das Rheingold* in the orchestral rehearsals at the beginning of July, I was apprehensive. Earlier scene changes, taking place in view of the audience, had included views of various stagehands going about their work, and noisily enough to compete with the orchestra; the exit over the rainbow bridge had never been rehearsed; the singers were growing impatient. But though Nimsgern was unable to sing Wotan because his throat was sore, and there were some imperfections in the lighting since Manfred Voss was still experimenting, an ordeal it was not. There were no technical disasters, and even the odd theatrical triumph here and there. The exit of the gods up a flight of steps placed behind the splendid cloth on which the rainbow bridge was painted, was as convincing a crossing of a rainbow bridge as could well be imagined. But the dress rehearsal would not take place for another fourteen days, each of which could usefully have been devoted to polishing *Das Rheingold*. During that fortnight there were stage and orchestral rehearsals of *Siegfried* and *Götterdämmerung*, and no more time for *Das Rheingold*.

Das Rheingold, an early rehearsal, with the painted cloth for the Rainbow Bridge.

Before the *Rheingold* dress rehearsal I asked Hall whether directors were nervous on such occasions, and he answered that he was, on this one. 'I hate the uncertainty. It's a gamble, and I don't like it. I just hope they laugh at the frog.' When the small frog (into which Alberich turns himself) appeared, operated at the end of a springy wire by a hidden stagehand, the audience did indeed laugh. In fact, errors at the dress rehearsal were few. The Rhinemaidens were entirely visible in the mirror, and the water was piped out of the tank during the second scene without a gurgle being heard. The giants never put a stilt wrong; and Wotan exited triumphantly over a rainbow bridge – something which had not been seen for decades. True, some lights still had not been set, the stage looked too dark in the Nibelheim scene (a visual problem compounded by over-generous use of the smoke machines), and the platform was in the wrong position to pull off the gold for Fafner to carry away, so that Manfred Jung had to improvise. But the show worked. The audience at the dress rehearsal seemed sympathetic. I felt a huge sense of relief.

Hall and Dudley were not elated. They felt that the technical management of *Das Rheingold* was so haphazard that although the show had worked at the dress rehearsal, it would not necessarily do so on the first night which was nine days later. They had been allotted only two hours to correct technical faults on the afternoon of the first night. No more time was available, for the platform could only be set up again on stage that same morning because of the previous evening's performance of *Die Meistersinger*, which was to open the 1983 Festival. Doing the *Ring* in the first place had been a gamble. The rehearsals of *Das Rheingold* gave Hall, Solti and Dudley an accurate indication of the odds against its succeeding.

11

Die Walküre: learning to love Brünnhilde

The soprano, Hildegard Behrens, who was to sing Brünnhilde for the first time in Bayreuth, was still breastfeeding her infant daughter when she arrived in Bayreuth on 29 April. With her hair cropped short, wearing a short smock and trousers, Behrens did not look like a prima donna; to begin with she did not sound like one either, for she was recovering from a bad cold. Since she was to perform in Munich the following week, Behrens hardly sang at all during her first rehearsals with Reiner Goldberg. Not realising that Goldberg had begun rehearsals earlier in the week, she had expected a couple of easy days during which Hall would talk to her about the production and Dudley would explain his set designs. But Hall put her to work immediately, plotting her moves while she walked about the platform with her score in her hand. The advice Hall offered was brief and to the point: he said he proposed telling the story of the *Ring* in 'a naïve, direct and poetic way'.

Behrens left for Munich after four days' rehearsal, and was not due back in Bayreuth until 15 May; during that brief interlude a remarkable rumour spread through the opera houses of Europe with the speed generated only by rumours of the highest class. Behrens, so the story went, was expecting another baby and had taken such a dislike to Peter Hall that she would use that pregnancy as an excuse for not doing the *Ring*. The news filtered back to Bayreuth, and Hall was incredulous. He had had some experience of extravagant operatic rumours; after all, he had heard reports that his wife, Maria Ewing, either had cancer and was dying or, alternatively, was already dead. Hall was sure he had established a close relationship with Behrens during their first few days of work together. Even so, the story nagged at him.

131

On 15 May, however, Behrens returned to Bayreuth, not pregnant and still on kissing terms with Hall. He was right about her reaction to him. 'I immediately found that we had an intuitive understanding of each other,' Behrens said later. 'There was nothing between us that was crampy or threatening.' Before long she and Hall had decided that they communicated telepathically: each seemed to know exactly what the other wanted. Hall had experienced such a sympathy before, with actors like Peggy Ashcroft, Judi Dench, Ian Holm and Paul Scofield, for instance, and with a few opera singers – Janet Baker, Frederica von Stade, and, of course, his wife, Maria Ewing. But this was not a common experience. Of all the gambles Hall and Solti took in Bayreuth, Behrens was the one that paid off most quickly and most generously.

Though Brünnhilde is the most testing role in the repertory of an operatic soprano, since she appears in *Die Walküre*, *Siegfried* and *Götterdämmerung*, Brünnhildes are not as scarce as Siegfrieds. (There were three other Brünnhildes in the cast at Bayreuth: Jeannine Altmeyer, who had just been singing *Die Walküre* in San Francisco, Agnes Habereder, and Anne Evans; the only other Siegfried was Manfred Jung.) But virtually every soprano who had embarked on Brünnhilde had begun cautiously with *Die Walküre*, adding the other two operas to her repertory during the next two or three years.

Behrens had not even thought about singing Brünnhilde until 1979; although she had sung Sieglinde, she had not heard much else from the *Ring*. Then, during an engagement in Monte Carlo she heard another soprano rehearsing the part. 'I thought: "This is my music."' Behrens did not seek out an opera house that would give her the role: she simply believed that the chance would turn up. So when Solti asked if she would sing all three parts of the cycle in which Brünnhilde appears, Behrens did not hesitate. 'I didn't even think consciously about the size of the part,' she says. She was even willing to sing in Puccini's *Turandot* in Vienna in the same summer, because she had promised she would. Solti did not consult her before extricating her from the Vienna engagement, but 'Oh,' she says, 'I was so happy they let me out.' She seems never to have found the prospect of singing Brünnhilde in Bayreuth forbidding.

Hildegard Behrens spent ten days at Tanglewood (the summer music festival in Massachusetts) in 1982 going through Brünnhilde's music with a pianist to get some idea of the length of the part; then she forgot it. During the autumn and winter of 1982–3 she was too preoccupied in giving birth to a daughter, and singing in operas by

Facing page: Hildegard Behrens with Hall and Guus Mostart in the main rehearsal stage room.

Schoenberg and Mozart, to think of Wagner. Besides, her experience is that she can only learn a part while actually rehearsing it. Before she travelled to Bayreuth, her main concern was not so much the length or difficulty of the part, as that she should enjoy the production. 'Learning it by heart comes with the moves, the length of a walk, the gestures, the reaction of the partners. Then it's nailed in the head. And once I get the music in my brain, I'm not afraid to sing it.'

Behrens was evidently not afraid of anything. Hall and Dudley knew before rehearsals began that she would be asked to make the most improbable entrance of all. At the end of *Die Walküre*, Brünnhilde has been put to sleep by Wotan on a mountain surrounded by fire, and she does not reappear until the third scene of the third act of *Siegfried*, when the hero himself walks through the fire to wake her with a kiss. The problem was that in the scene preceding Brünnhilde's reawakening, the platform was in a concave position, and the intention was to create the impression of a wall of fire by turning the platform through 180 degrees between Scenes Two and Three, settling it in a convex position so that, when it stopped, Brünnhilde would be sleeping in the same position in which she was last seen at the end of *Die Walküre*. The only plausible way for Behrens to make her entrance, if she were not to clamber up in full view of the audience, was for her to be strapped upside down on the underneath of the platform just before it turned, staying strapped in for a minute and a half as it assumed the new position. Hall mentioned this possibility to Behrens several times before the manoeuvre was attempted on stage, and she did not demur, especially when Hall cunningly said he feared it might be a little too dangerous for her. A harness was made, and the inflated rubber doll from the sex shop in Bayreuth made positively its last stage appearance when the harness was tested, before Behrens herself was asked to try. Predictably, Wagner stormed on to the stage, saying that such an entrance would be much too dangerous, and besides, how could Behrens possibly release herself quickly from any harness that was really safe? Anyway, he said finally, does she agree? Of course she did.

Wagner's last attempt to dissuade Behrens, once she had tried the manoeuvre, was to insist that she repeat it, under the supervision of a doctor and a nurse, on a machine specially constructed in the workshop, which would simulate the platform's 180-degree turn while measuring her physiological response. The instruments revealed no damaging side-effects, and her pulse rate was quite unchanged. Behrens was not just a good voice.

Facing page: The first trial, in darkness. Brünnhilde, harnessed, is inverted under the platform, and rotated to appear on the rock in *Siegfried*.

She was, however, clearly that; the quality of her top notes was evident right from her first entry in *Die Walküre*, singing 'Hoyotoho, hoyotoho', when she produced a fine clear, high B. The only question about her voice was: how good? I was told in Bayreuth that one effective way of judging the quality of a fine soprano is to think of it as a marble column. For a perfect dramatic soprano voice, there should be no cracks at all in the marble from the top to the bottom of the column, and this is so rare that sopranos who have met the requirement in the last seventy-five years can be counted on a few fingers of one hand. Using this analogy, the top of Behrens's voice is excellent; the bottom, when she sings from her chest, is good; but there are a few cracks in the middle. Her voice is not perfect, and it is not the huge instrument of a great vocal athlete like Birgit Nilsson who,

The resident theatre doctor examines Behrens after her first inverted journey; Hall, Dudley, Mostart and Kottke anxiously await his findings.

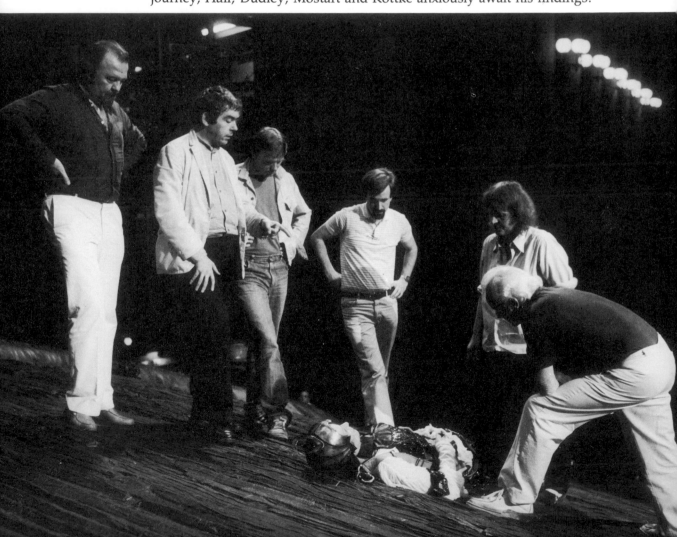

you feel, could knock you off your chair at 100 paces merely by opening her mouth, but it is ideally suited to the generous acoustic at Bayreuth. Moreover, she has qualities that other great Brünnhildes lack. She looks the part (how many Brünnhildes can appear successfully at rehearsal wearing blue jeans?), and she is a splendid actress, capable of sustaining Brünnhilde's personality through the whole range of passion, fearlessness, gentleness, jealousy, and generosity. Some singers found her habit of tucking her chin into her chest when she was singing bottom notes irritating, but that seemed a small price to pay for a performance of such conviction. From the start, she displayed a remarkable commitment to the part and to the production. Hildegard Behrens was the heroine of the 1983 *Ring* off the stage as well as on it.

Hers is not an intimidating physical presence; she was happy to stand unnoticed in line for coffee at the self-service counter in the Festspielhaus canteen, in her rehearsal smock and trousers or jeans. Under her cropped hair she has a finely boned face, with an aquiline nose and very slightly projecting front teeth; she is not conventionally pretty, but her face is expressive and repeatedly breaks into a generous smile as she looks intently at whoever is speaking to her. She is bilingual, her English coloured by the accents of Germany and New York City, where she lives with the American she variously describes as her husband and her lover. She drove to and from the Festspielhaus in a rather grubby car, and what passed for an entourage comprised her baby daughter and her studious-looking brother who helped to look after the child. Behrens was not in the least bit grand.

Her terse programme biography tells us that she was born in Oldenburg and studied at the Freiburg Academy of Music with Ines Leuwen. She made her debut as the Countess in *The Marriage of Figaro* at Osnabrück in 1972 before becoming a member of the Deutsche Oper am Rhein in Düsseldorf, where her debut was in the part of Agathe in *Der Freischütz*. She appeared subsequently in *La Bohème* (Musetta), *Lohengrin* (Elsa), *Wozzeck* (Marie), *Tannhäuser* (Elisabeth), and as Sieglinde. She sings regularly in Frankfurt, Munich and Zürich (Senta, in *The Flying Dutchman*). In 1977 she made her Salzburg Festival debut as Salome, conducted by Herbert von Karajan, and she returned there in 1979 when Karl Böhm conducted her in *Ariadne auf Naxos*. She played Leonora in *Fidelio* in Frankfurt and New York, Salome in London, and the Empress in *Die Frau ohne Schatten* in Paris. What we learn from the note is that Behrens had been singing professionally for a little more than a decade when she first sang Brünnhilde, and had concentrated on the heavier soprano roles in the German repertoire, dominated by Wagner and Richard Strauss. But there is not much flesh on those bones.

Inquiring in Bayreuth, I discovered that Behrens has a reputation as a 'free spirit', and that she has another child from an earlier alliance. I was also told that von Karajan claimed to have discovered her in Düsseldorf, and that she had fallen out with him when he insisted that the Dance of the Seven Veils in *Salome* should be performed by a double; Behrens wanted to do the dance herself. This was more interesting, but there was clearly only one person who was going to tell much more about Hildegard Behrens, and that was Behrens herself.

We walked up the hill and sat under the trees in the Burgherreuth, an agreeable restaurant above the Festspielhaus, and without any prompting Behrens immediately launched into the subject of the heroic principle. She defined it herself by means of the phrase inscribed on the tomb of the eighteenth-century German metaphysician, Immanuel Kant: *Moralische Gesetzt in mir; gesternt Himmel über mir*. Behrens's free translation was that the individual exists in the cosmos, but listens only to an inner voice that dictates right and wrong. That was her Brünnhilde, she explained, just as it inspired her Leonora in *Fidelio*.

The sixth child of two doctors, she thought she inherited this romanticism from her mother, who was born in Metz in northern France. From her father she learned to keep her feet warm and to love music. All the Behrens children learned two instruments, and her father composed a few of the pieces they played. At home, Hildegard was a pianist, but she did not at first consider becoming a professional musician. On the contrary, she decided to study law at Freiburg in southern Germany, but when she graduated with a law degree she realised that she never intended to use it (though she still casts an expert eye over her contracts). By then she had become a singer, first with the student chorus and then with the Freiburg Bach Choir, having spent much of her undergraduate years in the music school instead of the law faculty. She was uncertain about her prospects if she tried to sing professionally, but, she says: 'I realised that either I start singing with full impact or not at all.'

Her audition for Ines Leuwen was unpromising: 'She told me I sang like a young dog,' Behrens recalls. She did not find the environment in the department particularly sympathetic, but admired the teaching, which concentrated on breathing technique. (The breath is like the bow of an instrument, Behrens explains, and she discovered how different composers demand variations in breathing technique.) Her lessons were clearly learned well because Behrens was offered a professorship at Freiburg when she finished her five-year course. But she had been in Freiburg for ten years, there were no students for her to teach, and she had a child to support; so she joined the studio at the opera house in Düsseldorf to begin a professional apprenticeship. It was very brief. Within a few months she had made her debut at Osnabrück. In her second year in Düsseldorf she had a soloist's contract, and in her third year Herbert von Karajan, having attended an orchestral rehearsal for *Wozzeck*, offered her the part of Salome in Richard Strauss's opera three years later in Salzburg. 'Since I finished music school in 1972 I have never taken singing lessons. I am always working on my own. But I'm an Aquarius, which means I'm accustomed to being independent. And because I started late and had a child, I have always played all or nothing; it works or it doesn't work.' Her boldness enabled her to cope easily with her success.

The conservatism of other sopranos was not in Behrens's nature. During one of her first roles, for example, in Janacek's *The Cunning Little Vixen*, her colleagues took bets that her voice would be ruined by the clucking and screaming noises she made (she was playing a chicken). When she sang Elsa in *Lohengrin*, her coach told her to mouth the finale she sang with the chorus at the end of the first act. 'He told me to be careful, because it is a long part and I needed my energy. I said no, the music is wonderful and mouthing is a kind of cheating. I came to the conclusion that if I can't sing the whole thing, I'm not ready for it yet. I don't want to boast, but I found it a wonderful experience. If you stay on full impact, it's like an aeroplane. When the music gets higher, it doesn't need full energy to stay up there.'

Her attitude to the use of the deeper voice from the chest (as opposed to the high soprano known as the head voice), was no less unconventional. Behrens is scornful of singers who argue that constant use of the chest ruins the voice. She learned the technique from a tenor in Düsseldorf: 'He showed me how to practise it, and not be afraid. When I was warming up to sing in Frankfurt one day, they said they thought it was a tenor, because I carry the chest voice high, and the head voice down. It's just part of the talent of technique to find out how to do it, and if you watch yourself carefully, it's not dangerous at all.' In Bayreuth other singers were still willing to bet that Behrens's voice would not last, and, having talked to her about it, I was content to take the wager. Behrens herself confidently expected to be singing Brünnhilde for the rest of her career: 'That's why I'm so tremendously happy, because I love this role.'

Behrens sings only fifty to fifty-five times a year, so that she can spend time with her children in New York, and when she does sing, she prefers to work in productions in which she has originated her part. That was another reason why she was looking forward to Bayreuth in 1983: 'Hall is a Shakespeare director, so I thought he must be a very subtle theatre man.' The two of them quickly agreed that in the conflict between love and power in the *Ring*, it is Brünnhilde who literally carries the torch for love – the altruistic love of *agape* – before being dragged down into the human world of jealousy and hatred by the malign power of the ring. 'She is the one big sign of love and courage. Peter agreed to that, and I found everything was taken care of in the production. I could blossom. I thought Brünnhilde's emotions were always coming through like a laser, so that she should move decisively; it's in her character. We always agreed.'

In rehearsal, Behrens's concentration rarely faltered; there was no idle chatter with the other singers. When she repeated her moves, it was as though they had been programmed by a computer, so exactly did she always arrive in the right place. And her physical commitment was so complete that during emotionally tense scenes I could see her body shaking.

Behrens's relationship with Solti was equally frank. They discussed tempi together, worked out when Brünnhilde should sing to another character on stage and when she should sing directly to the auditorium. Solti corrected her when he thought she was losing the rhythm, and she corrected Solti when she thought the tempo was too fast. I remarked that she was the only singer I had seen do that in Bayreuth: was this a mark of confidence, or status? 'Part of it has to do with hierarchies,' she replied. 'Some singers fear the conductor because they're afraid he won't hire them again; that's a class difference between the employers and the employed. But we're making music together. I acknowledge the conductor's position, because he is responsible for the whole musical conception. But I must explain if the music is too fast for the emotional situation, because the wrong tempi can take the fire out of my singing. I remember I once sang Isolde and the conductor wanted me to do strange things and I told him: ''I'm eager to fit into the concept, but you have to let me be Isolde. It's my part. Otherwise I'm just an *apparatchik*, and you might as well let a computer sing it.'' I've always argued and discussed, with Solti, Karajan, everyone.'

Her energy seemed to raise the performances of many of the singers who appeared with her. She took her relationship with them seriously, believing that a fruitful partnership creates a chemical energy that improves all their work, and Hall's production required unusual energy from many of the singers – those sopranos and contraltos doing the Ride of the Valkyries, for instance.

Rehearsing the best-known scene in the *Ring*, Hall and Dudley worked from a single basic idea. When the curtain rose on Act Three of *Die Walküre*, the platform would be at the back of the stage as high as it could possibly go, facing the audience vertically, with four Valkyries strapped to it, looking as though they were on a mountain peak. As they sang a greeting to their four colleagues bringing on the dead heroes, recently slain in battle, the platform was to swoop forward before flattening out and settling on the stage floor. The Valkyries' harnesses came across both shoulders, and as the platform rose for the first time, they all slipped down as it moved into the vertical position. Safe though they were in their harnesses, they clearly did not *feel* secure; if none of them actually cried out it was probably because they were too frightened to do so. Then Anita Soldh, a cheerful Swedish soprano who, as Freia, was already familiar with the platform, told the others that if they all leant forward and out, letting the harness take the strain when the platform was vertical, they could get a firm grip with their feet. Trying that, and discovering it to be the case, some confidence came back into their voices, though their first 'Hoyotoho's' did sound rather more like cries of distress than of welcome. Next, they discovered that it was easier to get into the safety harness than out of it, because they had to unscrew, rather than unclip themselves. The simple clunk-click mechanism of a car seat-belt was not deemed safe enough, and there were heated discussions between stage staff, who insisted that any other method was *verboten*, and the Valkyries, who feared that they would be unable to rise quickly or gracefully enough from their sitting position when the platform landed. (A screw-clip that could be undone more quickly was eventually successfully incorporated into the harness.) Hall's requirements were intimidating, but the effect was certainly dramatic. Of the four Valkyries on the ground, two were also Rhinemaidens, and Diana Montague and Agnes Habereder, already experienced in swimming and singing, rather envied the Valkyries who were flying and singing too.

Hall was less certain about the entrance of the grounded Valkyries. He decided that Agnes Habereder, who arrived first, should be mounted on a rearing horse with the body of a dead hero

Die Walküre, Act III. Wotan and Brünnhilde, with (centre) the Valkyries.

across the saddle. The horse was a model, carried on the backs of two strong men (one of whom had carried a Chéreau giant on his shoulders), who could manipulate the neck and legs of the model to simulate the movements of a real horse. Because the lighting was concentrated on the platform, leaving the stage floor very dim, Hall proposed that the horse carrying Habereder should enter on a truck – a mobile platform – to make it more visible. Diana Montague was to drag on her dead hero, and the other two Valkyries were to arrive on the same horse, making a couple of return trips. The first run-through looked chaotic, but seemed as if it would make visual sense. 'We've cracked it,' Hall announced confidently.

Dudley had spent months wondering how to show the dead heroes, and now he announced that he had cracked that too: 'I've just written the most extraordinary thing I've ever put on a prop list – twenty naked men.' Richard Wagner's insistence on dead heroes was going to be taken fairly literally, with men lying at the front of the stage. The number of dead heroes was shortly reduced from twenty to seven, and the Festspielhaus had no trouble recruiting young men from the local university to make their stage debuts. But Dudley's simple solution provoked more concern among some of the Germans watching the rehearsals than he was aware of. Hall had seen the Valkyries as 'young, feminine and fairly sexy', but for many Germans the Valkyries are violent and ruthless reminders of a remembered past. Doris Soffel said that the naked corpses looked to her more like concentration-camp victims than dead heroes, and the

Die Walküre. Act III. Brünnhilde summons Siegmund to Valhalla, but he refuses to abandon the senseless Sieglinde at his feet.

third assistant on the production team, Dorothea Glatt-Behr, a Bayreuth veteran, commented that the booing which is such a tradition of the house might well begin when the naked heroes were carried in.

Hall's confidence about the look of the scene had been premature, for Wagner now announced that the horse would have to be screwed on to its truck, making it look ridiculously static; worse, the lighting, minimal though it was, revealed the truck as well as the horse. The truck was cut. The two strong men then found it difficult to manipulate the horse's neck and legs convincingly, so the horse was cut. Hall had to rely on his human properties, and the Valkyries did move gracefully, react positively and sing well. As they huddled together to hide Brünnhilde from Wotan, the stage picture was one of the most satisfying I had seen that summer. On the burnished silver platform covering, in their black leather costumes and carrying long spears, they managed to be both fearful and defiant as Wotan threatened Brünnhilde with the direst of punishments. (They claimed themselves that this was entirely coincidental, and that the under-rehearsed picture changed from performance to performance.) Like the Rhinemaidens, the flying Valkyries had been asked to perform physically demanding stage tricks, and, like the Rhinemaidens, all were proud of their audacity. Anne Evans showed the bruises inflicted by the safety harness she wore as if they were campaign medals. So, in a sense, they were.

Just a few scenes were simply acted out on the stage floor as if the *Ring* were any other opera. One of these was in the first act of *Die Walküre*, between Wotan's twin son and daughter, Siegmund and Sieglinde, and her husband Hunding, the most straightforwardly theatrical in the whole cycle, so that Hall could direct it in the manner most familiar to him. Siegmund was sung by Siegfried Jerusalem, a slim, good-looking tenor, who accurately expressed one definition of the fine Wagnerian actor: still when he acts, letting the emotion show through the music. Sieglinde was Jeannine Altmeyer, a fine-looking Californian, with a big, lyrical, soprano voice. Sieglinde's discovery that she loves her brother is one of the most operatic moments in the *Ring* and Hall was anxious that they should not exaggerate it. 'Love turns you both into poets,' he said. 'You're delighted, you're expressing things you did not know you had in you. Look at each other, and be still; the stiller the better, especially when you discover you're brother and sister (*'Deines Auges Glut/erglänzt mir schon'* – And your gleaming glance/I've seen it before). You must sound disturbed. It's not sentimental or radiantly happy; it's terrible as well as wonderful.'

144

Jerusalem and Altmeyer were an obliging pair of lovers, though Jerusalem did point out that they would have to look at Sir Georg as well as each other and Altmeyer was conscious of her extravagant gestures. 'Don't be an operatic lady,' Hall told her. 'But that's what I am,' she replied, truthfully. She confessed later: 'Now I'm afraid to move my arms in case it looks operatic,' and indeed the contrast between Jerusalem's studied stillness and Altmeyer's natural flamboyance was never wholly eradicated, despite all Altmeyer's efforts. She was one of the few performers in Bayreuth capable of comparing the styles of Hall and Chéreau, for whom she had played Sieglinde. In 1979, the fourth year of Chéreau's *Ring*, when he had time to concentrate on detail, she had worked with him for two weeks down to the last facial expression. The brutal first-year schedule made such concentrated work with Hall impossible, but even so she had been aware of some differences. 'In Chéreau's *Ring* Sieglinde had become hardened by misfortune. She was cold to Siegmund when he arrived, and wanted him to go, so her falling in love with him was more shocking. In fact, quite a bit of Chéreau's staging contradicted the music. He would tell me to turn away from Siegmund when the music was telling me to look at him. Peter Hall is more loyal to the musical directions, and I've found him easy to work with because he's patient and doesn't make you feel nervous.' The sole cause of real insecurity in 1983, she thought, was the shortage of rehearsal time. In San Francisco there had been three complete orchestral rehearsals on stage for her Brünnhilde. 'After that you feel so confident that you hardly have to look at the conductor.' Altmeyer's eyes did stray to Solti more than Hall would have liked, but it was uncertainty about the exact tempo that made her do so.

Working on the first act of *Die Walküre*, with Jerusalem, Altmeyer, and Matthias Hölle who sang Hunding, Hall could concentrate more than usual on developing motives and polishing the performances. There were no problems with the set, and no difficult props (though some of them did not actually appear on stage until the dress rehearsal). It was not unlike rehearsing a Mozart opera at Glyndebourne, and Hall felt liberated: 'The thing about this lot is that when you want to you can let them sing and correct them later.' But the tyranny of technical difficulties returned to plague him in Act Two. This begins with a long scene between Wotan and Fricka, who arrives in a chariot drawn by two life-like rams which came in on a truck. The scene is set on a high rocky ridge, which was indicated by polystyrene rocks scattered over the platform: but after plotting Wotan's and Fricka's moves around them, Hall decided they looked clumsy and cluttered the stage. The rocks were cut.

The carnage in this first scene of Act Two was modest compared to what happened at the end of the act, however. Wagner's detailed stage directions read: 'A flash of lightning illuminates the pass for a moment, and Hunding and Siegmund are seen fighting there. Sieglinde rushes towards the pass but suddenly, from above the contestants, a flash breaks forth so vividly that she staggers aside as if blinded. In the blaze of light Brünnhilde appears, hovering over Siegmund and protecting him with her shield. Just as Siegmund aims a deadly blow at Hunding, a glowing red light breaks through the clouds, in which Wotan appears, standing over Hunding, holding his spear diagonally out at Siegmund. Brünnhilde, with her spear, recoils in terror before Wotan. Siegmund's sword shatters on the outstretched spear. Hunding lunges his spear into the unarmed man's breast. Siegmund falls to the ground: Sieglinde, who heard his death sigh, falls with a cry, as if lifeless, to the ground. As Siegmund falls, the glowing lights on either side disappear at once; a cloud of thick darkness rolls forward; in it, Brünnhilde is indistinctly seen, as she turns in haste to Sieglinde. She lifts Sieglinde quickly on to her horse, and disappears with her. At this moment the clouds part in the middle, so that Hunding is clearly seen. Wotan, surrounded by clouds, stands on a rock behind him, leaning on his spear and gazing sorrowfully at Siegmund's corpse. At the contemptuous wave of his hand, Hunding falls dead to the ground. Wotan, suddenly breaking out in a terrible rage, disappears in thunder and lightning. The curtain falls rapidly.'

Hall's original intention was to take the stage directions literally. Hunding and Siegmund were to begin their fight backstage, and finish it on the platform, and Brünnhilde would indeed carry Sieglinde off on a horse – the same horse carried by two strong men and moved on a truck. One day, when the delays in staging this difficult scene became as boring to me as they were to the singers, I went backstage to see what was happening. There I found Hunding and Siegmund standing in front of a television monitor at the bottom of a ramp leading up on to the platform. This monitor gave them their cue from the conductor, and when it came, they stood and sang, before mounting the ramp and emerging on to the platform, each fighting for his life. Meanwhile, Brünnhilde clambered up a ladder on to the truck and then mounted her horse. The truck was trundled towards the platform by a group of stagehands, and when they manoeuvred it into place, Brünnhilde dismounted. On the other side of the backstage area, Wotan stepped on to an insubstantial platform mounted on the lifting mechanism of a fork-lift truck. He secured himself to a backrest, and was raised into

Facing page: 'Dies eine musst du erhören! Zerknicke dein Kind, das dein Knie umfasst.' Die Walküre, Act III. Brünnhilde and Wotan.

position above the platform, so as to appear from the clouds. The stagehands grunted, the fork-lift whined, the stage managers frantically muttered the cues. Backstage looked like a subway station at rush hour when the lights had failed. Watching it, I thought it impossible that the moves could ever be synchronised so that each character made a convincing entrance and exit on cue.

At the dress rehearsal the improbable became a nightmare. The truck carrying Brünnhilde's horse made an erratic entrance, and as they exited Brünnhilde and Sieglinde had so much difficulty mounting the horse – whose rear end now faced the auditorium – that a ripple of laughter went through the audience. Wotan's platform was lit from above instead of the side, so it could be seen clearly, and the same light illuminated the truck carrying the departing horse. A momentary view of the strained faces of Brünnhilde and Sieglinde triggered more giggles in the audience. The curtain could not have fallen rapidly enough.

During the interval Hall finally lost his temper. There had been a disaster earlier in the act when no cue had been given for the entrance of Fricka's chariot. Hall was angry about the stage management and critical of various lighting changes that had exposed the backstage manoeuvres. He said he had never been so badly treated in a theatre in all his life. At this, Dorothea Glatt-Behr, the third assistant director, burst into tears, charged Hall with ingratitude, and left. The horse was cut, and Wotan's fork-lift truck was cut: Hall felt he could not rely on the stage management to deal with either.

Act Three might have caused another bout of these technical problems, for the climax of the act was one of Dudley's most imaginative strokes. After Wotan had lit the circle of fire around the sleeping Brünnhilde, smoke curled out of the fiery red lights, and when Wotan left the plaform it began to rise, carrying Brünnhilde up into the sky. The effect reminded Wolfgang Wagner of a spaceship; I thought it looked like a circle of fire on a mountain top. Whatever interpretation spectators put on it, the technical requirement was for Brünnhilde to be strapped into her harness before liftoff, and it was clear that the sight of her belting herself on to the platform after she was supposedly asleep risked more laughter from the audience. Behrens dealt with the problem herself. The platform was never at a really dangerous angle, she said, so there was no need to be strapped in at all. She was not.

Shortly after this episode, Hall said thoughtfully to Dudley: 'Do you realise just how fortunate we are in our Brünnhilde?' Of course Dudley did; everyone in the Festspielhaus that summer realised how lucky they were in their Brünnhilde.

12

Siegfried: a tragedy too sad to contemplate

Tenors insist that Siegfried is a truly impossible role. In the first act the poor man exhausts himself forging the sword, Nothung. After a break, he resumes by killing the dragon Fafner and communing at length with a woodbird. After another interval, the tenor is back on stage for a long conversation with Wotan and then, in the last scene, he has to sing full out for twenty-five minutes with a soprano who has been resting in her dressing-room and comes on stage as fresh as April. Moreover, the part has to be sung in the most uncommon of fine male voices, a *Heldentenor*.

So Siegfrieds are rare creatures. But, having originally despaired of finding a tenor willing to sing both *Siegfried* and *Götterdämmerung*, Solti and Hall had 'discovered' Reiner Goldberg, the East German who sang for them in Bayreuth in August 1981. Goldberg had never sung Siegfried before; casting him was a risk, but if the gamble came off and they had a fine new Siegfried, they would have hit the jackpot.

Reiner Goldberg soon became a familiar figure in Bayreuth. He and Peter Haage, who sang the part of Siegfried's guardian, Mime, were the first singers to arrive at the Festspielhaus late in April, and at the end of rehearsals, when Haage returned to his caravan parked up the hill behind the theatre, Goldberg would walk down the hill to the singers' pub, the Wehenstephan, since the Festspielhaus canteen did not open until mid-May. In those early days, in the chill of late spring, Goldberg liked to wear a tracksuit and trainers. Not that he was an athletic figure. Bill Dudley, who had designed his costume, noted that Goldberg had put on weight since the famous audition in the summer of 1981. He was balder too, and even with his spectacles on he looked slightly myopic, his face round and unlined. But what made Goldberg instantly recognisable was his flat-footed, shambling walk, his legs apparently bearing only a distant relationship to his trunk. I had seen that walk on stage at Covent Garden the previous winter when Goldberg sang the part of Walther in *Die Meistersinger*. It was one of the two memorable things about his performance: the other was the voice – a fine *Heldentenor*. Guus Mostart, who was at the same performance, commented that Peter Hall would not find it easy to make a Siegfried out of Reiner Goldberg. Not impossible, of course, but difficult.

Mostart reported to me on my arrival that the first week's rehearsal with Haage and Goldberg had not been too bad. Goldberg had responded to Haage's excellent character acting as Mime, who brings up Siegfried in the forest after his mother Sieglinde has died in childbirth. When Goldberg re-forged the sword, Nothung, he had sung the scene full out, and the sound was very exciting. They did notice one problem when Hildegard Behrens arrived at the end of the first week, and they rehearsed the long last scene of *Siegfried* – one of the great climaxes of the *Ring*, when Brünnhilde and Siegfried fall in love. Hall and Mostart were aware that when Behrens sang Goldberg was often inattentive, looking around instead of at her. That Goldberg should concentrate and act to Behrens was a constant theme in the notes Hall gave him after those first rehearsals. Mostart translated those notes, for Goldberg spoke no English.

Hoping to understand Goldberg better, Mostart and Michael McCaffery, an imaginative young English stage and opera director whom Hall had asked to be his second assistant director, took Goldberg out to dinner during that week, and they found him disarmingly naïve. He chatted about Dresden, his girlfriend in Vienna, and his car, though he did not seem particularly interested in Siegfried. When Goldberg left Bayreuth to sing during the Berlin Staatsoper's tour of Japan, the production team were still nervous about his performance; but they felt he was not unpromising, and he certainly could sing. Hall decided that he must make the best of Goldberg's innocence; it was the one obvious quality he shared with Siegfried. He had already become known, affectionately, as 'the plank'.

During the Japanese tour a colleague of Goldberg's defected, causing Wagner to fear that the East Germans might retaliate by refusing Goldberg permission to sing in the West. But that was never really likely. The East Germans regard their fine singers as a useful source of foreign exchange, and once Goldberg established himself as the Bayreuth Siegfried he would be worth at least $10,000 every time he sang the role in the leading opera houses of the world.

While Goldberg was in the Far East, more singers arrived in Bayreuth, and some were curious to hear about his rehearsals. Those who had seen him thought they detected a serious imperfection in Goldberg's vocal technique: the voice was excellent, but it did not appear to be anchored to the skills all professional singers learn, like pacing themselves during a long role, and relaxing before reaching a vocal climax. For a part like Siegfried, the most arduous in the whole operatic repertoire, these techniques are essential requirements. Goldberg's grasp of them could not be properly tested until the dress rehearsal in the middle of July, but the speculation about him was only just beginning.

I was in London when Goldberg returned to Bayreuth late in May to begin work with Solti, and when I went back myself in June, Goldberg was the subject of the most dramatic news. Solti had now discovered that he did not know the part properly, in either *Siegfried* or *Götterdämmerung*. His singing contained serious musical errors, and yet when Goldberg had worked with Solti in London in January, with David Syrus accompanying him at the piano, he had seemed to know the part perfectly. The only explanation Syrus could offer was that Goldberg must have been able to see the score, he, Syrus, was playing from, and read the bits he did not know.

Solti decided that his only option was to teach Goldberg the part himself. He had started his career as a *répétiteur*, and here he was, in Bayreuth, aged seventy, back where he began, sitting at the piano and teaching Goldberg his part line by line. Charles Kaye judges that Solti spent thirty hours working alone with Goldberg. Solti worked with Goldberg most days in late May and early June, which was hard on the other singers, many of whom had come to Bayreuth partly because of the prospect of being coached by Solti. Doris Soffel had expected four hours' coaching from Solti, and got one and a half – her case was not untypical. None of the singers blamed him; they appreciated his predicament; but it was no less frustrating for all that. It was frustrating for Solti too, who had to act as social as well as musical disciplinarian, trying, for example, to stop Goldberg smoking.

I first saw Goldberg rehearse in one of the large rooms that flank the auditorium, when Michael McCaffery suggested that I come along because, he said, 'We're teaching Reiner how to walk.' I did not immediately realise that McCaffery was being entirely serious. He and Hall had worked hard to adjust Goldberg's bodily equilibrium, to get him to walk straight and naturally – as a hero ought to do – but his deportment had so far proved an intractable problem. The scene being rehearsed was from Act One of *Götterdämmerung*,

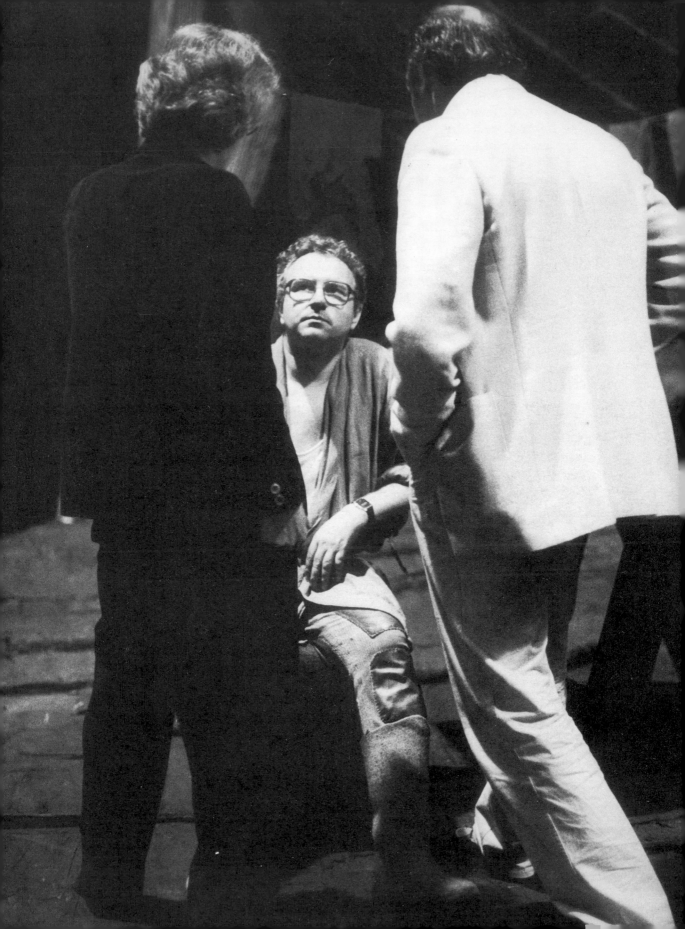

when Siegfried meets Hagen, Gunther and Gutrune, and drinks from the drugged drinking-horn that makes him lose all memory of Brünnhilde. Goldberg was wearing a short towelling dressing-gown, hung loosely over his chest, and patched leather trousers, but it was his nervous mannerisms that drew my attention. He gulped each time before he sang; he ran his hand through his greying hair; pushed his spectacles back on the bridge of his nose; scratched his chest. Goldberg seemed mesmerised by David Syrus, who was conducting, and had to make a conscious effort to look another singer in the eye. He took the drinking-horn from Gunther much as he would have taken a glass from a waiter, and his embrace with Gutrune was no more than tentative. Goldberg seemed anxious to please, however, making one entry wearing his helmet sideways on his head and grinning amiably. *'Bitte, Reiner,'* said McCaffery wearily.

Reiner Goldberg. Left. Hall explains, while Dorothea Glatt-Behr translates. Right. Guus Mostart patiently repeats stage notes and instructions.

During that rehearsal when Solti arrived, and started to conduct, Goldberg began to work harder. When he sang full out – which singers rarely do in that sort of rehearsal, because they concentrate on moves and motive – the sound was splendid, and my first impression was that he would not be a disaster at all. He did occasionally display the kind of naïvety Siegfried shows when, for instance, he takes the drug that brings about his downfall. But he would clearly need much more rehearsing; Solti, taking McCaffery aside, said as much and asked him to do it. The next day, it was the scene from *Götterdämmerung* when the Rhinemaidens warn Siegfried of his impending fate. Goldberg had taken off his spectacles in Solti's honour – he was waiting for the contact lenses that had been ordered for him – but he still needed prompting from the piano, and he was coughing. That was the day when Goldberg sang, 'I have nothing with me to give', and Solti, at the music rehearsal following the stage rehearsal, said, *'Jawohl, mein Herr.'*

I thought I sensed in Goldberg at those rehearsals a nervous insecurity, brought on by his imperfect knowledge of the part and the difficulty he found in acting. This impression was enhanced by a furious outburst from another singer, who reported that Goldberg had not only announced that he was the finest tenor in the world, but that he had no need of Solti's coaching. Perhaps Goldberg may have the finest *Wagnerian* tenor voice in the world (he could not compete with, say, Placido Domingo in other parts of the repertory) when he is giving a concert performance with the score open in front of him. But the suggestion that he needed no aid from Solti was so preposterous that it could surely have been made (if it was made) only by a man extremely unsure of himself.

By June, Hall and Solti had already begun to talk about replacing Goldberg. Hall was concerned that his performance was beginning to infect others, but neither he nor Solti was at all keen to call in Manfred Jung who was Goldberg's cover. Jung had been in Chéreau's *Ring* and they were determined on a new cast; and Goldberg's voice still rang like a true *Heldentenor*'s. Had there been any other singer with Goldberg's qualifications – a Bayreuth debut, and the voice – there would have been a new Siegfried, but there was not. In a situation report on 13 June, Hall commented: 'He's hanging on by his fingernails.'

Michael McCaffery, who was working longer hours with Goldberg than any of his colleagues, thought that this heavy emergency schedule was actually causing a deterioration in Goldberg's performance. 'He has a run-through on stage in the morning, works

Götterdämmerung. Prelude: The three Norns weave the rope of life, on the Valkyrie rock. The rope breaks — the final catastrophe is approaching.

(*overleaf on left*): *Götterdämmerung.* Act I, Scene 1: Gunther and Gutrune sit enthroned in the Hall of the Gibichungs.

(*overleaf on right*): *Götterdämmerung.* Act II, Scene 1: On the shore near the Gibichungs' Hall, Hagen (*below*) and Alberich plot the destruction of Siegfried.

Previous pages: Götterdämmerung.
Act II, Scene 4: Brünnhilde:
'Hilf meinem ewige Eide!'

Götterdämmerung. Act III, Scene 1:
The Rhinemaidens try to
persuade Siegfried to return the
ring to them, warning of the evil
which lies within it for him.

Götterdämmerung. Act III, Scene 2: The hunting party; Siegfried recounts his adventures to Gunther (*seated*).

Götterdämmerung.
Act III, Scene 3:
In the Gibichungs' Hall.

Top: As Hagen tries
to reach the ring; the
hand of the dead
Siegfried rises
threateningly,
watched by Gutrune
and Brünnhilde.

Bottom: Brünnhilde
kindles Siegfried's
funeral pyre; the
Twilight of the Gods.

with Solti in the afternoon, and by the time he does another run-through in the evening he's forgotten everything,' he said. McCaffery noted that the quality of Goldberg's performances on stage so depressed Hall that he had become reluctant to give notes himself at the end of rehearsals, and felt Goldberg might take Hall's advice more seriously if it were delivered personally. But Hall was developing an obsession about Goldberg. He said little during rehearsals, leaving most of the work to McCaffery, and when he did speak to Goldberg he sounded like one party in a crumbling marriage talking to the other. One evening he jumped on to the rehearsal stage and hissed at him: 'Why do you always walk as though it's only because I've told you to?' But Hall said this in English; Goldberg would not have understood what he was saying – the absence of a common language made it harder for him to appreciate the exact nature of Hall's dissatisfaction. No doubt this contributed further to the erosion of his confidence.

At a stage rehearsal on 14 June Goldberg was clearly trying much harder. McCaffery thought it was because he had heard rumours in the Festspielhaus that he might be about to quit, either voluntarily or not, and was determined to allay them. That evening he was gesturing like an actor, and on one occasion Hall called out: 'That's good.' Nevertheless Goldberg was so awkward that I wrote in my notebook: 'I begin to think that the Bayreuth audience will not be looking at *Siegfried*, but laughing at it,' and I soon discovered that Hall and Dudley shared this fear. Hall was particularly concerned about the scene in the second act of *Siegfried* in which the dragon has to be slain: 'The audience has to believe in the dragon, and they will only do so if Siegfried appears to believe in it too. If he doesn't, he might be laughed off the stage.' After the rehearsal that evening, Hall had thirty-five separate notes for Goldberg, and intended to give them to him personally, but he gave up after the sixth, because he judged that Goldberg wasn't listening.

Hall woke early the following morning, and found his decision had been taken while he slept. He telephoned Solti, who was taking a short break in London: 'If we have Goldberg, we don't have a *Siegfried*.' Solti, in reply, sounded unhappy but philosophical, and they agreed to take a decision when he returned to Bayreuth the following day. Having got that off his chest, Hall was more relaxed, like a man remembering a nightmare rather than living it. He recalled then that Guus Mostart had said a week earlier that Goldberg should go so that they would have time to rehearse Manfred Jung. 'Tactically, Guus was right, but I still hoped for improvement.'

155

That afternoon, sitting having coffee, I saw Mostart, McCaffery, and the third assistant, Dorothea Glatt-Behr, talking earnestly to Wolfgang Wagner. When they broke up McCaffery strolled over and said: 'Great drama.' Earlier in the afternoon, Goldberg had been scheduled to rehearse the forging scene in Act One of *Siegfried*, a difficult business at best because of the variety of props he has to use. (Swords at various stages of forging have to be produced at the correct moment in the process.) Goldberg had arrived ten minutes late, and when he began to work had ignored the acting instructions. To McCaffery's criticism, Goldberg replied that, having been a smith before he became a singer, he knew how to forge metal. McCaffery pointed out that he was forging a sword for the audience at Bayreuth not a client in Crostau, at which point, Goldberg, declaring he was not interested in that kind of detail, walked out. Hearing the story, I assumed that it would be the pretext for Goldberg's summary dismissal. I was quite wrong.

Goldberg's next appointment that afternoon was a music rehearsal with David Syrus. He was ten minutes late for that too, but he sang beautifully, which was what mattered to the music staff. The conflicting demands of music and production staffs are one of the characteristics of an opera house. This is not because musicians blindly admire singers who cannot act, or directors ignore the sound of the voice: it is a matter of priorities. Musicians regard some voices, like those of Luciano Pavarotti or Montserrat Caballé, as being so superb that ungainly physical appearances do not matter. Hall, on the other hand, preferred not to work with singers who disdained acting, no matter how excellent the voice. Led by Syrus, the music staff at Bayreuth agreed that Goldberg's voice was so fine that his inability to act was a price worth paying, and there was a historical precedent for this sanguine view. The greatest pre-war Siegfried, perhaps the best of all, was Lauritz Melchior. Apparently, at the dress rehearsal before his Bayreuth *Siegfried*, Melchior was still carrying the score to check his lines, and, poor man, he could not act even if his life depended on it.

When Solti returned, he conducted a rehearsal for a scene that included Goldberg, the end of the prelude to *Götterdämmerung* when Siegfried gives Brünnhilde the ring – a wonderfully emotional musical moment. It was well sung by Goldberg and Behrens, but Hall was unmoved. Sitting in the auditorium, he told Valerie Solti that *Siegfried* was a catastrophe and *Götterdämmerung* not much better. 'I can't go on with him,' Hall said. Later he told Dudley, who cared almost as deeply about Goldberg's ungainly performance, that either he, Hall, or Goldberg would have to go. This was an indication of Hall's degree of depression rather than his intentions, however. The next day he and Goldberg were both still working in Bayreuth: Solti continued to prefer the vexing reality of Goldberg to the prospect of the reappearance of Manfred Jung.

Goldberg did receive a warning from Solti, who told him that Hall was deeply disappointed by his work and that he would go if it did not improve. (This warning caused a brief disturbance in the otherwise excellent relationship between Hall and Solti. By not associating himself with the criticism, Solti was thought by Hall to have been less than frank about his own misgivings.) By 24 June, when Goldberg was due for a few days off in Berlin, he had thoroughly alienated Solti too, and Hall reported Solti as saying that they should ask him not to come back. That was an opinion, not a decision, however; and Goldberg did come back and started to work harder again on stage, looking a little more like Siegfried. Once more he was reprieved, and a new deadline was set. This further delay was justified by the knowledge that Manfred Jung was scheduled to sing Loge in Bayreuth, and other parts elsewhere in Germany, so that he would not have been able to rehearse *Siegfried* before the end of the month anyway. On 1 July the deadline was extended for another seven days, when the first full orchestral rehearsal of *Siegfried* was to take place. Hall and I lunched together early in July, and I said that Goldberg had now been reprieved so often that it seemed inevitable that the blow would never fall. 'I suppose it's a gamble I can afford to take, because it's too late now anyway to rehearse Manfred Jung properly,' he replied, sombrely. (Wagner was rarely involved in these talks between Hall and Solti, but the crisis did produce one of his best lines of the summer. As he listened to Solti in the pit, Wagner turned to Charles Kaye and said: 'OK, let's send Goldberg home. Solti can whistle through the part.')

At the first orchestral rehearsal of *Siegfried*, Solti's patience seemed to have been justified. Goldberg relaxed into the music, and the hours of stage rehearsal paid off. McCaffrey had said he would be good in Act One, and Hall now declared he was better than that: very good, he announced. The music staff were delighted, and complimented Goldberg enthusiastically.

I saw the run-through of the Second Act of *Siegfried*, and the improvement was so marked that I noted, 'Goldberg is not only still with us, he even seems to be of us.' But later in the rehearsal a deterioration set in: all the old mannerisms came back, plus a new one. Every few minutes Goldberg, who was sweating profusely, paused to wipe his brow. It was very hot, but none of the other singers did so. 'Too many people have been telling him how marvellous he is,' growled McCaffrey. The next night, during the run-through of Act Three, things were worse, and the familiar musical errors began to creep into his performance again. Despite all the coaching, Goldberg evidently still did not know the part properly. Hall's gloomy conclusion was that something really would have to be done the following morning, with no more delay.

Something was. Almost three years earlier Solti and Hall had agreed that it made dramatic nonsense to have two different singers playing Siegfried in *Siegfried* and *Götterdämmerung*, but on the morning of 9 July they decided to ask Manfred Jung to take over the role in *Götterdämmerung*. As he told me of the decision to drop Goldberg, Hall commented ruefully: 'It's the curse of the *Ring*.' An anouncement was made by the Festspielhaus that Goldberg was indisposed (he did have a sore throat), and Solti told other singers that he had returned to Berlin to recuperate. But Goldberg never left Bayreuth. He stood in the wings the following day to watch Jung walk through his part for the first time. Formally, he declared in a letter to Wagner that though he did know the part of *Götterdäm-merung*, he would consent to sing in *Siegfried* only.

Siegfried, Act I. The forging of Nothung. Goldberg (Siegfried) and Peter Haage (Mime).

Before the dress rehearsal of *Siegfried*, McCaffery took Goldberg through his part, with Hall lurking in the background. McCaffery's notes were basic and simple: 'Reiner, you must concentrate when you hear the Valkyrie theme; look surprised when you see Brünnhilde's horse. But stay still.' Hall muttered to McCaffery: 'I hope Reiner realises there's nothing on the stage but him and Behrens. It's very brightly lit, and every fidget is noticeable.' By the end of the run-through Hall steeled himself to show as much confidence as he could in his Siegfried. 'For the first time I felt you were really talking to her,' he said. Since they had been rehearsing the scene since the beginning of May, this was hardly a compliment.

Just twenty-four hours before the dress rehearsal, his first appearance in front of a Bayreuth audience, Goldberg rehearsed the forging scene yet again; Solti was there, and so was Hall, who looked tired and unhappy. McCaffery, seeking comfort where he could, said he thought Goldberg had dealt with the various props as well as he had ever done. Goldberg, who seemed transfixed by Solti's hands, fluffed a few lines – and immediately sang full out as if to compensate. At the end of the rehearsal Solti comforted his *Heldentenor*: '*Sehr gut, Reiner, sehr gut.*' But as Goldberg left the room Solti turned to Hall and said they both deserved the Victoria Cross for conspicuous courage.

The dress rehearsal of *Siegfried* took place on 19 July before an audience that was familiar with the style of this *Ring* since *Das Rheingold* and *Die Walküre* had already been performed. Siegmund Nimsgern had made his debut in *Rheingold*; Behrens hers in *Die Walküre*; now it was Goldberg's turn. Outside the Festspielhaus there was a feeling of anticipation; inside a sense of acute apprehension. Goldberg appeared oblivious of this in his dressing-room, singing full out snatches of the forging scene – a fine, rich sound that had become instantly recognisable in the Festspielhaus.

The curtain rose at 6.05 p.m. on Mime's foundry, with Peter Haage trying to forge a new sword from the pieces of Nothung he had found years earlier beside the infant Siegfried. My first impression was that the orchestra was playing too loudly: this scene is one of the loudest in the *Ring*. After three or four minutes Siegfried made his entrance, dragging a bear, which distracted me for a moment. The bear's costume had been completed only the day before, so no one had seen it on stage, and it looked wonderfully like a real bear. Siegfried's first words are: '*Hoiho, Hoiho, Hau ein, hau ein. Friss ihn, friss ihn, den Fratzenschmied*' (Bite the lazy smith). They were barely audible, and I assumed that the orchestra was still playing *forte*. But as the dialogue between Siegfried and Mime went on, it became clear the problem was not the orchestra. Goldberg's voice sounded limp and strangled; the column of air that supports a singer's voice seemed to have collapsed. After Goldberg's first exit, Guus Mostart slipped out of the auditorium and went backstage to ask him if he was all right. 'He said he was, but his hands were shaking, like that,' said Mostart, showing both hands quite out of control. Goldberg's next scene, when he forges Nothung, sounded better; not as good as I had heard it, but recognisably Goldberg. The acting was clumsy, but not catastrophic, though some of the mannerisms were creeping back: he made as if to adjust the spectacles he no longer wore, and wiped his forehead. Mostart stopped at Hall's table in the canteen during the first interval and said that Reiner had never acted that scene better. But Hall was inconsolable; he thought it had been terrible. 'What should I do?' he asked. 'I've played every card, and I can't resign now.'

Goldberg's technical shortcomings had been noted by his colleagues throughout the summer. His voice was simply a remarkable natural instrument. Other singers develop their voices like finely tuned machines, so that when they are nervous – and they all are – the voice takes over from the brain and carries them through the worst of their nerves. That Goldberg had no such technical insurance against a disaster became clear during the second act.

This actually began remarkably well. Dudley's set was magnificent: the trees looked like trees; the pond in front of Fafner's cave steamed and bubbled for the first time. Nimsgern and Becht both sang particularly well in the fifteen minutes before Siegfried and Mime enter. But when Goldberg began to sing, I could see members of the audience in front of me stiffen; then there was an audible murmur in the house. Singers often 'mark' a part during rehearsal to save their voices, but Goldberg was not marking.

Before he killed the dragon, Goldberg looked into the wings and nodded, as if to assure someone he was continuing; seconds later he moved over to the edge of the platform, and had he walked off it, no one would have been surprised – shocked perhaps, but not surprised. Goldberg seemed to giggle when the dragon appeared; he made little of killing it, and a mockery of the murder of Mime, which caused a nervous titter to ripple through the house. Towards the end of the act, when the woodbird speaks to Siegfried of the glorious bride waiting for him on the mountain top ringed by flame, Goldberg was omitting so much of the text that Solti had to manoeuvre the orchestra like a tank on treacherous ground to catch him up. (As an example of conducting opera *in extremis*, Solti's performance was given top marks by another conductor who was listening – a rave, perhaps, that he would rather not have earned.) As we left the auditorium at the end of the act, I commented to my neighbour, who had watched many of the rehearsals with me, that we had just seen a man destroying himself in front of our eyes. It was questionable whether the performance would continue.

During the interval Solti and Hall visited Goldberg in his dressing-room, accompanied by Wagner and a couple of members of the music staff. Did he want to continue? they asked. Goldberg said he saw no reason why not: he had glandular problems in his throat, but there was nothing really wrong with his voice. They trooped out unhappily, agreeing that they might as well go on. Hall reported Solti's reaction: 'He said "Bloody opera, bloody opera, I'll never do an opera again."' Next, too many of the party crowded into the lift, which stopped between floors. During the pause Solti's companions learned about swearing in Hungarian. For his part, Hall was more determined than ever that Goldberg should go now, even at such a late stage, and none of his assistants argued with him. Hall was still unsure, however, what he could do if Solti disagreed.

The third act was a nightmare, apart from those periods when Nimsgern, Anne Gjevang as Erda, who is the mother of the earth, and Behrens were singing. Goldberg was merely going through the motions, and there were no more murmurs from the audience, just embarrassment. My conductor acquaintance commented that he expected either Solti or Goldberg – or both – to give up, but they kept going to the bitter end. There were a few cries of 'Bravo' as the curtain fell, for Behrens perhaps, who deserved them. Hall went to the conductor's room after the performance, still assuming that he would have to argue the case for Goldberg's removal. Not so: Solti simply said that was it, and suggested Manfred Jung should start rehearsing in the morning.

The news spread slowly through the few restaurants in Bayreuth that were open after the performance, surprising none of those who heard. One of Goldberg's colleagues worried about the reaction in East Berlin when Goldberg returned. McCaffery pondered, without being bitter about it, on the time he had wasted, and thought it a pity that the decision had not been taken earlier so that Manfred Jung could have been properly rehearsed. His first performance in *Siegfried* would be *the* first performance. The only person involved in the affair who seemed oblivious of the sense of doom was Goldberg, who went to the canteen and drank a couple of beers.

Goldberg was called to Wagner's office in the Festspielhaus the following morning to meet Wolfgang, Solti and Hall. Barely able to speak, he explained that because of his voice, he would be incapable

The end of *Siegfried* Act III, Reiner Goldberg's last appearance on stage at Bayreuth 1983.

of singing the first cycle of the *Ring*, but would be fit for the second and third cycles in August. Wagner told Goldberg that he would not be required to sing at all: an announcement would be made that he was indisposed, which was true in a way, and he would be paid for the performances he was not able to sing. He should, Wagner suggested, leave for Berlin without delay.

That morning Manfred Jung appeared for his first *Siegfried* rehearsal. Jung was cheerful; Hall was laughing, like a man freed from an obsession. And the extent of the tragedy of Reiner Goldberg had not really sunk in, perhaps because it was too sad to contemplate.

13

Götterdämmerung: a panic at the end

Götterdämmerung is the most operatic of the four parts of the *Ring* cycle, perhaps because it was the last to be written. The score was not finished until 21 November 1874, by which time Wagner was already planning the first production of the *Ring* in Bayreuth; it contained music for a large chorus as well as the existing cast of gods and mortals; there was even a trio in the second act, the first time in the whole *Ring* that more than two principals sing simultaneously. All the elements of great drama are contained in the text – love, jealousy, hatred, death and transfiguration. The climax of both the score and the text of the *Ring* is achieved with the themes of redemption through the love of Brünnhilde and Siegfried, the destruction of Valhalla, and the lifting of the curse of the ring when it is at last retrieved by the Rhinemaidens. At the end of a successful performance of *Götterdämmerung*, the audience should be in tears. In 1983, great drama had begun somewhat earlier, and tears had been shed, metaphorically at least, before the curtain parted for the first performance on 30 July.

On 24 April, Manfred Jung's commitment to Bayreuth in 1983 had been merely to understudy Siegfried. Three months later he was scheduled to perform Loge in *Das Rheingold*, and both Siegfrieds. He would now be on stage much longer than any other performer, but he seemed not to mind: he rejected the suggestion that another Loge should be found, to ease his burden. He could be forgiven for regarding his ability to step into quite so many breaches at once as an instance of his dedicated professionalism. Jung did not boast that he was the finest Wagnerian tenor in the business, but he was the one a remarkable number of opera houses relied on, and the list of cities in which he had appeared was longer than that of any other singer in the programme: Tokyo, Toronto, Chicago, Zürich, New

163

York, Berlin, Barcelona, Cologne, Frankfurt, Gothenburg, Brussels, Lisbon, Jerusalem, Karlsruhe, Rome, Montreal, and Salzburg. His eminence, achieved more by hard work than an inspired talent, was no less laudable for that. When other singers were drowning in litres of beer, Jung would be in bed, like an athlete in training for a world championship. He is stocky, fair-haired, and not unconscious of his seniority, for he first sang in Bayreuth in 1970, as a member of the chorus. He remained there for three years, and by 1977 he was a soloist. At the end of the decade he was established as Siegfried in the Boulez–Chéreau *Ring*, and after that had sung Siegfried all over the world, more than thirty times in all. There was no question about his knowing the part.

Jung arrived, crumpled, by car, from Nuremberg after a flight from Düsseldorf where he had sung the previous evening, to take part in his first *Götterdämmerung* rehearsal on 11 July. He was pitched straight on to the stage to sing with Hildegard Behrens in the prelude to the opera, a scene in which Siegfried, having given Brünnhilde the ring for safe-keeping, leaves her, to perform various unspecified heroic deeds. There were three people on stage that morning: Siegfried, Brünnhilde, and Michael McCaffery in a red tartan shirt, holding the score in which all the moves had been logged. Before each move, Jung glanced towards McCaffery, whose gestures told him whether he should be kneeling on one knee or both, whether he should be holding Brünnhilde's hand, and where he should make his exit. Jung's knowledge of the part, even though he was learning his moves and marking the part with his voice, seemed to reassure Behrens. The duet they sing in the *Tagesgrauen* – the dawn – brought tears to my eyes for the first time that summer. Irrational though it was, the substitution of Jung at this appallingly late stage actually made the production team more confident about struggling through the rest of *Götterdämmerung* – all four hours of it.

Work on the prelude had begun with the customary technical difficulties, since the three Norns, who open the opera and bring us up-to-date with Wotan's decline, were perched on ledges on the vertical platform. They were all Annes – Anne Gjevang, a Norwegian contralto who had already distinguished herself as Erda in rehearsals of *Das Rheingold* and *Siegfried*; and two British singers, the mezzo-soprano Anne Wilkens, and the soprano Anne Evans. There were predictable delays in early rehearsals as they strapped themselves into position and learned to manipulate the golden rope they were to weave as they told their tale. Anne Evans, sitting perilously twenty feet above the stage floor, once appeared to be about to fall backwards through the hole that had been made in the platform to accommodate the Norns, and as they wriggled into their positions one member of the music staff turned to another and said: 'Surely they're not going to *sing* like that?' But the Norns were made of sterner stuff than some of the musical coaches. They did sing like that, even if the positions in which Hall placed them did not accord with his self-imposed rule of operatic production: that the music will sound better if the body is well placed and centred, because the singers will feel more comfortable. (It was a 'rule' Hall ignored regularly in this production.)

The Norns' physical discomfort did not prevent Solti from subjecting them to a line-by-line examination of their singing. I was in the pit when he conducted a piano rehearsal for the Norns scene, and his comments show how little Solti was willing to leave to chance or idle inspiration. To Anne Wilkens, singing *'Dämmert der Tag schon auf'*: 'Make a little comma before the *auf*.' To Anne Gjevang, on the line *'dem Stamm entgrunte'*: '*Stamme*, I want to hear the "m" as if it had an "e".' Wanting Wilkens to adjust the level and rhythm on a line, he said: 'Tic, tic, tic, shhh.' To Wilkens, as she sings *'Weisst du, was aus ihm wird?'*: 'Try to speak that line.' To Anne Evans: 'That could be softer, more *pianissimo*.'

At Covent Garden, when he was musical director there, Solti, who has an expressive, bony face (especially angular in the light of a conductor's podium), was sometimes known as 'the screaming skull' because of his manner of imposing discipline on singers. In Bayreuth, more than a decade later, Solti's face was no less expressive (the viola players had a great view of his molars as he issued instructions), but he hardly ever shouted at singers. The musical discipline, though no less strict and detailed, was imposed more gently.

With the orchestra it was different. As Solti learned its strengths and weaknesses, he praised the former generously and became intolerant of the latter. As one group of brass players left a rehearsal session early, they were arraigned, first privately, and then publicly in front of their colleagues. David Syrus told me that, like some of the singers, many of the musicians felt nervous about Solti at first. They had to learn his technique of conducting, which is more energetic than precise. Unlike other conductors, who mark clearly two or four beats to the bar, Solti's gestures are intended to convey expression as well as tempo, and the players in Bayreuth were not always sure what he wanted, so that the music staff noted a lack of cohesion in the early rehearsals. At that stage, Solti was concentrating on clarity of sound, and he was helped in this by the dry

Götterdämmerung, Act I
downstage: Aage Haugland (Hagen)
enthroned: Bent Norup (Gunther) and Josephine Barstow (Gutrune) discuss
the expected arrival of Siegfried.

166

l. to r. – Manfred Jung (Siegfried); Aage Haugland (Hagen) and Bent Norup (Gunther) swear the vow of blood brotherhood.

acoustic in the Festspielhaus, which enabled him to insist that short notes be played accurately. Consequently, the thrilling dynamic sound listeners expected from an orchestra conducted by Solti was absent in the early rehearsals. Syrus counselled patience, hoping that the sound would improve during performances, when the conductor and the orchestra were better acquainted with each other. With the extra rehearsal time Wagner had found for Solti to work with the orchestra, the process of finding the right sound was protracted, and Solti's manner was not popular with all the players. Some of them regarded a Bayreuth summer as an agreeable working holiday, and a few were not up to his exacting standards. Solti himself knew how to deal with the recalcitrants; they would not be asked back the following year. 'I'm making mental changes. I know who I want,' Solti told me. 'But 99 per cent basically respected my authority; there was no question because they know very well that I know the pieces, there is an experience behind it, and let's face it, there is some musical talent, also.'

The relationship between Hall and Solti remained cheerful and equable. Before rehearsals began, Wagner had regarded a clash between the two as inevitable. It was not that he knew either Hall or Solti well; he just believed that arguments were in the nature of the relationship between the conductor and the director. No doubt he shouted at the conductor when he himself was directing, and most conductors would cheerfully return the insults. Indeed, Wagner enjoyed describing his relationship with Hans Knappertsbusch, who, he recalled, once saw Wolfgang and his brother walk across the stage and, pointing at them, said to the orchestra: 'Now you know why their grandfather was such a horse's arse.' (This is a free translation from the German.) But Hall and Solti discussed issues together patiently. When Hall judged that Solti was changing the tempi so frequently that the singers were finding it difficult to make their moves correctly, he told Solti so; but he did not shout. And when Solti felt that a singer had been positioned so that he or she could not see the conductor for too long, he asked Hall to alter the move; he did not instruct. 'This is take and give, and you can't do it any other way,' says Solti. Though each was generally too preoccupied with his own problems to interfere with the other's, Solti did recognise that one of Hall's particular troubles was Wagner. He took Hall aside one day in July and asked him if he could possibly say something pleasant to Wagner, to improve their relationship. Hall replied that he could think of nothing pleasant to say.

The length and complexity of *Götterdämmerung* are enough to try the most harmonious working relationship, so it was fairly certain to cause further ill-humour between Hall and Wagner. There are two scenes in the prelude, three in the first act, five in the second act, and three in the third, calling for eight scene changes, the locations ranging from Brünnhilde's rock to the interior and exterior of Gibichung Hall. For this theatrical ordeal, Hall had fifteen days' stage rehearsal, including the dress rehearsal: an average of one day's rehearsal for each scene. I was so incredulous that I checked this with the rehearsal schedule, and discovered that I had ignored another eight days' work in the rehearsal rooms. Counting those days too, there were 1.533 days to rehearse each scene of *Götterdämmerung*: not exactly conducive to smooth progress and even tempers.

Götterdämmerung actually fitted together with remarkable speed, despite some dreadful hiccups. The worst day I experienced came at the end of June, when Act Three was being rehearsed. This starts with Siegfried's meeting with the Rhinemaidens under a waterfall, which was to cascade down into a small pool in which the Rhinemaidens swam. Dudley hoped that a combination of dry-ice vapour falling from the edge of the platform and shards of glittering fabric behind the vapour would create an impression of falling water. But when the scene began, the vapour from the dry ice was so thin that it floated in wisps instead of falling in a stream; a failure which exposed the nakedness of the Rhinemaidens and the glittering fabric in the background. The scene looked like something mounted for a cheap strip-show. Hall's composure disappeared: 'Shit, shit, shit!' The scene would work only if enough dry ice was piped on to force the vapour to fall evenly. Would there be enough? No one was sure.

During the next scene (which ends with Siegfried's death) the front of the platform moved down to the stage floor and the back was raised, to create a small hill; but the birch trees surrounding the forest clearing dangled six inches above the platform. There had been a misunderstanding between Dudley and the workshop about the length of the trees. They were beautifully made, but, divorced from their roots, they looked ridiculous. No one knew whether there would be time or money to put them right. The entrance of Gunther, Hagen and the Gibichung hunting-party was delayed because the steps by which they entered at the rear, over the brow of the hill, had been placed in the wrong position. When they finally made their entry, I had my first look at part of the Bayreuth chorus. I had heard that this was the best chorus in the operatic world, comprising singers drawn from all over Europe and from America, and expectations in 1983 were higher than ever, for the chorus

Götterdämmerung, Prelude. Siegfried and Brünnhilde.

master, Norbert Balatsch, had weeded out some weaker voices the previous summer. Hall had told me how much he had enjoyed rehearsing with the chorus: 'It was the highlight of the summer,' he said after his first three days' work with them. But at first sight it seemed inconceivable that the male singers who made up the hunting-party could belong to the best chorus in the world: they were inattentive, truculent, and idle. After Siegfried's death, when his body is carried off through the trees as the platform rises, the angle of the platform as it moved upward became so steep that Bent Norup, playing Gunther, seemed in danger of losing his footing – possibly tumbling off the platform altogether. The next scene change, during which the forest is transformed into Gibichung Hall, the platform becoming a roof and great wooden beams rising on lifts from under the stage floor, was slow and noisy. Bill Dudley finally lost his patience with the chatterboxes from the costume department when they started to tell him how marvellous Siegfried's death had been in the Chereau *Ring*. My own impartiality collapsed as a member of the music staff – not one directly involved with the *Ring* – started to giggle during a stage disaster. Had he been sitting next to me, I should have kicked him, but he was only within verbal range. When Bill Dudley and I conducted a miserable post mortem on the disasters, he diagnosed the malaise as a fundamental and mutual lack of appreciation: 'They think we're amateurs and we think they're amateurs, and the trouble is we're both wrong.'

We had not allowed for the extreme variations in the emotional temperatures of the theatre, however. An orchestral rehearsal of the second act of *Götterdämmerung*, shortly after the debacle, revealed all that was good about Bayreuth. The chorus, in costume, was a revelation. Hearing them sing with clarity and power, and seeing them act as though each was playing his own role, banished any doubts about their being best in the world. The orchestra sounded livelier, and Manfred Voss's lighting made Dudley's set look like a Victorian painting, as he had intended. In all, Hall and Dudley looked forward to the orchestral rehearsal of Act Three the following day with a great deal less foreboding than usual.

And much of that rehearsal was no less satisfying than Act Two had been the previous day. The dry-ice vapour began to flow more freely; the birch trees in Siegfried's death scene were growing longer by the day; the rising platform for Siegfried's funeral march looked suitably eerie and distant; the orchestra was playing better and better. But these visible and audible improvements were set against the brittleness of the relationship between Hall and Wagner. The day had begun inauspiciously, when Wagner's only comment on

Previous page: Götterdämmerung, Act I. Brigitte Fassbaender (Waltraute) pleads with Hildegard Behrens (Brünnhilde)

the spirited run-through the night before was that the set would have to be cut because it was too heavy to change in the interval between the two acts. In the afternoon, when Hall was sitting in the auditorium presiding over a technical run-through of the last scene of *Götterdämmerung*, Wagner stalked up to the production desk and said loudly, in front of Hall's colleagues and Voss's team of lighting technicians, that Hall had only forty-five minutes left of this last technical rehearsal before the dress rehearsal, and that what was happening on stage was the worst solution to the end of *Götterdämmerung* that he had ever seen in his theatre. The remark might even have startled Wagner's Welsh mother; it certainly shook Hall. As usual, he said nothing to Wagner. There was not much to say. 'I almost went then, but I wasn't going to play Wagner's game,' he said after the rehearsal.

Wagner's offensive was not over. During the orchestral rehearsal that evening, Hall noticed that the torch with real flame which Brünnhilde was to snatch from a Gibichung to throw on to Siegfried's funeral pyre had been replaced by a miserable-looking plastic model. At Hall's request Michael McCaffery went backstage and discovered that the real-flame torch had been locked in a prop cupboard by Wagner personally, and that only he could open it. Hearing this, Hall told McCaffery to approach Wagner, who was sitting watching the rehearsal in the auditorium, and get the flaming torch back. At this request, Wagner strode up to the production desk and began to shout. The audible words from where I was sitting were: *'Es ist mein Haus.'* (I discovered later that his complete sentence was: 'This is my house, and I don't wish it to go up in flames.') Hall finally raised his voice: 'This is my rehearsal; would you shut up and go away!'

Offensive as Wagner's public comments were, it was true that Hall had problems with the end of *Götterdämmerung*. Richard Wagner's voluminous stage directions read: 'Brünnhilde has placed the ring on her finger, and turns to the pile of logs on which Siegfried's body is laid. She seizes a great firebrand from one of the vassals and flings it on the pyre, which quickly breaks out into bright flames. Brünnhilde sees her horse, which has been led in by two young men. She hastens towards it; she mounts the horse, and leaps with a single bound into the blazing pyre. The flames immediately blaze up so that they fill the whole space in front of the hall, and appear to seize on the building itself. The men and women press to the extreme front in terror. When the whole space of the stage seems filled with fire, the glow suddenly subsides, and only a cloud of smoke remains; this drifts to the background and lies there

173

on the horizon in a dark bank of cloud. At the same time the Rhine overflows its banks in a mighty flood which pours over the fire. On the waves the three Rhinemaidens swim forward and now appear above the pyre. Hagen, who since the incident of the ring, has observed Brünnhilde's behaviour with increasing anxiety, is seized with great alarm at the appearance of the Rhinemaidens. He hastily throws aside spear, shield and helmet, and rushes like a madman into the flood. Woglinde and Wellgunde twine their arms around his neck and draw him with them into the depths as they swim away. Flosshilde, swimming in front of the others, joyously holds up on high the esteemed ring. Through the cloudbank which has settled on the horizon, a red glow breaks out with increasing brightness. By its light the Rhinemaidens are seen, swimming in circles, merrily playing with the ring on the calmer waters of the Rhine, which has gradually returned to its bed. From the ruins of the fallen Hall, the men and women in great agitation watch the growing firelight in the heavens. When it reaches its greatest brightness, the Hall of Valhalla is seen, in which gods and heroes sit assembled. Bright flames seize on the hall of the gods. When the gods are entirely hidden by flames, the curtain falls.'

Hall's difficulty in negotiating this obstacle-course was obviously not unique. Richard Fricke, who had been Richard Wagner's assistant in 1876, confessed before the very first performance of *Götterdämmerung*: 'I fear that all the beauties of the earlier parts will be ruined by the ending.' Most recently at Bayreuth, Chéreau had used the climax to make a political statement: as the gods burned in Valhalla, the chorus turned and stared accusingly at the audience, presumably implying that they shared the weakness of Wotan and the others. True to his original intention, Hall was hoping to be as faithful as possible to Richard Wagner's stage directions. But the orchestral rehearsal cruelly exposed various imperfections in the staging of that last scene. There was so much smoke on stage that for almost a minute all sight of Brünnhilde was lost. Brünnhilde's horse still looked like an animal that found walking difficult, never mind leaping on to a funeral pyre. The Rhinemaidens, who were naked in the water tank at the back of the stage, were only partly visible because the platform obscured half the tank and the mirror. Hagen, who was to drown in the water tank, was quite invisible, and his last despairing words *'Zurück vom Ring!'* (Keep away from the ring!) were inaudible, even when sung by the commanding bass voice of Aage Haugland. The Valhalla cloth dropped late; the sun that was intended to rise over the burned castle did not look like a sun; and the family of Gibichung who climbed up the platform as

Top: *Götterdämmerung*, Act II. Brünnhilde, with Hagen and Gunther (back view).
Bottom: Act III. The death of Siegfried. *'Rache rieten sie mir'*. Aage Haugland (Hagen), Bent Norup (Gunther) and Manfred Jung (Siegfried).

Götterdämmerung, Act III. *'Ruhe, ruhe, du Gott.'*
Brünnhilde.

Hall's symbol of the continuity of human life looked exceedingly unconvincing. The family was cut, but after the dress rehearsal the other problems were still unsolved.

Hall, knowing that there would be serious problems in the last scene, had asked for a technical rehearsal with the Rhinemaidens and Hagen in the tank at the end of the dress rehearsal. (A prelude to extra rehearsals after the dress rehearsal was the appearance of Wagner on stage bellowing 'Raus, raus' at the audience, and unwittingly stirring unhappy memories, especially among the New Yorkers present.) Hall appeared backstage after the dress rehearsal, only to find that Wagner had sent the performers home. When Hall asked how he could have a technical rehearsal without them, Wagner tore off his coat and offered to double as a Rhinemaiden; then he began to pull Dudley's coat off his back so he might do the same. There was no technical rehearsal. Hall cut the tank, and he cut the mirror – a hard decision because the tank had been intended to make as big a splash at the end of the *Ring* as it had at the beginning. But, Hall explained, his climax had not worked because there had been too many imponderables. 'I was hamstrung by the tank. We always said it was worth it to get the Rhinemaidens back, but the price we were paying was the inability to construct a decent funeral pyre, or to have real fire.'

Guus Mostart, having worked with Hall before, had already experienced his willingness to take prodigious risks and remake the end of an opera just before it opened. I was reminded of one of Moran Caplat's laws of operatic production: 'It does not matter how much rehearsal is scheduled, there is always a panic at the end.' But taking risks at Glyndebourne, where Hall could concentrate his attention on one opera, was not the same as a last-minute transformation in Bayreuth. The schedule contained no rehearsals at all for *Götterdämmerung* between the dress rehearsal on 21 July and the first performance nine days later. That schedule was already being hastily rewritten to accommodate a few hours' rehearsal for Manfred Jung to learn the essential moves in *Siegfried*. Hall's changes to the last scene of the *Ring* meant finding even more time: he obtained another four and a half hours in all but only two hours were on stage, and those were on the actual day of the performance, when the *Götterdämmerung* set would be reinstalled.

The chorus and Brünnhilde were shown how Hall wanted the scene reworked, on a rehearsal stage on the morning of the opening performance of *Das Rheingold*. The removal of tank and mirror had created more room backstage, and Hall proposed moving the funeral pyre and making it larger, a decision that provided him with one conspicuous bonus. Because of extra space, Wagner had lifted his ban on the use of real flames. That ingenious fire (which burns inside an elongated and invisible glass bowl) and the new pyre were promised for Saturday. The strong men and their horse still survived in this scene, and since they would now have more room for manoeuvre, Hall hoped that the horse might finally rear up before carrying Brünnhilde to join Siegfried on the pyre. He was *hoping*; it was too late for anything more positive than that.

Three days later Hagen and the Rhinemaidens received half an hour's instruction on their part in the last scene, which had been shifted from the back to the front of the stage. Aage Haugland, the Danish bass who sang Hagen, was to lever his intimidating bulk from underneath the platform once it had settled on the stage (its curved shape meant that there was always a four-foot gap between the stage floor and the middle of the front edge of the platform). Having sung *'Zurück vom Ring'*, he was to be dragged back under the platform by the Rhinemaidens, as if they were drowning him, and Birgitta Svendén was to crawl forward to 'retrieve' the ring, which she would already be holding in her palm. The Rhinemaidens would then hold the ring aloft to celebrate its return. The general idea was clear enough, but they tried out their new moves in a small rehearsal room without the platform. They would only know whether the idea really worked by rehearsing it on the stage, a few hours before the curtain went up.

At 11 a.m. on the morning of the first performance of *Götterdämmerung* Gibichung Hall was set on stage. The soloists – most of whom had never before been called for a rehearsal on the day of a performance, when they like to be free to concentrate on the ordeal to come – arrived at 11.20, and stood about while the rostrum on which Gunther's and Gutrune's thrones stood was brought on to the stage. 'I thought you'd cut it,' Mostart shouted from the stage to Hall in the auditorium. 'I haven't made up my mind, and I can't decide until I've seen it,' Hall replied. There were four and a half hours to curtain time. I sat in the auditorium with Hermann Schreiber, the author who was expert on the subject of rehearsals in the Festspielhaus, and asked if such a last-minute reorganisation of a climax to an opera was unique. He replied that the French director, Jean-Pierre Ponnelle, sometimes worked on the day of the performance, but only on lighting. Wieland Wagner had once called a rehearsal before a performance of *Das Rheingold*. No one had ever attempted to do as much as this.

Repeating the moves learned in the rehearsal room, the chorus were clearly conserving their energy for the evening's exertions, and the repeated run-through of their exit, as they fled from the fire, was woefully slow, since Gibichung Hall had to be reset each time. But Dudley noticed that a beam designed to break away from the main construction as Gibichung Hall collapsed was doing just that, a detail he had not expected to see until the following summer; and the real fire on the funeral pyre was splendid. By 12.40, Hildegard Behrens had arrived and the rostrum had been cut. Once Behrens and the chorus had a rough idea what they were to do, the platform was turned over; it ceased to be the roof of the Hall and was lowered on to the stage so that Hagen and the Rhinemaidens could try out on stage what had been mapped out in the rehearsal room. Dudley was immediately impressed with the reworking but Hall said: 'I haven't got time to worry and look, and wonder whether it's going to work or not.' His idea for the last scene was promising enough, although it was no longer faithful to Wagner's stage directions, but it really needed five or six hours of rehearsal.

The very last element in the closing scene, when Valhalla collapses, was first rehearsed with barely fifteen minutes to go. Because the platform was lower than originally planned, the cloth on which Valhalla was painted needed to fall further than before, and the bar holding it in the grid became visible. Hall's powers of invention were exhausted and he turned to Mostart: 'What can we do, Guus?' Mostart thought a combination of the smoke and lighting might mask it, but he was not sure, and there was no time to experiment. With only three minutes left, Manfred Voss lit the platform to make it look as if the sun were rising. The final lighting cue was given with thirty seconds to go. At 1.00 p.m. precisely Hall, Dudley, and Mostart left the theatre, limp and emotionally exhausted. The re-worked scene was most imaginative, but there was no way of knowing whether the changes would work as planned that evening. Walter Huneke was more upset than exhausted. Unlike Wagner, he made no critical judgements about the artistic quality of Hall's last scene; his concern was that the stage staff should know what was expected of them. 'If only they'd given me more time,' he growled. Hall and Dudley had had nearly three years to plan the *Ring* cycle, and three months in which to rehearse it, but they had never had enough time.

14

A very hot Festival

The 1983 Bayreuth Festival had opened on Sunday 24 July, six days before the agitated finale to the *Götterdämmerung* rehearsals. The town had adjusted to the annual influx of visitors by doubling the price of hotel rooms and putting up flags along Siegfried Wagner Allee on the hill leading to the Festspielhaus. But the people who had come to see the *Ring* – because almost everyone in the audience sees the complete cycle – hardly impinged on the orderly life of Bayreuth. Many opera-goers, especially the veterans, chose to stay in hotels in the surrounding countryside. Richard Wagner had wanted his Festival to be held in a town that offered an audience no distractions, and I described Bayreuth as 'characterless' in an article in the *Sunday Times* that July. The local newspaper, the *Nordbayerische Kurier*, replied good-naturedly that Bayreuth had been a most delightful provincial town before the Allies bombed it in 1945. What can be said without fear of contradiction is that Bayreuth is a peaceful urban location that offers no distractions to a music festival.

The town did not wholly ignore the Festival. A local bank mounted an informative exhibition about Richard Wagner's death in Venice a hundred years earlier. Record companies hired shop windows, including one in the Parsifal Apotheke, to advertise their artists. Pictures of conductors and singers were plastered over billboards, and one morning I swear I saw a woman place an automatic camera on a tripod in front of a poster of Peter Hofmann, the glamorous German tenor singing Parsifal, set its timing mechanism, and take a picture of herself kissing the pictured face full on the lips. One of Solti's friends claimed that a chocolate medallion embossed with the profile of the great man himself could be bought at a local confectioners. Still, the Festival does not take over Bayreuth as, say, Edinburgh's does. Most local people – waiters, barmen, and hoteliers excepted – were in bed, as usual, before the *Ring* performance ended.

There was, however, one common topic of conversation between residents and visitors. This was not Richard Wagner, or Wolfgang, or Solti and Hall (who were known formally in Bayreuth as Sir Solti and Sir Hall). It was the heat. The temperature began to rise during a succession of sunny days in July, and by the end of the month it had become a phenomenon. Flags hung limply. The flower beds wilted in Richard Wagner Park, even though they were watered faithfully each morning; and the grass was streaked with patches of brown. One day during the first week of the Festival the temperature reached 96 degrees Fahrenheit, which was – depending on who you talked to – the hottest day in Bayreuth since the turn of the century, since Richard Wagner's death, or ever. (The only respite was on the opening day of the Festival, 24 July, when the grandees arrived to watch Wolfgang Wagner's production of *Die Meistersinger* in the downpour which, it seems, traditionally greets the first day of the Festival.) For a whole week, the heat was relentless, and the Festspielhaus's primitive cooling system – spraying water over the roof of the auditorium – could not hope to keep down the internal temperature. Outside, it was so hot that the audience sheltered from the sun as if it were rain, staying in the cafeteria or the restaurant until it was almost time to enter the auditorium. Those outside huddled in the shade of the building, and spectators who braved the full heat of the day by standing on the terrace to hear the fanfare that announces the beginning or the resumption of performance, would have looked more suitably dressed in tennis gear than evening clothes. No one went as far as that, but the proportion of men wearing black ties was reported by seasoned observers to be falling, though men in ordinary suits were still exceptions to the rule. Once inside the auditorium, however, many men took off their jackets and rolled up their sleeves. It was no weather for sartorial niceties.

Backstage, where there was no similar relief for the performers, temperatures regularly rose above 100 degrees. In the pit it was even hotter, and Solti and the players were acutely uncomfortable. Sweat poured so freely down Solti's face that he was occasionally unable to read the score. At least he and the orchestra did not have to wear tails: Solti conducted in a sweatshirt and trousers. A few of the singers, Hildegard Behrens among them, seemed impervious to the heat, as though the fear that is a prelude to all performances – but most particularly to a debut in Bayreuth – had made them immune to simple physical discomfort. But others inevitably succumbed, and flagged. High temperatures made Hall's liberal use of smoke even more of an irritant to the singers. (It was number one of

184

their list of dislikes in the production, followed by entrances and exits on the platform, and the unreliability of cues from the stage managers.) The most envied members of the cast were, of course, the three Rhinemaidens, who wore no costumes at all while they took a dip in their pool.

The best reading in the programme for the opening day of the Festival was the small print, which listed the people who do not appear, but without whom, as they rightly say, no performance would be possible. There are hundreds of them. Anyone phoning the Festspielhaus can enquire whether the call is being taken by Irene Neese or Gunda Lodes, and be sure, incidentally, that both come from Bayreuth, since the home town of each staff member is also recorded. Thus it is possible to calculate that only four of the 188 instrumentalists who play at one time or another during the Festival come from outside Germany – from Lyons, Korea, Prague, and Toronto. The chorus is a genuinely international group, drawn from ten European countries and the United States of America, though foreigners are heavily outnumbered by Germans. This is not the case, oddly enough, among the stage crew, ten of whom are imported from Prague, eight from Austria, and one each from Poland and the United States; they easily outnumbered the fourteen Germans on the crew. (Wagner even squeezed in a programme mention, obscure though it was, for Mike Barnett, the engineer who designed the platform.) Once the Festival was under way, I spent a day in and around the Festspielhaus watching some of the unsung participants at work.

At 9.00 a.m. on performance days there was already a small knot of people outside the ticket office, which opened an hour later, each with a handwritten sign saying 'Suche Karte?', hoping for returns, or for tickets to turn up on the black market. (Some always did, sometimes at double the face price of DM 180, for a stalls ticket, DM 720 for the complete cycle: at rates of exchange current in the summer of 1983, a ticket for the cycle cost £180 or $270, which was not unreasonable by comparison with most metropolitan opera houses.) The lady who sold stamped envelopes as souvenirs was by that time placing them neatly in a rack by the book and record stall, which, being flanked on either side by a public lavatory, is an excellent location for catching the passing trade. Across the road, in a kiosk built into the front of the Festspielhaus, shutters were taken down and the sale of postcard-pictures of the current performances began.

The stage crew arrived at 9.00 a.m. too, to dismantle the set from the previous performance; the day I was there early, most of the evidence of *Die Walküre* had gone by 9.30 a.m. A section was removed from the platform so that it could form the wall and entrance to Mime's forge, and by 10.30 a.m. new platform coverings for Acts One and Two of *Siegfried* had been fixed, and the crew were beginning to hang the trees that appear in the background of the set. Lighting technicians had arrived and were starting to place their lamps.

In the press office on the first floor of the office-block, Dr Oswald George Bauer, who doubles as Bayreuth's dramaturge and press officer, was already giving the first of the interviews (in German, French and English) that fill his working day. A studious, bespectacled figure, Bauer came to Bayreuth from a university drama department and is a considerable Wagner scholar. One of his tasks is to commission articles for the Festival programme, which are very serious, very long, and often rather obscure. (I noticed the following sentence in a piece by Claude Lévi-Strauss, the French anthropologist: 'Through its recurrences, the motif does not only reveal two systems of correlations; it further suggests that those should also be paralleled in order to reach a deeper level of meaning which is at the root of the fragmentary meanings that each system individually revealed.' Perhaps the prose lost something in translation from the French.) When he first came to Bayreuth, Dr Bauer intended to involve himself as little as possible in the distribution of tickets to journalists, but a little had turned into a lot. In 1983 he received more applications from music critics than ever before, about 200 in all, only 110 of whom could be accommodated in the first cycle. Half of these came from German-speaking countries; most of the rest were from Europe and the United States, but he had also received applications from Australia and Japan, India, South Africa, and South America. And the output of these critics is astonishing: Dr Bauer's office collected twenty-seven box-files of reviews for Patrice Chéreau's *Ring* in its first year.

At 11.00 a.m. four technicians from the Decca recording studio arrived on stage to rig microphones for the performance that evening. The sound from stage and pit was fed into a battery of sound-mixers in a temporary studio that had been crammed into a rehearsal room (to accommodate the tape machines a hole had been knocked through the wall to an adjacent lavatory). These Decca engineers had a job unique in the record business. Most recordings of live performances are haphazard affairs, relying on luck as much as judgement, but Decca, for whom Solti records, had decided in this case to leave nothing to chance. They recorded *everything*, beginning with the orchestral rehearsals, and hoped in two or three years to produce a complete *Ring* that duplicated exactly the sound heard in the auditorium. Each morning the technicians reset the stage microphones, and checked the thirteen microphones in the pit. After a month, they were finally coming to terms with the platform, whose slight hiss, when it moved, they had originally despaired over. (Fortunately, Solti only whistles during rehearsals.)

Towards midday the crowd of would-be ticket holders began to trail away from the ticket office, where three brave ladies had spent two hours politely repeating that they had nothing to sell. The business of actually selling tickets takes place early in the winter, since all tickets are balloted for and sold by mail to prevent local people cornering the market. When it had put all the applications on the computer, the ticket office calculated that it would take six *Ring* cycles, not three, in 1983 to meet the demand. Many of those who had hung around hopefully all morning left the Festspielhaus only to change, so that if something were to turn up at the last minute, they would be dressed to take advantage of it.

At 1.00 p.m. two stagehands arrived to check that everything had been properly set by the morning shift. One of these was a slim Californian in his early twenties named Christopher Thomas. A graduate in theatre arts from UCLA, Thomas is a zealous Wagnerian, and had already worked with the stage crew for three years. Since he is fluently bilingual, he had been asked by Huneke to come to Bayreuth and, before long, was performing the duties of a stage manager as well as a stagehand. Later in the summer Hall would introduce Thomas flamboyantly as the man without whom he could not have done the *Ring*. On performance days, however, Thomas was back on menial duties: vacuuming the stage floor and the wings, and checking the props and the hydraulic system that opens the curtains. (The curtain is one aspect of the auditorium that Richard Wagner would not recognise: Wieland Wagner replaced his grandfather's rising curtain with one that parts in the middle, as he thought it would improve the acoustic.) Finally, Thomas checked the smoke machines to make sure they contained the correct mixture of paraffin and water, which is heated and then released by compressed gas, to produce smoke. At 3.00 p.m. exactly the firemen from Bayreuth's fire department, whose bright red *Feuerwehrwagen* stands outside the Festspielhaus throughout each performance, arrived to check the metal fire curtain dividing stage from auditorium. This brief task gave them ample time to troop down to a long table in the canteen and consume quantities of beer before the performance began at 4.00 p.m.

Shortly after the firemen left, the stage crew began to take their places, dressed completely in black so as to be as little visible as possible during scene-changes that took place in view of the audience. This crew's shift ended with the last scene change of the evening. By the time the curtain closed they had all gone home, leaving Thomas and his colleague to hold the curtain during the calls, and tidy the set. They were the last to leave the stage. Only the chefs and waitresses in the Festspielhaus restaurant laboured on, patiently, until the last plate of smoked duck had been eaten by a dinner-jacketed patron, the last mug of dark beer drunk by one of the crew.

The first horn fanfare for *Das Rheingold* sounded at 5.45 p.m. on 25 July, summoning to their seats an audience that contained an unusually high proportion of professional opera-goers: critics, administrators, and singers who were not performing that evening. I sensed an atmosphere as much of curiosity as of anticipation. Gossip about production problems, such as Reiner Goldberg's precipitate departure, and the edgy relationship between Wagner and Hall, had flourished in the hotels of Bayreuth. A few spectators were confidently forecasting disaster before they had heard a note.

Hall and Dudley had spent the afternoon in the canteen, in the customary mood of theatre people on the first night: apprehension verging on funk. Hall had been asked to wear a dinner jacket in case he and Dudley took a curtain call at the end of the performance. (There was no point in asking Dudley to wear a dinner jacket; he did not have one – never had. When he appeared, it would be in his light seersucker jacket and the black boots he wore most of the summer.) But both Hall and Dudley resisted the idea of a curtain call that evening: they knew that Patrice Chéreau had made an appearance on the first night of his cycle in 1976, in his jeans, as a defiant response to the booers, but their understanding was that the Bayreuth custom called for director and designer to take their curtain call only after *Götterdämmerung*. (They discovered later in the week that Wolfgang Wagner had taken calls after each performance in his *Ring*s.) There was, however, another reason for their reluctance to take calls after *Das Rheingold*. A final technical rehearsal promised for that afternoon had not taken place because the set for Scene One was not on the stage in time, and Hall, finally conceding that the scene changes could not be performed in view of the audience, asked that a curtain be used during the changes. He felt he wasn't responsible for technical disasters that might occur. Dudley added gloomily: 'It's going to be a busk tonight', theatrical jargon for an improvised, unpredictable performance.

As it turned out, their fears were groundless. The first performance of *Das Rheingold* was not entirely free from technical errors, but they were insignificant. The water reflected in the mirror was as exciting as Hall and Dudley had always hoped, and the Rhinemaidens dazzled most of the audience, some of whom could not believe they did not have non-singing doubles in the tank. The giants were, indeed, more like giants than in any other Bayreuth production, and with the climax on the rainbow bridge, the story of the *Ring* had begun to unfold impressively. Had Hall and Dudley taken a bow after *Das Rheingold* there would, I suspect, have been widespread applause. A couple of boos did ring out when Solti appeared (with a natty Mao jacket over his sweatshirt), but they were soon overwhelmed by cries of 'Bravo'. The mood of the production team that evening was one of elated relief.

Das Rheingold, Scene 3. Wotan, left, and Loge try to persuade Alberich to part with the Nibelungs' gold and the ring.

This page:
Top: *Die Walküre*, Act III. The Valkyries.
Bottom: *Die Walküre*, Act III. *'Loge! Loge! Heiher.'* Wotan directs the fire to encircle the rocks.

Facing page:
Top: *Die Walküre*, Act I. The confrontation in Hunding's hut. Jeannine Altmeyer (Sieglinde), Matthias Hölle (Hunding), Siegfried Jerusalem (Siegmund).
Bottom: *Die Walküre*, Act II. Fricka confronts Wotan.

This humour lasted through the first act of *Die Walküre* the following day. Hunding's hut was a splendid visual continuation of the naturalism of *Das Rheingold*, and both Siegfried Jerusalem and Jeannine Altmeyer were liberally applauded. At last feeling free to pay attention to the music, I asked my neighbour, a skilful young Swedish conductor I had met in Bayreuth, for his opinion. He was impressed by the clarity with which Solti developed the musical themes, so that they always complemented the story as it unfolded on the stage. 'What's so good is Solti's architecture. He is very disciplined, but very romantic at the same time.' Clearly, Solti had established a satisfactory balance between the pit and the stage. Among the instrumentalists who impressed my conductor friend were the violas, the cellos and the basses, and one marvellous horn player (it was Gerd Seifert, from the Berlin Philharmonic Orchestra). 'Not so good are the two clarinets, and the trombones, unfortunately, because they are so important to Wagner's music.' After Act Two he noted that the violins had begun to blossom. The only fundamental fault he isolated was that some of the instrumentalists were out of tune, particularly in the brass and wind sections. It is, of course, difficult to tune an orchestra when so many of the players can only hear the section closest to them, and perhaps the heat did not help, but when the orchestra is out of tune the singers' job naturally becomes more difficult. But this deficiency did not diminish my friend's great pleasure in Solti's conducting: 'I've read the score, and I hear what I've read,' he said.

On stage, Hildegard Behrens had made her entrance in Act Two, and was splendid right away. But, visually, the act confused the audience. Of the naturalistic effects, only Fricka's chariot, drawn by two black rams, had not been cut. Consequently, the stage looked as bare as anything Wieland Wagner had designed, contradicting the naturalistic settings that had appeared before, and distracting from the unfolding of the story. In Act Three, the anxiety caused by the naked dead heroes was less what they symbolised than whether they could be seen at all, they were so dimly lit. The most disturbing visual failure of all, however, was the circle of fire at the end of Act Three, when smoke billows from the glowing red lights and the platform rises, carrying the sleeping Brünnhilde to the top of her mountain. Unfortunately, hardly any smoke emerged, leaving the lights looking like a glowing ring on an electric cooker. Bill Dudley, standing at the entrance to the stage after the performance, was distraught: 'What happened to the smoke?' he asked, repeatedly. In the auditorium, there had been boos from twenty or so people at the end of *Die Walküre*: 'Trying to ignite the blue paper,' Hall said. The reception had seemed muted; backstage the reaction was quite the opposite. Voss was impatient at last-minute requests for lighting changes, and told Mostart so, bluntly. McCaffery was worried that Hall's refusal to take a curtain call was creating unnecessary hostility. Dudley said sadly, 'When's the fun going to start?'

It certainly did not begin with the performance of *Siegfried* two days later. *Siegfried* was beginning to attract ill-fortune like an operatic version of *Macbeth*. On the morning of the performance Siegmund Nimsgern, who had suffered in the heat during *Die Walküre*, telephoned to announce that the glands in his throat were swelling and that he might be able to sing only the first of the three acts. Immediately, Nimsgern's understudy, a gentle and polite Dane called Bent Norup, whose role was Gunther, was called to rehearse Wotan's moves in Act Two with Hermann Becht. But a superficial knowledge of Act Two was not to be enough, for shortly after lunch Nimsgern's voice failed completely. I saw Norup arrive to sing his first Wotan in Bayreuth an hour later, looking very subdued: there is never any time to rehearse understudies properly at Bayreuth.

Before the performance began, Wagner appeared in front of the curtain and announced that Wotan would be sung by Bent Norup, 'who knows the part well'. Wagner's remark dismayed Solti: Norup knew the words and music well enough, but after a few minutes' rehearsal of one act, he could hardly be said to know the production. Manfred Jung, too, had had only three rehearsals with Hall since taking over from Reiner Goldberg, during which he could only sketch in the moves. Two of the three chief protagonists in *Siegfried* were stepping on to the stage in Hall's production for the first time. It seemed as if the curse of the *Ring* had struck again.

There was booing after the first act, which Wagner insisted was directed at him because of the late replacement of Goldberg. Perhaps it was, but Jung behaved as though the boos had been meant for him, and when he took his curtain call he gave the audience a withering stare. It was inconceivable, surely, that the boos could have been directed at Norup, though some observers thought they were. He was evidently nervous; his eyes rarely left Solti's hands, his movement was minimal, and his involvement in the acting slight, but without him there could have been no performance at all.

Jung and Norup navigated the second act without floundering, which was as much as could be expected. Jung had competition from the stage staff when he was about to kill the dragon, since one could be heard saying 'Achtung' – sound advice though that might

The last night of the first cycle of the 1983 *Ring*. Centre l. to r. Hall, Solti, Dudley, Behrens, Habereder, Jung.

Curtain calls after *Götterdämmerung*. l. to r. Behrens, Solti, Norup, and Norbert Balatsch (chorus master).

be, it does not appear in Wagner's text. There were no more boos at the end of that act, but Hall's hope that the story of the *Ring* would be revealed intelligently and simply had been dashed.

The third act benefited from the reappearance of Behrens; and Jung, who had carefully saved the best of his voice for his scene with Brünnhilde, sang confidently. But the dramatic tension was in the music, not the acting. There were no boos at the end of *Siegfried*, but most of the audience felt let down, and some were bored. No one in the auditorium was as gloomy as Hall and Mostart after the performance, however. They did not complain about Jung and Norup; they appreciated their luck in having two such professional singers available to salvage the performance. But various details of the staging had been either incorrect, or ineptly done, and Mostart had already put a three-page list of technical errors on Wagner's desk. 'I wouldn't mind if I never came back,' Hall said sombrely. I suggested that it was unrealistic to expect everything to be right in the first year. 'I don't care,' said Mostart. 'I want it to be perfect.'

196   *Facing page:*
Wolfgang Wagner knows
a star is born

Götterdämmerung approached perfection more nearly than any other part of the cycle. The new climax that had been cobbled together that morning had looked as though it needed much more rehearsal, but in performance it was technically faultless, in spite of the fact that Voss had to do all the lighting cues manually from his small box at the back of the auditorium, with Mostart at his side giving vocal cues to the stage managers on his microphone link. As the curtain closed there was a moment of silence, shattered by a single cry of 'Bravo', soon swelled by many others. The singers were enthusiastically applauded, especially Behrens, who looked radiant. A posy of flowers was thrown at Solti, who picked it up as he acknowledged the cheers and thunderous applause.

Peter Hall and Bill Dudley took their first curtain call together with the whole of the company, conductor and orchestra, soloists and chorus. As the curtain opened to reveal both of them smiling, Wagner's *Ring* suddenly became a blood sport. The boos, at first as loud as the applause, soon began to drown it. Hall and Dudley still smiled; indeed Dudley turned to Solti as the boos began and whispered: 'Don't worry, Sir Georg, it's only rock and roll.' Hall, Dudley and Solti then took their own call and the boos became even louder. Solti turned to Dudley and presented him with his posy of flowers, which Dudley was still carrying as he and Hall took another curtain call on their own. They found this a bizarre experience; Dudley said they could hear the boos and see the applause, which appeared to be coming from more than half the house. Hall smiled serenely; Dudley did a little tap dance as he waved and smiled. 'At least they didn't throw anything,' he said as the curtain closed. Bayreuth veterans, immediately analysing the reception, concluded that it was not as bad as Chéreau's 1976 opening, or Goetz Friedrich's *Tannhäuser* a few years earlier.

Neither Hall nor Dudley was hurt by the booing. They had been expecting it, and they felt it bore little relationship to the *Götterdämmerung* the audience had seen. Both judged that they had put on a good show that evening, anyway, and went off to the canteen for a drink before leaving for England next morning. Hall talked no more of 'not minding if he never came back'. As he got up to leave, he touched Dudley fondly on the shoulder, and said: '*Ça commence.*'

15

The curse of the *Ring*

Hall and Dudley left Bayreuth without saying goodbye, since both expected to return for the last of the summer's three *Ring* cycles, at the end of August. As we turned on to the Nuremberg autobahn, Dudley commented that for the first time he was sorry to be leaving Bayreuth; but Hall was quite exhausted, and anxious for a rest in the Sussex countryside. Both learned by telephone from Guus Mostart, who stayed on at the Festspielhaus, of an appreciative reception for the second-cycle performances, when hardly a boo was heard – an indication that the character of the audience had changed.

After the first cycle there were fewer people in the audience who were there because opera is their business, though there was no lack of familiar faces. The perfect Wagnerite, Bernard Levin, reported in *The Times* that among the English contingent alone he observed a former Prime Minister, a Secretary to the Cabinet, a Royal Duke, a former Minister of the Arts, a genius, and a saviour of Venice. Famous, infamous, or anonymous, members of the audience at the second cycle were notably less volatile than those at the first – perhaps because there was less to be volatile about. Technically, the performances were smoother, and there were no last-minute changes of cast. Siegmund Nimsgern finally conquered the nerves which had contributed to his inability to sing in the first performance of *Siegfried*. He gave Solti an anxious moment when he said he feared his voice might not be capable of coping with the third act of *Die Walküre*, but, having been persuaded to try, he found that it was, and subsequently improved with each performance. I also noticed a shift in attitudes in reports that filtered back to London: a pair of first-time visitors to Bayreuth, drawn by the Solti–Hall *Ring*, reported their delight at driving through Bavarian forests so dense that they would not have been surprised to see Siegfried emerge on the roadside tooting his hunting-horn; others described the pleasure of picnicking in the grounds of Wahnfried. No such relaxations had been permitted the production team during their months in Bayreuth, for they had arrived in the Festspielhaus at 10.00 in the morning, and had been lucky if they left in time for a proper dinner.

But the curse of the *Ring* had not lifted. In the third cycle, at the end of August, after most expectations had been satisfied by *Das Rheingold* and *Die Walküre*, Manfred Jung succumbed to the strain of his hyper-active summer. Though unwell before *Siegfried*, he agreed to sing nonetheless, and all he got for his pains was a barrage of ill-mannered abuse at the end of the first act. Wagner, outraged, came out in front of the curtain, silenced the audience, and then delivered a lecture: they were extremely lucky to be watching *Siegfried* at all, he said; Jung was not well, and there was no reason why he should continue singing if his reward was such hostility. Warming to his theme, Wagner added that casting Siegfried was difficult enough at the best of times, and that if audiences were abusive, there would be no more *Ring* productions at Bayreuth. Wagner's message was received and understood, and after both succeeding acts Jung was warmly applauded. But the part of the audience that had tasted blood turned on Solti instead, and for the first time in the summer he was brutally booed. One suggested explanation was that Solti had not lowered the volume of orchestral sound to help Jung sing more comfortably. Perhaps this was so; I was no longer sure by then that rational excuses could be found for the behaviour of the hostile minority.

In *Götterdämmerung* Siegfried was sung by the third tenor to sing the role in that one summer, the 61-year-old American Jean Cox. Having had only a couple of hours to familiarise himself with the complicated sets, Cox sang the first two acts competently, but was reduced to a vocal whisper in the last act. It was the smoke, he remarked crossly. He refused to take a curtain call, so the hostile elements turned on Solti again, and when Wagner made another appearance they booed him too. Wagner is philosophical about the behaviour of the Bayreuth audience, holding (as he explained to me one day) that there are only two places where people can express their feelings without there being any negative consequences in social, financial, class, or job terms: a football ground, and the theatre. A famous industrialist, he said, could shout in the Festspielhaus in a way he would never think of doing in his factory, and Wagner insisted, 'When the audience leaves the theatre politely, that is the worst thing of all.' This theory was not especially sympathetic to English ears, perhaps because they are too familiar with the hooliganism of football crowds, and hear in the hysteria of a part of the Bayreuth audience a destructive passion that, in

Germany, has not always been confined to the theatre. Hall described it as 'fascist' (with a small 'f'), and the ferocity of the booing certainly emphasised a gap between German and English cultures. Indeed, it occurred to me that had Richard Wagner's ghost taken a curtain call, some people might have booed him too.

At the end of the third cycle, the booers were perhaps also frustrated at not having Hall and Dudley to shout at. Shortly before the summer's last performance began, Hall's exhaustion became a serious illness, and he suffered a recurrence of a virus infection in his eyes that plagues him whenever he is run-down. His doctor warned that unless he rested, Hall might even lose his sight. With Hall unable to go to Bayreuth, Dudley decided not to interrupt his work in London either. (He was in his element, designing a pantomime – *Cinderella* – for the National Theatre.)

Mostart represented Hall in the meetings during the third cycle in which cast changes for the 1984 summer's *Ring* were discussed. Some changes were inevitable with so untried a cast, for not all Solti's and Hall's experiments had succeeded. Some voices had proved too light, even in the Bayreuth acoustic, and among those who would not return were Donner, Froh and Fasolt from *Das Rheingold*; some of the Valkyries; and Gunther and Gutrune. Josephine Barstow, who had been Maria Ewing's late replacement, had only intended staying one year anyway; but Jeannine Altmeyer, who had decided to concentrate on her San Francisco Brünnhilde, was persuaded to repeat her Sieglinde in 1984. Manfred Jung was not asked to repeat his marathon performances: Solti wanted Jung only to sing Siegfried in *Götterdämmerung*, so there would be a new Loge, and another Siegfried for *Siegfried*, if one could be found. It was no surprise when one was not, and Jung was contracted to sing both Siegfrieds in 1984.

The recasting having been discussed, Solti talked to Wagner about some of the disagreements of the summer. Why, he asked, had Wagner so obdurately refused to commit himself about the production? Wagner replied that he never did commit himself; his function was to advise, and he in this case had not been asked to do so. In public, Wagner was unfailingly loyal to Solti's and Hall's work, as was his custom. But his support in public did not necessarily reflect his private thoughts; since he was so reticent, I could piece together his real opinion only by inference after our talk during the rehearsals. Wagner had said then that Hall's and Dudley's work was in the same tradition as Patrice Chéreau's, both productions being a reaction against the abstraction of Wieland's *Ring*s, and his own. Dudley, he continued, was developing a 'totally different picture language' by his use of modern technology to develop the platform; it derived, Wagner thought, from the optical restlessness of the cinema. Talking to Hermann Schreiber, Wagner also said that Dudley had some of the visual genius of Wieland (of course, he said nothing of the kind to Dudley himself).

Wagner was concerned, however, that the *Ring* should not just be a sequence of stage pictures. He was not persuaded that a romantic *Ring* based on the original stage directions was sufficient as a conception. 'It is never quite right to stick to the 1876 stage directions, because if Richard Wagner had had the money his 1877 *Ring* would have looked different.' Wagner told me he was still looking for the 'thin red line' – the thread – that ran through the whole of the Hall–Dudley production, and, without realising it at the time, I then heard the fundamental criticism of Hall's *Ring*; that it lacked an overall conception – a personal philosophy, be it social, psychological, or ideological. This charge was pressed most relentlessly by German critics; and Hall even had intimations of it before the first performance when an interviewer had asked him why, since Richard Wagner had been revolutionary, Hall felt he could ignore the politics of the *Ring*. Hall gave his answer to that question during the press conference that is traditionally held during the first week of the Festival: 'If Wagner had wanted to write a political piece about the barricades in Dresden he would have done it, but he wrote a piece about gods, and giants, and gold, and enchantment, and spells, and about the corruption of power, and morality.' (Hildegard Behrens was less diplomatic with an interviewer who suggested that the *Ring* really ought to urge nuclear disarmament: 'Don't you think that people have been threatened all the time in their existences?' she replied fiercely.)

Hall was shocked, however, by the ferocity of many of the German critics, who reacted as though Hall had arrived at a formal party wearing shorts and sneakers: it simply was not done to arrive in Bayreuth without a 'conception'. Worse still, it was Hall who eventually provided them with the stick they happily beat him with. This took the form of a statement of intent to help critics review his *Ring*. Oswald Bauer had asked Hall to provide one but he had felt disinclined to provide any such thing; when he worked in the theatre, he preferred the critics, like the audience, to make up their own minds about the intentions and merits of a production. My only positive contribution to Hall's *Ring* was to suggest that I put a statement together, based on various interviews we had had. He agreed. Later both of us wished that we had done nothing. Since the statement was used as the basis of so many reviews, here it is:

202

I have been asked by the Festspielhaus to write a brief introduction to this production of the *Ring*.

I believe that Richard Wagner elevated a fairy story into an adult myth, and that the craggy naïveté of the text for the *Ring* is at one with the period in which Wagner wrote the music. The romanticism is in the music, and I have tried to reflect that by remembering nature in the *Ring*; its background is the weather and the cosmos, it takes place on mountain tops and in water. The shelters built by human beings are all vulnerable to the power of nature – to fire and a river in flood.

Naturally I am interested in the political side of the *Ring*, but I think this has been so emphasised in recent years that the sensual side – not only the sexuality of Siegmund and Sieglinde, but the pure love of Brünnhilde – has been overlooked. I have concentrated on the complete narrative story of the *Ring*, and this is complex and contradictory. It can, and perhaps should, mean different things to each individual who sees it. In his polemical and absorbing *Ring* in 1976, for instance, Patrice Chéreau told us that the revolution is coming, but the *Ring* does not say that to me at all. The revolution fails, and what the *Ring* tells me is that life goes on, seasoned by some forgiveness, some humanity, and some love; Fortinbras gives us the same message at the end of *Hamlet*.

If there is an intellectual inspiration for this *Ring*, it is not neo-Marxism, or Freudianism, or abstract expressionism. I suppose the production is most influenced by the Cambridge critic, F. R. Leavis, who taught me always to examine the text, and to have faith in it. In Wagner's text and music, I find a classical story of the conflict between power and love; of how heroic love eventually redeems characters who have been corrupted by power. This might sound simple but I believe in naïveté in the theatre. I would like this production, visually and in its actions, to make sense to a child.

Consequently, I have been as faithful as possible to Richard Wagner's stage directions, which are very specific. When the text calls for Rhinemaidens to swim in water, I want the audience to believe they are swimming in water. When the action moves between the various Kingdoms of the *Ring* – the mountain tops, the valley of the Rhine, and Nibelheim, under the earth – I want the audience to sense the journey.

With the highly mobile and visually beautiful platform, designed by William Dudley, I hope we achieve that feeling of movement. The mobile platform allows us to transform the naturalistic settings of the earth's surface to the real world of the gods. There should be no contradiction between the realism of the scenes involving the mortals, and the more abstract mountain top inhabited by the gods. And when Wagner asks for giants, a dragon, a huge worm, or a frog, we have tried to provide them. The realism helps us understand Wagner's nightmare metaphor.

Doing all four parts of the *Ring* in a single summer, as only Bayreuth does, is, of course, quite impossible. My experience is that, no matter how well prepared a director is, his ideas do not really take shape until he works with people on the stage. On the other hand, the idea of doing a complete cycle straight away appeals to me, because the whole story is told consecutively in one week. This is a great advantage over a *Ring* that is revealed gradually, in annual episodes. The emphasis on narrative means that each of the characters knows only his part of the story, and this narrative style is intended to create spontaneity, clarity and innocence. This is how I have tried to tell the story of the *Ring*.

Various passages provided fuel for the attack that was launched on the *Ring*. Objection was taken to the description of Wagner's text as naïve, and Hall, realising that it was not a word in the lexicon of Wagnerian critics, withdrew it when he spoke at the press conference. An English critic, Tom Sutcliffe of the *Guardian*, picked on the reference to F. R. Leavis: 'One might imagine that Leavis took a neutral view of the text – instead of evaluating the work on moral grounds, with the aid of footnotes. To cite Leavis in the context of a simple, romantic *Ring*, is pure flannel.' Not, however, when a director is describing his loyalty to an author's intentions. Nor did the idea that the story could be told simply meet with widespread sympathy. 'Hall's evident failure to produce a coherent view of the *Ring* rankled the highly critical, proprietary audience as the week progressed,' wrote Michael Walsh in *Time* magazine. Donal Henahan, the *New York Times*'s critic, who appeared to have spent a perfectly miserable week in Bayreuth, wrote: 'It is as if Hall, as director, having decided against imitating all recent interpretations of the *Ring*, found himself with an empty bucket. . . . Hall seems to have no more interesting idea than to throw together in jarring juxtaposition styles drawn from a century of Wagnerian history.' The critic of the *Frankfurter Allgemeine Zeitung* was crisper: 'The whole production appears to be heading for quite a disaster,' he wrote after *Die Walküre*.

The critics' quest for a conception became so obsessive that Hall himself decided that he must provide something more for them at the press conference. 'I understand many people in this room cannot see the concept. I can only say I have a strong concept about the *Ring*. I think it is a morality opera about good and evil; it's strongly philosophical, strongly psychological, strongly political, but only after it's a myth. And I've tried to put on stage a myth.' That, however, was not enough for the Wagnerians. It occurred to me that we were listening to a debate between two irreconcilable ideas of the theatre. On one side were the conceptualists, on the other were textualists, and the debate between the two was as unproductive as a confrontation between Marxists and Democrats. (Indeed, the debate in Bayreuth sometimes was between Marxists and Democrats.) Hall's stance as a textualist was not unsupported. In the *New Yorker*, Andrew Porter wrote: 'Operatic directors with "conceptions" in the form of reinterpretations, distortions, partial glosses or misconceptions are the curse of our day.' In *The Times*, Bernard Levin made a similar case, and went on: 'Wagner's great tale . . . will speak clearly enough to an audience when the director has the courage – as Hall has had – to let it do so, to seek the truth in the relationship, in the characters, in the symbolism, in the struggle of strength that cannot be waged through force, in the Shakespearian understanding of the human heart that runs through this most heroic of dramas. . . . It is a measure of Hall's success that I cannot remember having seen or heard a *Ring* in which the leitmotifs made Wagner's points, with all their complexity and many-sidedness, in a manner at once so urgent, so clear, and so illuminating.'

The conceptualists' case was based on memories of the work of Chéreau, and Wieland Wagner; and in Wolfgang Wagner's insistence, restated in the programme for the Festival, that the *Ring* should be continually reinterpreted so that it had contemporary relevance. They totally rejected the idea that the *Ring* could be told simply, as a story. They never seemed to realise that what appears to be the easy way of directing the *Ring* is possibly the most difficult of all, because the demands that Richard Wagner makes on a director are so extravagant. Critics are perfectly entitled to comment only on what they see, and to ignore problems in rehearsal that cause imperfections in performance. Even the harshest critics, however, might sympathise with Hall's comment that 'doing all four parts of the *Ring* in a single summer is, of course, quite impossible'. But some critics did not. Guus Mostart and Christopher Thomas had the droll experience of picking up on their two-way communication system an East German radio broadcast which was stating that Hall's remark was an admission of failure. By the standards Hall brought to Bayreuth, perhaps it was. By Bayreuth standards it was not. It is, after all, Wolfgang Wagner himself who counsels his audience to wait until the second year's performances to judge a production, since the Festspielhaus is a workshop in which a director's work grows from necessarily imperfect beginnings, just as both Chéreau's and Wieland Wagner's had done.

Naturally, few critics liked all they saw, though some liked much more than most. John Higgins in *The Times* judged that 'for three-quarters of its length this new *Ring* is visually stunning', and concluded that Solti, Hall and Dudley 'could be well satisfied with their work on the *Ring* – the fairytale that needs time and polishing to come true.' The critic of *Die Zeit* shared the satisfaction that Hall and Dudley had felt after the first performance of *Götterdämmerung*: 'Of all the parts of the *Ring*, this is the most impressive. It is really well thought out, lively, has stature, and here the singing and the acting are thoroughly convincing. The third act of the drama provided something that has been lacking so far: poetry. It also demonstrates particularly well an interesting characteristic of Peter Hall, at least in the more active scenes: a graphically operating direction which corresponds with William Dudley's liking for geometry. Whether consciously or not, it is an aesthetic order-movement concept.' (So there *was* a concept after all.)

In the *New Yorker*, Andrew Porter – the only English-speaking critic who writes at the same long length as the Germans – was considerably tarter: 'Hall's initial plan was right, but in its execution there was many a slip. . . . In brief one might say that this *Ring* floundered on an unhappy combination of missing principals; ill-conceived and as it turned out impractically ambitious designs; and, on Hall's part, over-confidence, misjudgement and, perhaps, inexperience. (This last is an odd word to use of him, but how else can one account for the bungled stagecraft in a theatre famous for its technical efficiency?)' One can partly account for it by demonstrating that the theatre is not as efficient as it is reputed to be, but the formidable technical demands made by the platform were a theme in a number of reviews, a theme developed at some length by Max Loppert of the *Financial Times*: 'The most significant [reason the production went off track] I believe, is that the entire tetralogy has been made reliant on a single piece of immensely sophisticated stage wizardry. The platform is obviously a brilliant piece of technological invention, even if the unveiling of it was noticeably less than trouble-free. Yet the structuring of a complete *Ring* upon a single gadget may at some point have taken precedence from all the other component parts, visual and dramatic, that go to make up a balanced production.' Though it may well be that the platform was moved too much during scenes, it did allow the astonishing transformations Wagner insists upon between scenes – from the bed of the Rhine to the top of a mountain, from Gibichung Hall to Brünnhilde's cave – to take place with magical effect. The errors which were evident when the platform moved during scenes would almost certainly be remedied by moving the platform less often, and the same is true of the smoke, the superabundance of which was much commented on. (In the *Sunday Times*, David Cairns said the smoke made Gibichung Hall look like an old-fashioned railway station.) Whether it would be possible to dispense with the gauze, which irritated a good many members of the audience, depended on how well the arms of the platform could be masked; a problem that would have to wait until the summer of 1984.

For Solti's conducting, praise was especially generous. The boos heard during the third cycle were the first hint of criticism, for the critics had been laudatory almost to a man. (I came across no women critics in Bayreuth.) Most heard what Solti hoped they would hear – a broader, less excitable reading of the *Ring*. Joachim Kaiser, a distinguished critic who writes for the Munich newspaper, the *Suddeutsche Zeitung*, commented that Solti's conducting had the lyricism of a Karajan and the dynamism of Böhm; praise even a modest man could never forget. One of the few dissenting voices was Andrew Porter's, in the *New Yorker*: 'He sentimentalises tender episodes, and he trivialises excited passages by charging through them.' Porter is a devotee of the English conductor, Sir Reginald Goodall, who conducted the *Ring* in Porter's own fine translation at the English National Opera in London, and whose slow, measured tempi have been, for Porter, the standard by which he judges all *Ring*s. Loppert shared his doubts.

The singers, however, received very mixed notices, and Solti was criticised for having chosen a mainly new cast that included an unusually large number of light voices. But this is a point on which neither Hall nor Solti could conceivably win, since they would have been attacked for being conservative if they had selected familiar voices, just as they were attacked for not being conservative when they tried a new cast that was not wholly successful. There being no absolute standard of judgement, it is worth noting how many of the singers were complimented on their work: I read no harsh words about the Rhinemaidens or the Norns (indeed, their excellence was much remarked on), of the Valkyries or the basses – Fafner and Fasolt, Hunding and Hagen. Hermann Becht and Peter Haage (the brothers Alberich and Mime) were admired as much for their acting as their voices. Jeannine Altmeyer's 'enormous soprano' was widely acclaimed, and Siegfried Jerusalem received warmer notices for his Siegmund than for the Walther he sang in *Die Meistersinger*. Doris Soffel was generally liked in *Das Rheingold*, less so in *Die Walküre*. This list embraces more than three-quarters of the members of the new cast; unfortunately, it does not include the principals. Generous critics noted how little rehearsal Manfred Jung had had, but even so they were not enthusiastic about the voice; and while they conceded that it was not entirely fair to judge Siegmund Nimsgern until they had heard him sing in *Siegfried*, most thought him insufficently god-like in *Das Rheingold* and *Die Walküre*, though a few heard potential in the voice. Only Hildegard Behrens was seen as a great new *Ring* performer. She provoked inspired lunacy in Levin, who began his article in *The Times*:

> At about seven o'clock in the evening on Monday of last week, in the middle of Act II of *Die Walküre*, Hildegard Behrens embarked upon the long dialogue in which she brings the tidings of death to the doomed hero, with the words *'Siegmund seh auf mich'* ('Siegmund look on me'). At that moment a puff of white smoke was seen to emerge from the Festspielhaus chimney, and the vast throng on the terrace, many of whom had been there, patiently awaiting this moment, for anything up to thirty years, fell to their knees; some were openly weeping, and a few of the more elderly ones, mostly French, expired on the spot, their faces wreathed in beatific smiles. Then the Cardinal-Secretary, Herr Wolfgang Wagner, stepped on to the balcony over the main entrance and gave the traditional blessing, *Urbi et orbe*, and pronounced the fateful words, so long unheard in these parts: 'Habemus Brünnhildam'.

The more sober judgement of Levin's colleague, John Higgins, was that Behrens's first Brünnhilde was a great performance. All was acclaim – except for Andrew Porter, that is, who thought that Behrens had been over-praised: she was an attractive, arresting, and intelligent actress, he said, but her voice lacked the power, the amplitude and the glory that a Brünnhilde needs. (It is, of course, conceivable that Andrew Porter might be wrong.)

The reviews were rather like the booing at the end of *Götterdämmerung*: disappointing, but not as bad as Chéreau's. Just as the audience was converted to the Chéreau *Ring*, so it is likely that the critics will eventually become kinder to Hall and Dudley. Hall always claims that he gets no satisfaction from reviews: 'One's mates say it's lovely, or the critics say it's wonderful, and that gives

you a glow for half a day; the reverse gives you a pain for half a day.'
But producing the *Ring* is an unusually intense and long-lasting
emotional experience, and I believe the pain of those reviews lasted
for more than half a day. Dudley, who read just one review, and
that only by accident (it appeared in the *Observer*, headlined 'Why
the *Ring* went Wrong'), noticed that his friends talked sympath-
etically to him, as though the Bayreuth summer had been a disaster.
But Dudley's friends are mostly *Guardian* and *Observer* readers who
had not read *The Times*. Solti has a long memory for bad reviews, but
on this occasion there were few critics he would want to add to his
blacklist. As for the critical German reviews of the production, Solti
simply dismissed them: 'That they didn't like it is what to expect,
because we don't play *Weltanschauung*, and they cannot imagine it
without something read into it.'

Hall and Solti judged the quality of their own work by what they
themselves saw, and heard; before we left Bayreuth, at the end of
the first cycle, I asked each of them for his own assessment of the
1983 *Ring*.

Hall felt that he had 'under-achieved' in Bayreuth. I asked why. 'I
think we spent too long arguing with the management. I think we
weren't carefully enough planned to start with. We made too many
changes. I think the Goldberg episode was a disaster that wasted a
lot of time that should have been spent creating the work. I think
one should never try to do all four parts of the *Ring* in one year. My
instinct to pull out when Wagner said he would not let us do two
parts one year and two the next, was right. If we hadn't had casting
problems it would have been a help, but I still think it would have
been agony.'

And what mistakes had he made?

'Optimism, by which I mean a determination not to compromise,
because we thought they could get it right. They didn't. I actually
thought that they would solve the problems created by the
platform, but they didn't. And I actually thought that if we allowed
rough-and-ready cueing at first, they would eventually improve,
but they didn't. There are several scenes I want to restage because I
don't like them. I don't like the green "Avebury" ring in *Das
Rheingold* because it restricts movement. I don't like the first scene of
Gibichung Hall. I'm not content with the Ride of the Valkyries,
though I don't quite know why, and I don't know what to do
instead. But there are things I want to do in every scene if I can
stomach coming back. I've got to tell myself to take the long view,
because doing the *Ring* here is like pushing a ton of rocks up a hill.
But when you think of what the *Ring* means in Bayreuth in terms of

the passion of the audience, I would say it's gone better than I expected it to, actually, all in all.'

And his view of Wagner's *Ring* having finally directed it?

'In some respects it's a malformed masterpiece, but now I love it.'

Solti did not share Hall's melancholy. He believed he had won his struggle to find the correct balance in the Festspielhaus pit. 'I think I achieved the presence of a Wagner orchestra. I hated the very refined, far-distant sound; that was like people playing in Bad Berneck [a village twenty kilometres north of Bayreuth]. I just didn't like it, and I have a very good witness for my sound – Wagner himself. I am certain he hated that thin sound. I am certain he would not have played any of his operas except *Parsifal* with that cover on. I got frightened with *Götterdämmerung* and put the cover back on, but maybe next year I will take it off.

'I know a few people think my interpretation is broader and therefore slower now, but the astonishing thing is that the playing time of this *Ring* is faster than my recording. So it is rubbish that I am slower. What it is: I am faster in the faster scenes, and in the broader scenes, broader. That is my experience now, and I have a little more wisdom, musical and psychological – how to build – which I didn't know fifteen years ago.

'At the end of each performance I had the feeling I couldn't go on any more. It was not just the exhaustion, it was the heat. People have no idea what the suffering is in that pit. I asked myself many times: "Why the hell do you do it?" I lost five kilos this summer, though that made me very glad; but when they took my pulse after every act it was only 80, and normally I am 72. So I know now I am strong as an ox, and I have endurance.

'As for the production, it is not 100 per cent yet, but I didn't expect 100 per cent in the first year. We have to seriously rethink a few points and there are two scenes I don't like, but that is very little for such a huge, complex piece.'

Since Solti had been intimately associated with both Hall and Wagner, I asked him finally why he thought the relationship between the two had been so poor.

'Purely psychological and nothing else. It's a human problem, because both are slightly stubborn. Peter too. Peter didn't put Wagner into his confidence, or at least he says "I tried, but he didn't want it." I don't think he tried. And Wagner felt totally unused in his capacity as director of the Festspielhaus, therefore he hated the whole thing. He is so anxious to be put in our confidence. The origin of the poor relationship is I think that they cannot communicate. Neither speaks the other's language, and this is terrible. Can you imagine what it would be like for me to work in English with a Yiddish orchestra? This is not an artistic point, but it is essential.

'But I want to defend Wagner on one point: when he said simplify for the first year because we won't complete it, I understood. Peter thought he was making difficulties for the sake of making difficulties. But he knew his technical possibilities better than we did. We overestimated them. We were too ambitious. That was wrong, and he tried to say that to us, but he said it in a different language. Now we know what the problem is: he must be put into our confidence. That is the whole story. And we can cope with it much better next year.'

After the first performance of *Götterdämmerung*, when Hall and Wagner, Solti and Dudley posed together for a photograph by Roger Wood, the tensions that had built up during the summer seemed to have slackened. Solti, having risen from the bed in his darkened dressing-room on which he slumped after each performance, gave a lively and cheerful smile for the camera. Hall and Dudley were still slightly bemused by the booing, though neither was depressed. Wagner was in a mildly manic mood. The last photograph Roger Wood took was of Hall and Wagner, leaning across the table to shake hands. They were smiling broadly at each other, as if they would like to mean it one day: a hopeful augury. And a month later, Hall no longer wondered whether he could 'stomach' a return to Bayreuth the following summer. Rested and fit again, he saw the first year's work as 'a success', but felt that with some recasting and more hard work, the production would run more smoothly in 1984.

To return to the analogy I used in my first chapter, that to create a new production of the *Ring* in Bayreuth is like an attempt on Everest without oxygen, Hall and Solti had glimpsed the peak through the smoke on this their first expedition, and now they believed they might scale the whole mountain the following year. After all, many of the errors that the critics had identified in performance were just as obvious to the director and designer, the conductor and the management. Having been diagnosed, they were susceptible to treatment. There would still be Wagnerians in the audience for whom Hall's emphasis on the text was insufficiently conceptualised, but Bayreuth would also see a new generation of *Ring* devotees taking their places, as had been the case during the five years of the Chéreau *Ring*. Enraptured comments from non-professional opera-goers in 1983 had made it clear that there was an enthusiastic audience for the most straightforward, least bombastic production of the *Ring* anyone is ever likely to see in Richard

211

Wagner's theatre. As Hall had said cheerfully to Dudley after *Götterdämmerung* opened: '*Ça commence.*'

But did that mean they really would eventually scale the peak? By the end of the summer I had begun to wonder whether anyone could. The *Ring*, the most demanding of all great works, provokes an emotional intensity that sometimes seems to border on insanity. When I asked Wolfgang Wagner whether he had ever known a director who was satisfied with his production, he grunted thoughtfully, then laughed and shook his head. Peter Hall, for once, agreed with him. 'There is no definitive production of any great work, no definitive *Hamlet*, no perfect *Ring*.' Directors become addicted to great works of art, and having done them once, begin to imagine a new production. Perhaps the proper lesson to be learnt is that in the assault upon so great a work, the emotions of performers and audience are so deeply engaged that no one can agree exactly where the peak is, or how high it is, let alone how best to tackle it. Having watched a *Ring* being made, I think I can now define a work of art: it is truly great only when it can never be perfectly produced. Hall was right at the beginning: doing the *Ring* is impossible. How brave, how bold, are those who try.

30th July 1983. The first cycle of the *Ring* is over. Relief unites all four makers of the production. l. to r. Dudley, Hall, Solti and Wagner.

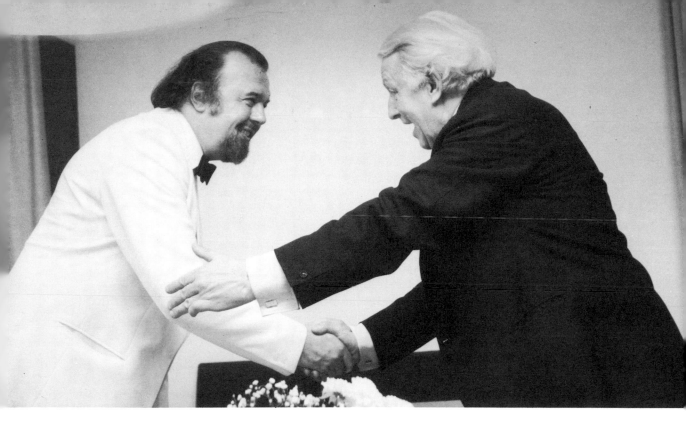

Postscript

In the spring of 1984 Sir Georg Solti had not been sleeping well. He felt tense and he was worried about his heart. At seventy-one he was not, perhaps, as strong as an ox. In mid-May his doctor confirmed Solti's own diagnosis – he had been working too hard. There was a simple cure for that: the doctor recommended that Solti should not work in Bayreuth in the summer of 1984.

Acutely aware of the disappointment and disruption his withdrawal would cause, for the orchestra, the singers and the production team – never mind the ticket holders – Solti was unwilling to give up completely. He suggested to Wolfgang Wagner that he should attend the rehearsals and conduct the first cycle during the 1984 Festival. This would enable Sir Peter Hall and himself to explain their scheme to the singers joining the cast that summer. The offer was generously meant but it placed Wagner in a compromising position. Asking a reputable conductor merely to finish off the second and third *Ring* cycles was offering crumbs from a maestro's table. So, late in May, Wagner announced in Bayreuth that for reasons of health Sir George Solti had asked to be released from his contract. His place would be taken by a promising German conductor named Peter Schneider who had been working in Bremen.

The news of Solti's withdrawal was further evidence, if any was needed, of 'the curse of the *Ring*'.

Appendix

The story of Wagner's *Ring*

In the first opera, *Das Rheingold*, Alberich, head of a family of dwarfs from Nibelheim, steals gold from the Rhinemaidens, a deed which can only be achieved by renouncing love. Alberich then makes a ring from the stolen gold which gives its owner great power. Wotan, the god, tricks Alberich into surrendering the ring, whereupon Alberich puts a curse on whoever owns it. The story would end there if Wotan immediately followed the sound advice offered by Loge, god of fire, to return the ring to the Rhinemaidens, allowing the gods to seek fulfilment through love instead of power. But Wotan gives the ring to the giants Fafner and Fasolt in payment for building his great new castle, Valhalla. Alberich's curse strikes immediately: Fafner kills Fasolt in order to become the sole possessor of the ring. Developing musical themes illustrate the ring itself and Wotan's authority (invested in his spear and symbolised by Valhalla), underlining the message about the corruption of power and the contamination of greed.

In *Die Walküre*, the second opera of the cycle, the themes become broader as the story unfolds, and include the effects of Wotan's own shortcomings: his delight in wandering and in philandering. His promiscuity is formidable, and no fewer than eleven of his children now appear: nine are his warrior-maidens, the Valkyries, led by his favourite daughter Brünnhilde. The others are the twins Siegmund and Sieglinde, who fall in love; a relationship that is not only incestuous but also adulterous, since Sieglinde is already married to a mortal called Hunding. Wotan sympathises with the lovers, placing them under the special guardianship of Brünnhilde and giving them a magic sword, Nothung. This infuriates his wife Fricka (who is not the twins' mother); she insists that Wotan uphold his own law against incest and withdraw his protection from the twins.

Siegmund decides to kill both Sieglinde and himself before Hunding finds them. Moved by their love, Brünnhilde disobeys Wotan and saves Sieglinde. Hunding kills Siegmund because Wotan intervenes at the last minute to shatter the magic sword Nothung, which would have saved his son. Brünnhilde gathers up the broken bits of sword and gives them to Sieglinde, sending her away into the forest to bear her child, whilst she faces the wrath of Wotan alone, her sister Valkyries being too frightened to help her.

Brünnhilde's punishment for defying Wotan's authority is to be put to sleep on a mountain top, ringed by fire; she can be awakened only by the kiss of a hero fearless enough to walk through the flames. By the end of *Die Walküre*, Wotan, the lawmaker, has seen one of his children die and lost two more as a result of enforcing his own law, yet his authority has been diminished by his initial reluctance to act. Although a god, Wotan has tried to have his cake and eat it, with no more success than most mortals.

The subject of the third part of the cycle is Siegfried, the child of Siegmund and Sieglinde (who died in childbirth). Both Wotan and Alberich see in Siegfried, the innocent and fearless hero, the means by which they might regain the ring. So too does Alberich's brother Mime, who has brought Siegfried up in his forge in the forest. Fafner, the giant, has now turned himself into a dragon to protect the ring and is vulnerable only to the sword Nothung which Siegfried has reforged. Siegfried kills the dragon and takes the ring. He then kills Mime and the power of the ring enables the anarchic young hero to shatter the symbol of Wotan's authority, his spear. Finally Siegfried strides through the fire to find the sleeping Brünnhilde. They fall deeply in love.

In *Götterdämmerung*, Siegfried gives the ring to Brünnhilde for safe-keeping. Alberich then incites his son Hagen to help him regain the ring, which Hagen does with the help of his half-brother and sister, Gunther and Gutrune. Hagen drugs Siegfried who forgets his devotion to Brünnhilde and falls in love with Gutrune instead. Siegfried then tricks Brünnhilde into marrying Gunther, and takes back the ring. On discovering Siegfried's treachery, Brünnhilde betrays him to Hagen, revealing how Siegfried may be killed. Hagen promptly slays him. Brünnhilde, finally understanding that Hagen has tricked them both in order to regain the ring, orders Siegfried's funeral pyre to be lit and rides straight into it, redeeming both of them by her love. Wotan and the other gods, who chose power, not love, are immolated in the flames that destroy Valhalla. Hagen is drowned by the Rhinemaidens, who repossess the ring; its curse is lifted when it is returned to nature, where it belongs.

Der Ring des Nibelungen

CAST LIST

Das Rheingold

Wotan	Siegmund Nimsgern
Donner	Heinz-Jurgen Demitz
Froh	Maldwyn Davies
Loge	Manfred Jung
Fasolt	Manfred Schenk
Fafner	Dieter Schweikart
Alberich	Hermann Becht
Mime	Peter Haage
Fricka	Doris Soffel
Freia	Anita Soldh
Erda	Anne Gjevang
Woglinde	Agnes Habereder
Wellgunde	Diana Montague
Flosshilde	Birgitta Svendén

Die Walküre

Siegmund	Siegfried Jerusalem
Hunding	Matthias Hölle
Wotan	Siegmund Nimsgern
Sieglinde	Jeannine Altmeyer
Brünnhilde	Hildegard Behrens
Fricka	Doris Soffel
Gerhilde	Anita Soldh
Ortlinde	Anne Evans
Waltraute	Ingrid Karrasch
Schwertleite	Anne Wilkens
Helmwige	Agnes Habereder
Siegrune	Diana Montague
Grimgerde	Ruthild Engert-Ely
Rossweisse	Anne Gjevang

Siegfried

Siegfried	Manfred Jung (Reiner Goldberg in rehearsals)
Mime	Peter Haage
Der Wanderer	Siegmund Nimsgern
Alberich	Hermann Becht
Fafner	Dieter Schweikart
Erda	Anne Gjevang
Brünnhilde	Hildegard Behrens
Waldvogel	Sylvia Greenberg

Götterdämmerung

Siegfried	Manfred Jung
Gunther	Bent Norup
Hagen	Aage Haugland
Alberich	Hermann Becht
Brünnhilde	Hildegard Behrens
Gutrune	Josephine Barstow
Waltraute	Brigitte Fassbaender
1. Norn	Anne Gjevang
2. Norn	Anne Wilkens
3. Norn	Anne Evans
Woglinde	Agnes Habereder
Wellgunde	Diana Montague
Flosshilde	Birgitta Svendén

215

Index

217